H^{to}eal, Proclaim, ^{and}Teach

"Jared Dees makes an important and necessary contribution to the New Evangelization. Coupling sound theology with personal witness, evangelization with strong catechesis, and pastoral concern with creative outreach, this is an engaging and inspiring read. Accessible, thorough, and yet spiritually deep: This is an excellent book!"

Julianne Stanz
Director of New Evangelization
Diocese of Green Bay

"Here is a promising antidote to the discomfort many of us feel toward evangelization. Dees offers a perceptive reading of contemporary culture, a spiritual grounding rooted in deeply pondered human experience, and a rich theological framework based on the ministerial priorities of Jesus. This is an exciting resource for all parish leaders, providing a wealth of practical suggestions for weaving evangelization throughout parish life."

Zeni V. Fox
Professor of Pastoral Theology
Seton Hall University

"For all the discussion these days about the New Evangelization, there seems to be a surprising amount of confusion about what it is. Jared Dees takes us beyond all the clutter and chatter to set out the basics, returning us to the very ministry of Jesus. *To Heal, Proclaim, and Teach* is an extremely readable, entirely practical guide for anyone interested in this critically important topic. Great book; we love it!"

Rev. Michael White and Tom Corcoran
Authors of *Rebuilt*

"What must we do to awaken the sleeping giant that is the Catholic Church? Jared Dees offers a compelling vision. He shows us how to engage and transform Catholic hearts through Jesus' healing love, inspired preaching, and experiential teaching. Everyone involved in the New Evangelization will want to read this book."

Bob Schuchts
Author of *Be Healed*

"Dees's conversational tone, stories from his own personal and professional faith journeys, examples of vibrant ministries, and practical tips make this a wonderfully engaging and helpful read for any Catholic minister who takes seriously Christ's call to go and make disciples."

Sr. Theresa Rickard, O.P.
President and Executive Director
RENEW International

to Heal, Proclaim, and Teach

The Essential Guide to Ministry in Today's Catholic Church

JARED DEES

AVE MARIA PRESS AVE Notre Dame, Indiana

Founded in 1865, Ave Maria Press is a ministry of the United States Province of Holy Cross.

www.avemariapress.com

Paperback: ISBN-13 978-1-59471-619-5

E-book: ISBN-13 978-1-59471-620-1

Cover and text design by Andy Wagoner.

Printed and bound in the United States of America.

Library of Congress Cataloging-in-Publication Data
Names: Dees, Jared, author.
Title: To heal, proclaim, and teach : the essential guide to ministry in today's Catholic Church / Jared Dees.
Description: Notre Dame, Indiana : Ave Maria Press, [2016] | Includes bibliographical references.
Identifiers: LCCN 2015043283| ISBN 9781594716195 (pbk.) | ISBN 9781594716201 (ebook)
Subjects: LCSH: Evangelistic work--Catholic Church. | Church work--Catholic Church.
Classification: LCC BX2347.4 .D44 2016 | DDC 253.088/282--dc23
LC record available at http://lccn.loc.gov/2015043283

CONTENTS

Preface
SPIRITUAL NOT RELIGIOUS

On January 10, 2012, twenty-two-year-old Jefferson Bethke clicked *publish* on a YouTube video that was about to go viral. He made a bet with his roommates about how many views it would get—a hundred views, maybe a thousand—but none of them came close to predicting what was about to happen. The video, titled "Why I Hate Religion but Love Jesus," is a poetic rap expressing Bethke's love for Jesus but disdain for religious legalism. In two days it had more than two million views. Two weeks later YouTube showed it had more than sixteen million views, and by early 2015, it approached thirty million.

This video resonated with so many millions of people because Bethke was able to articulate in a five-minute video what a growing number of people try to express by calling themselves "spiritual but not religious." This self-characterization is incredibly common today within every generational, ethnic, and cultural grouping in the United States.

There is no questioning the real decline in numbers facing the Catholic Church in some parts of the United States today. In many areas of the country, numbers of self-identified Catholics are decreasing at rapid rates. According to a recent Pew Research Center study, the number of people self-identifying as Catholics decreased from 23.9 percent in 2007 to 20.8 percent in 2014.[1] That equates to a loss of about 3.4 million Catholics in just seven years. In many places the pews are increasingly empty. Baptisms, marriages, First Communions, Confirmations—you name it—they are on the downturn. People are not satisfied with their churches, so they go elsewhere or they do not go at all. During the same period between 2007 and 2014, the number of Evangelical Protestants grew by about 2.4 million and the number of religiously unaffiliated (spiritual but not religious) grew by a staggering 19.2 million people.[2]

Many of these unaffiliated spiritual seekers put a higher priority on youth sports events, watching professional sports, recreational activities with friends or family, personal downtime, or simply sleeping in on Sunday mornings than they put on going to Mass. They have not stopped believing in God—in fact, many will be back in church on Christmas and Easter—they just do not find much inspiration or joy in organized religion on a weekly—let alone daily—basis. In many areas of our country, church after church is being forced to close or consolidate now that once-full pews are growing empty.

One possible response is to blame an uncontrollable consumer culture and simply admit defeat. Many have pointed to the various "-isms" for the shift away from religion (secularism, relativism, individualism, etc.) and express an incapability to overcome such powerful movements. But another possible response is to look at ourselves as Christian leaders and the work we have been doing to see if there is something we can do differently to meet the spiritual—indeed, religious—needs of Americans today. Take a look at one of the most powerful verses from the middle of Jefferson Bethke's rap:

> But now that I know Jesus, I boast in my weakness.
> If grace is water, then the church should be an ocean,
> Cuz it's not a museum for good people
> it's a hospital for the broken.

Compare that verse with the words of Pope Francis in his 2013 interview with Father Antonio Spadaro in *America* magazine titled "A Big Heart Open to God":

> I see clearly that the thing the Church needs most today is the ability to heal wounds and to warm the hearts of the faithful; it needs nearness, proximity. I see the Church as a field hospital after battle. It is useless to ask a seriously injured person if he has high cholesterol and about the level of his blood sugars! You have to heal his wounds. Then we can talk about everything else. Heal the wounds, heal the wounds. . . . And you have to start from the ground up.
>
> The Church sometimes has locked itself up in small things, in small-minded rules. The most important thing is the first proclamation: Jesus Christ has saved you. And the ministers of the Church must be ministers of mercy above all.[3]

I believe Bethke and Pope Francis are both pointing to an essential change that we need to make as leaders in the Church. We have to heal wounds, and we have to go deeper with our proclamation of salvation in Christ. It may be that the reason we continue to see so many Catholics leave the Church is that many people do not find in the Church a source of healing for their pain. They do not hear people in our churches preaching a message that inspires or connects with their deepest hopes, dreams, and needs. It may even be that our focus on conveying doctrine, without first laying a foundation for understanding it, renders the Church easy to leave for many and keeps others from ever entering its doors.

The Church can either be a community of people that welcomes the sinner and helps heal the wounds of sin and isolation, or it will be a place where sinners are condemned and turned away, forced by our lack of mercy back into their spirituality of individualism. It can be a community that proclaims the Good News of salvation in Jesus Christ, or it can be an institution focused on scolding (sometimes condemning) outsiders for denying its doctrines. For many of us on the inside, especially those of us in leadership, the Church *we* know and love welcomes the lost and proclaims salvation, but the great challenge we face day in and day out is helping others see and experience what we do so that they develop a hunger to come and see more.

WHAT ABOUT RELIGION LOOKS SO BAD?

Let's face it: religion is a tough sell—even to the curious. To outsiders, religion often seems dominated by rules—rules that are pretty tough to follow. *They* ask *us* to totally transform our lives and turn away from what is comfortable and makes us feel good. The time commitment once each week (sometimes more) may seem like nothing to us, but for many people Sunday morning is prime time for all sorts of other activities. Religion can feel confrontational or can seem an unnecessary hassle. Probably most people who don't go to church are hardworking good people who just want to get a break by sleeping in, playing golf, watching football, getting caught up on things around the house, or just enjoying downtime with loved ones.

The vast majority of people who grew up going to church and do not go anymore are not ardent atheists. They are not anti-Church or anti-God. Remember, they see themselves as spiritual people who believe in God. They may not get anything out of going to church on Sundays, but they do like to pray, especially in times of crisis or when they feel profoundly grateful. Most of these people want to do what is right, and they want to enjoy life. Religion, however, puts restrictions on them without providing much payoff. To them, it adds unnecessary rules and meaningless actions to their already too-busy lives. Religion seems to take the fun out of life.

As Christian leaders whose lives have been transformed by Christ, we know differently. We are spiritual *and* religious because we know the joy of intimate relationship with Christ and the benefits of following God's laws and getting involved in a community of fellow believers. We are at church not out of an obligation but because we *want* to be there. We want to give thanks to God for his gifts, and we know we cannot live the life we want to live without his help. Many of us have tried to find fulfillment outside of the Church but ultimately cannot find a better source of hope. Our attempts to find happiness elsewhere have failed. We have found hope and an incredible source of peace and joy in God and within the communion of the Church.

Do you see the difference? We believe what we believe and do what we do because we *want* to. Religion is a part of who we are, something we choose over and over again to remain with. Our religious practice brings with it certain obligations, but they are obligations we choose to accept as members of the Church. Those who consider themselves open only to spirituality see religion as an obligation put upon them by others. This is why many of them still go to church occasionally when Mom and Dad visit, on Christmas and Easter, or for other special occasions such as weddings, Baptisms, and funerals. Often these people attend more because of sentiment than conviction.

The challenge before us, then, is to show others why Christian beliefs, teachings, practices, and laws are worth understanding and embracing. It is to show our brothers and sisters that just being spiritual is not enough; there is further commitment necessary when choosing a Christian life. But even before inviting others to discipleship, we need to help restore for them trust in organized religion, which continues to be degraded by a tendency to preach and teach without first attending to compassionate mercy and love. Many religious leaders—certainly within Catholicism, but also within other Christian communities—have too long neglected that to which Pope Francis now calls us. We must return our way of ministry to our biblical roots and the example of Jesus himself by becoming "ministers of mercy above all."[4] This is the key to genuine, life-changing evangelization.

IT DOESN'T HAVE TO BE SO HARD

As I write this book, I have in mind many conversations I have had with parents who are in tears over their grown children's separation from the Church. They have tried everything. Every conversation these parents have had about God is brushed off and unwelcome. If their children come to church with them, it is out of coercion or a murky sense of guilt, not free choice. If they believe there is a God, they are not all that interested in worshiping him, especially not in church. On the brink of hopelessness, these parents turn to God in prayer, feeling helpless and guilty for failing to raise their kids to become practicing Catholics. They cannot even with confidence claim their children are Christians.

I also have in mind the professional and volunteer ministers who are struggling to reach people at all different ages and progressions along their faith journeys. In many places the pews are emptier and emptier each year. New ministries, such as youth nights and adult faith-formation series, often do not attract enough participants to sustain them. Children's programs may be steady in attendance, but the parents of these children do not bring their kids to Mass on Sundays. Often, once those kids receive the sacraments, they don't come back to Mass or any other parish activity. In other places churches are filled to overflowing, but ministry leaders can't help but feel that what they do primarily is barter in the sacraments. They set up hoops, parishioners jump through, and sacraments are received. But then what? Too many ministers are left wondering how many people come to truly know Christ because of what they do.

There are, of course, sparks of success in many corners of the Church, but nearly everywhere there are too many Catholics who *aren't* in church this can bring great distress to ministers striving to do more. These leaders try new things but never quite know what is working, except for prayer, which faith tells them always works.

As a result, some members of the Church have unfortunately become passionately frustrated and even angry with the current situation. In reaction to the many uncatechized kids and adults, members of this group hold tight to the fervent beliefs and doctrines of the Church and try to share their love of these teachings every chance they get. It is usually with good intention but often with negative results. The spiritual-but-not-religious crowd often reacts by taking offense and turns further from the Church, sometimes growing passionate as well—passionately frustrated with the people in the Church!

What, then, shall we do to bring people back or attract them for the first time? How might we who are engaged inspire them to know and love God *and* Church? You will find in this book a process for evangelizing ministry that works. It is a process that Jesus himself used to make disciples. It is the process that his apostles used to grow the Church and that the great saints throughout history have followed ever since. It is the same process that many successful individuals, parishes, and Catholic ministries are using today to foster growing numbers of disciples and conversion experiences in the people they serve.

With this process, you will not have to feel hopeless anymore. Instead of turning to God in prayer as a last resort, you will trust in his work, trust in the process, and thank him in prayer for his great intervention. Or, instead of putting all the trust in your own actions to inspire faith in others, you will look to the process and turn to God in faith that he will work through you and others in each stage along a person's journey.

Evangelization is not a mysterious set of activities that only people with charismatic gifts are able to do. It is about so much more than great preaching or good teaching. It is something we all can do in every day of our lives if we begin with mercy offered as healing to those who hurt. The most common form of evangelization, in fact, doesn't feel like something extraordinary at all. As you will find, we are all *called to* and *able to* make disciples, and we don't have to be great preachers, teachers, or miracle-workers to do it.

Introduction
WHAT IS EVANGELIZATION?

Every Sunday millions of Christians throughout the world say "I believe" as they recite the words of the Nicene Creed. *Believe* is a word that has taken on all kinds of meanings today. We might say, "I believe in ghosts," meaning, "I believe that ghosts exist." We can say to someone, "I believe you," as in, "I believe that what you are saying is true." We often say, "I can't believe that!" when something shocking has happened that is difficult to comprehend. In almost every case other than in the context of the creed, we say "believe" in reference to the acceptance of an idea or perception. The "I believe" we say in the creed, however, is very different.

In the original Latin, "I believe" is the single word *credo*. It can mean "believe in," but it can also mean "trust in." The Latin word originates as the compound of two words: *ker* or *cor*, which means "heart"; and *do* or *dheh*, which means "to put, place, or set." When Christians recite the creed, what we are really proclaiming is that we place our hearts in God. It is commitment to a someone (not just a something) with whom we can have a relationship. It is so much more than a simple acceptance of ideas, perceptions, or truths. When we recite the creed, we pledge our very hearts to God. This should have an enormous impact on the way we live every day and a profound influence on how we think of ministry, particularly in the way we evangelize.

WHAT IS EVANGELIZATION?

What exactly is the purpose of evangelization? What are we try-ing to accomplish? Why should we want to do it? What exactly *is* it? Simply put, evangelization is the way in which we show others why and how to trust in God. It is the process by which we help others learn to pledge their hearts continuously to Christ. From the outside, this might feel selfish and imposing. Today more than ever people take offense even to the idea of openly sharing religious beliefs with those who do not already accept them. They have become hypersensitive to proselytization and religious fundamentalism because they have seen and experi-enced the negative effects of these.

At the same time, the word *evangelization* has been naturally adopted by the secular world. An increasing number of "brand evangelists" can be found in companies and start-ups today. These individuals practice a form of marketing that is focused on word of mouth. They create messages that spread among people who love a product or a company. The goal is to craft a message and a reputation among people who already love a product and get it to spread to others.

Christian evangelization, on the other hand, is about so much more than spreading an idea or defending a reputation. Christianity spreads not because of convincing arguments, but because of heartfelt encounters with Christ that transform lives. Christianity calls for more than the acceptance of ideas alone; it exists as the result of and in response to an encounter with a living God. As Pope Benedict XVI wrote, "Being Christian is not the result of an ethical choice or a lofty idea, but the encounter with an event, a person, which gives life a new horizon and a decisive direction" (*Deus Caritas Est*, 1).

If, when we think about evangelization, we think only of the beliefs and stories of Christianity and not about the benefit to the other person, then our perception is much too narrow. We evangelize to enter into the deepest needs of our neighbors in order to help them find solutions to their deepest desires. Evangelization is about the heart, wounded by sin and separation and yearning for something more. This kind of evangelization—one that puts the needs of others first—is the only one that really works. It is the ministerial approach used by Jesus himself. It is this kind of evangelization that will not cause us to feel guilty or unsure of ourselves. We never have to feel bad about evangelization in this sense, because it keeps the needs of others at the forefront of our concern.

Evangelization is not primarily about teaching doctrines and communicating ideas. Learning and assenting to the doctrines of the Church and committing to a life of discipleship do not *lead* a person to conversion. Rather, these *result* from conversion. In order for a Christian to proclaim "I believe," he or she must first experience a transformation in mind and heart. With that transformation comes the recognition that we are loved by God and will do everything we can to love God back. The doctrines and teachings help us to love God, but they only make sense when built upon that firm foundation of love.

Understanding and accepting Church doctrines is a process that takes time and internal motivation. It cannot be done with a simple intellectual assent. We accept the doctrines because of an intimate relationship that we have formed with Christ and the Church. This is what we mean by the word *faith*. The *Catechism of the Catholic Church* describes faith as a response to God's revelation by which "man completely submits his intellect and his will to God," and, further, "with his whole being man gives his assent to God the revealer" (142–43). In order to have faith, we must have a change of both mind *and* heart, a reorienting of our lives toward God, which leads to ongoing conversion. This

means we have to share more than ideas when we evangelize.
When we invite another into relationship with Christ, we have
to *love*.

HOW TO EVANGELIZE

Evangelization, if it is to be effective, is always the challenging
work of entering into the depths of another human being's experience and walking with him or her into the light of a better
tomorrow. It is more than teaching about doctrines. It is more
than spreading ideas. Ministry is always about serving another
human being in that person's greatest need and deepest longing.

I always thought the new evangelization—the appeal to
Catholics to evangelize even those who have already been
baptized but have now fallen away—was about getting better
at knowing and sharing my "faith" (i.e., Catholic doctrine and
theology) with others. As it turns out, the new evangelization—
and, in fact, *all* evangelization and all ministry—calls for a much
greater sacrifice than acquiring knowledge and building up the
skills of articulating what we believe. It calls us, as disciples, to
get comfortable with being uncomfortable, to be vulnerable
rather than knowledgeable, to be interested *in* others rather than
simply interesting *to* others.

As dedicated Catholics and ministers, most of us have had
striking, unexpected transformations in faith or lifelong religious
experiences that have made an incredible impact on our lives. At
some point we felt the call to share the love of God we encountered in those experiences—to serve the Church in children's or
youth ministry, adult faith formation, or liturgical ministries; as
volunteers in soup kitchens; or in numerous other ways. We feel
compelled to share the joy we know in Christ, but the question
is, how do we actually do it effectively without scaring people
off or, worse, pushing them away?

There is no reason to think that our situation is any different from every other era in the history of the Church. In each century, the Church has had to overcome seemingly insurmountable challenges in making new disciples. Many great saints became beacons of hope during those times and showed us how to spread the Gospel amid adversity. In fact, while the methods they used to spread the Gospel may have differed, the process they used to bring people into the Church can be traced back to Jesus himself.

We all know in a general way what Jesus did. We can cite specific stories of his miracles, meals, preaching, and teaching. But twice in the Gospel of Matthew we find a concise summary of the threefold ministry of Jesus Christ: **"Jesus went around to all the towns and villages, teaching in their synagogues, proclaiming the Gospel of the kingdom, and curing every disease and illness" (Mt 9:35; see also Mt 4:23).**

Here Matthew lays out for us a clear summary of what Jesus did: he healed, he proclaimed, and he taught. Each action is a distinct and effective form of ministry with people who are at various points in their faith journeys. Jesus responds to the need before him and ministers accordingly, depending on where each individual or group is along the path to conversion and eventual discipleship. Healing, proclaiming, and teaching are all just as essential today as they were at the time of Jesus' ministry.

Many Catholic ministers and volunteers are very comfortable with being good teachers of doctrine. Most of the well-attended ministries in Catholic parishes focus on catechesis and preparation for the sacraments. For the most part, the goal of these meetings or classes is to pass on the teachings of the Church. We know, however, that many participants in these programs are poorly catechized and even unevangelized. As Saint John Paul II observed in his apostolic exhortation *Catechesi Tradendae*,

"A certain number of children baptized in infancy come for catechesis in the parish without receiving any other initiation into the faith and still without any explicit personal attachment to Jesus Christ" (19). This is why all of us who are responsible for catechesis should recognize that it is only one aspect of the larger responsibility of evangelization.

Thankfully, Jesus gave us a model for ministry that makes evangelization possible. Take note of where Matthew says Jesus taught. He taught in the synagogues. He taught people who were already committed to being spiritual *and* religious. The crowds, however, whom he met in the cities and villages, heard a different message. They were interested in knowing God and probably even considered themselves to be spiritual. Why else would they come to hear what a great spiritual sage like Jesus had to say? To them, he proclaimed Good News about the kingdom of God, which he preached with words and proclaimed by the way he lived. Like Jesus, we must offer those who are not yet fully committed disciples a different message than those who are already disciples. To them we must offer an initial proclamation that expresses God's infinite love for us—a love that requires a response of faith.

To be able to hear and understand that message, however, individuals need to experience love in their own lives. This is where healing ministry comes in. I will explain later how healing is an essential part of evangelization, not because of the occasional physical miracles that may occur, but because of the inner healing of emotional brokenness. When wounded hearts are healed in the context of a personal encounter with Christ, through the ministry of his disciples, the other parts of the evangelization process can effectively take place.

TO TEACH OR NOT TO TEACH

I have nothing against teaching religion. In fact, it has been my entire life's vocation. After graduating college, I immediately entered the classroom as a religion teacher and continue to serve as a catechist today. I have seen firsthand that focusing too heavily on professionalism and perfectionism as a teacher is one of the easiest ways to turn people away from Christ. Let me share an example of this common mistake.

When I was a new Catholic-school teacher I found my role as educator to be the easiest place to hide. As a recent college graduate, I was young and self-conscious about my age. I developed a real complex about it that started with the very first time I met my new students and their parents. At our first open house, at least five parents and a handful of kids smiled dismissively when they met me and said, "You look too young to be a teacher."

From that moment on, I hid behind the veil of professionalism, and the effects were truly unfortunate. This was never more clear than during a moment in my second year of teaching when one of my eighth-grade students came to talk to me about his girlfriend, Rachel, a classmate. She was noticeably distraught in recent days and not her usual happy, bubbly self. It turned out that her parents were getting a divorce. Knowing that my parents had been through a divorce, her boyfriend turned to me for guidance.

He caught up with me between classes and said, "Could you talk to her, Mr. Dees? You said your parents are divorced, and I thought you might be able to say something to her." He was brief because he didn't want her to know that he told anyone.

Over the next few days I looked for a chance to talk to Rachel, but I'm sad to say I never did. I didn't know what to say, and I was afraid. Part of it may have been my own painful memories of my parents' divorce; I'm not quite sure. But I justified the lack of action in the name of professionalism. I told myself it was not my place to say anything—that I should be the teacher, not the friend. I told myself that it was my job to teach about religion and history and not get involved in the personal lives of my students. How very sad for a Catholic-school teacher, especially a *religion* teacher!

This is a scenario playing itself out in many different ministries in our Church today. It is easier to teach a speed-lesson about the Sacrament of Baptism to new parents than it is to sit with them one-on-one to talk about their biggest hopes and greatest fears as new parents. It is easier to grudgingly issue certificates of completion to engaged couples who have met the minimum diocesan requirements for marriage without ever getting to know why they are getting married in the first place or what they dream of becoming together. Attend enough classes, complete a program, attend the annual retreat, and you qualify for your First Reconciliation, First Communion, and the Sacrament of Confirmation.

Church leaders today are sometimes more focused on completing a curriculum than actually getting to know the needs of the people they are serving. For instance, some of our homilies might catechize adults about the sanctity of marriage and at the same time ignore the profound pain that separation and divorce have caused many people in the pews. Our RCIA ministries may try to cram in every paragraph of the *Catechism of the Catholic Church* in a multiweek lecture series that ends up dissipating the desperate hunger for the kingdom of God that catechumens and candidates brought with them. Our marriage-preparation programs can become a series of classes that display bite-sized introductions to big-time issues such as the significance of families of origin, finances, communication, unrealistic expectations, hopes, and fears, the value of Catholic teaching on contraception, the problem with cohabitation, and what *sacrament* really means. We teach teenagers in Catholic schools about Church history and Catholic morality despite the fact that many of them do not even believe in God, or mistrust or simply do not see the point of religion.

I write all this not as a complaint but as a confession. I spent too many years focused on teaching people about the doctrines that I love rather than loving the people that I taught. I am the guy who started a website called *The Religion Teacher* because of my passion for our Catholic beliefs. Teaching has long been an integral part of my identity. Over the years I have gotten good at it. I was bad at first—really bad—but I got better, and now I feel confident that I can teach a lesson I know my students will remember. In the process, though, I became so focused on the craft that I lost sight of the needs of the children in front of me.

Teaching about Church doctrines can be inspiring and influential. It really can. Our beliefs certainly can make a lasting impact on people who hear about them in the proper context. The problem is that teaching alone is not enough. Teaching is safe, comfortable, impersonal, and objective. It is not risky. It does not necessarily require us to share any part of ourselves. As teachers, all we need to do is pass on what we have learned in the clearest way possible. If they can remember and repeat back to us what we have taught, then we can reasonably say that we are successful. The truth is, however, there is so much more to evangelization than this.

We in Catholic leadership, in ministries complex and simple, are left with a choice. We can continue acting only as teachers resenting those who don't "get it," all the while wishing there were more people at Mass on Sundays. Or, we can do things differently. We can give first priority to healing the wounds of those in need, connect the Good News of salvation with the actual hopes and dreams of the people we serve, and only then try to teach them.

FIRST, HEAL THE WOUNDS

The process of evangelization begins with the ability to see the pain in our brothers' and sisters' hearts and find ways in which we can help them find healing. It requires a disposition of mercy that looks beyond our own desires for protection and fears of losing what we have.

Think for a minute about the way Jesus attracted and led people to conversion. Jesus was a teacher, yes, but did he always lead with a lesson?

Take, for instance, the calling of the first disciples. How did Jesus win over the doubting fishermen? When he met them, the men were struggling to catch fish. Again and again their nets came out of the water empty. It seemed as though they would go home completely empty-handed from a long day at work. But, upon Jesus' instructions, they put out into the deep water one last time and, to their amazement, found their nets bursting at the seams with fish.

Jesus saw their pain and met their needs. He did not lead with a lesson. He started with their pain. The soon-to-be disciples saw that Jesus was the source of this miracle, and upon his command they followed him. They committed to a relationship with him before they ever heard a lesson from him.

Or take the woman at the well. Jesus met the woman, identified her most painful source of guilt and shame, confronted it head-on, and helped her find mercy instead of harsh judgment. Out of that healing encounter came her conversion. She went away recognizing Jesus as the Son of God and proclaiming his work in her life to the other people of Samaria.

A similar story is repeated again and again throughout the gospels. A person is healed by Christ but, more importantly, finally feels loved and accepted instead of feeling rejected by others. As a result of a healing encounter, he or she follows Jesus and spreads the Gospel.

The lesson here is clear: healing is the first step in evangelization.

How on earth can we imitate the healing power of Jesus? Should we learn how to become miracle-workers? Sorry, but you will not find a manual for magical healing in this book, nor will you discover the ways in which you can become an evangelical miracle-worker, slaying people with the Holy Spirit onstage before large crowds. No, the healing power you will learn in this book is much, much more difficult and much more effective.

In order truly to help heal the pain of our brothers and sisters, we have to enter into it. We have to feel a compassionate desire to help by walking with them in their pain and helping them navigate a way toward healing mercy and toward salvation. This takes time, emotional investment, and a lot of vulnerability on our part.

The healing we provide through our ministry isn't some kind of medicine that takes away the pain. In some cases, the pain never goes away. What we do is lead others to the source of our own personal healing and strength, the Lord Jesus Christ. Unlike Jesus, who healed physical pains as miracles and proof of his divinity, we don't often offer the alleviation of physical pain. But as Jesus also did, we take on and experience their pain together with them. Through compassion we offer a healing touch, a merciful presence to those who are hurting. In the face of suffering, we are the *Body* of Christ.

THEN, PROCLAIM THE GOOD NEWS

Jesus is the Savior; he brings salvation through his unconditional love for us. Jesus, the Son of God, came to this earth and suffered just as we suffer but to the point of a humiliating death on a cross. Then he rose again and ascended into heaven, paving the way for us to experience our own salvation today. Through Baptism, we enter into the kingdom of God and continue to dwell in Christ both in this life and the next.

Salvation is something we get to experience right now, reaping the benefits of the Christian life, and also after death, when we will be united with God and others in the perfection of heaven and entry into the kingdom of God.

This is the heart of the Gospel that always comes with us when we enter into the pain of our brothers and sisters. We cannot magically heal a person's deepest pain, but we can bring redemptive love to sit alongside that pain. We enter into the woundedness of others and show them the way we found healing in Jesus Christ our Savior and Lord. In other words, we help our brothers and sisters to find healing, and we show them who provides that healing by proclaiming the Good News of salvation.

We all want to find healing and freedom from something in our lives. For some it is a physical ailment, but much more commonly it is the pain of isolation, loneliness, rejection, betrayal, inadequacy, oppression, and other such emotional hurts. When the joy of the Gospel is proclaimed in the context of the pain someone is experiencing, and the hope of something different is offered, then a door is opened to a meaningful, healing encounter with Christ.

Instead of turning to Christ, however, many people look elsewhere seeking deliverance from their pain. Some people turn to addictive behaviors involving drugs, alcohol, food, sex, money, and power. For many others, though, it is the simple satisfaction of short-term relief found in entertainment, social media, or smartphones.

The Gospel brings hope, but it is a hope that claims a stake on our lives. It demands of us self-giving love. When we proclaim the Good News, we cannot hide the fact that the kingdom of God requires great sacrifice from us. Its rewards are often not immediate as it calls us out of ourselves to work for the greater good of reconciling the world to God. Disciples of Jesus put others before themselves, as do the honored guests in the parable of the wedding feast (see Lk 14). People who pursue the kingdom, such as those in the parables of finding the pearl and the hidden treasure (see Mt 13), find the kingdom so valuable that they sacrifice everything else just so they can take part in it.

Once people accept the true promise of the kingdom, things start to fall into place. They begin to taste the peace that comes from giving rather than receiving. They see the failure of other habits and addictions to bring joy and fulfillment and begin to see that only their faith in God will give them rest. Curiosity is sparked and questions follow. Questions are answered in conversations, in books, in lectures, in classes, and in churches on Sundays. Only at this point in a person's journey of conversion is teaching truly effective. It is effective at this point because the person is now motivated to learn and ready to ask more questions. He embarks on a journey of discovery, and we, as teacher-evangelists, can finally introduce him to the doctrinal beauty of the Church.

THE CHURCH EXISTS IN ORDER TO EVANGELIZE

Church leaders have talked and written and read about evangelization so much in recent years that we have placed it in a category of actions all to itself—as if evangelization were one mode

of acting and speaking that ministers undertake completely
separate from the work of other ministries. It would be a very
big mistake to think that only those with offices and titles that
include the word *evangelization* are responsible for it. It can be
easy to separate, in our minds, the good work of managing soup
kitchens or planning weddings or educating children in Catholic
schools from the work of evangelization. But all ministries must
be characterized by an evangelizing spirit, and all efforts at evangelization must be rooted in the ministerial priorities of Jesus.

Evangelization is not something we do in order to proscly-
tize or urge people along a series of steps on a faith continuum
toward discipleship. No, evangelization is built into our very
being as ministers and especially as disciples and servants of
God. We are always evangelizing, even if the primary work we
do has no explicit link to spiritual conversion, education, or open
sharing of our beliefs about God.

Pope Paul VI wrote in *Evangelii Nuntiandi* (Evangelization in
the Modern World) that "the Church exists in order to evangelize" (14). All Catholics are called to evangelize no matter what
we do for a living. With that said, all of us, whether a parishioner,
pastor, youth minister, retreat leader, choir director, eucharistic
minister, DRE, catechist, teacher, or missionary have one primary goal: to lead others into an intimate and transformative
encounter and ongoing relationship with Christ. Evangelization
is a part of who we are as Christians. It is integrated into everything we do. It is not some separate class of actions that only
particular individuals in the Church are able and supposed to do.
It is not reserved to those who make a living as ministers within
the Church, but rather evangelization is the rightful ministry of
all the baptized.

When I talk about parish ministry in this book, I am talking
about evangelization. When I talk about evangelization, I'm

talking about ministry. There is no ministry that is not intended to be evangelizing (characterized by proclamation of the Good News in word and action). And there is no evangelization that is not rooted in the threefold ministry of Jesus to heal, proclaim, and teach.

ARE YOU READY?

This book is divided into four parts. Part I examines the foundations of evangelization found in the Bible and in the Church's documents. Part II explores each aspect of Jesus' threefold ministry (healing, proclaiming, and teaching) and tries to clarify what each means for us today. We will look at saints who have exemplified these forms of evangelization in the past. Their stories will provide a clear vision for what imitating the ministry of Jesus entails and why it still works so well today.

In part III we bring the healing, proclaiming, and teaching framework to the front lines of ministry in the Church today, and I offer practical examples of how to become evangelizers in our everyday lives and ministries. We look at ways in which we can put ourselves in positions to be continually evangelized so that we can go heal, proclaim, and teach people one-to-one and in groups.

Finally, part IV applies the threefold ministry framework to various age groups with case studies of ministries and movements seeing the most success today. We will examine best practices in Catholic evangelization today and provide practical ways in which ministers of every generation—whether children, teens, or adults—can implement the heal, proclaim, and teach approach. In addition to this book, you can find a collection of resources, including video trainings and printable tools, at healproclaimteach.com.

PART I

FOUNDATIONS

1
NEW TESTAMENT ROOTS

Suppose we look at the New Testament as a field manual for evangelization. Within its pages, we have story after story of people's lives being transformed from distant seekers to dedicated disciples. If we look at these stories and the many examples of conversion in the New Testament, we start to see similarities between the situation in Israel two thousand years ago and the situation we are in today.

The Bible gives us more than a historical record of the actions and words of the person who founded Christianity. It is a pathway that leads us to encounter that person. It provides us an opportunity to meet and come to know the living Word of God. It is not just *words* about God. We look to the Bible as the source and inspiration for *all* the work that we do in the Church. To claim the Bible as the source of our inspiration, we can model our ministries after the disciples and the apostles and consider ways in which we can bring people today into relationship with Christ. Or we can imagine ourselves as the people who experienced transformative encounters with Christ and consider how we can engage those who need that experience today.

We can also, if we are willing, consider the ways in which we have become like the scribes and Pharisees who rejected and killed Jesus. This isn't easy to do, but if we truly take the risk of seeing things from the perspective of the Pharisees, we can start to see that their intentions, though misguided, grew from their hope of holding on to their religion. They were afraid, just as many of us today are afraid, of losing a hold on the common beliefs and practices that they always knew and loved.

As we take a close look at various groups of people in the Bible, consider how you might have acted in their situations. This chapter is a kind of lectio divina for a present-day evangelizer. It is meant to guide you in reflection on particular people in the New Testament in order to inspire you to think and pray about how you can become a better disciple. By imagining ourselves in the shoes of these figures, contemplating each person's feelings and motivations, we can learn from them and grow in our own efforts to evangelize, not just in our ministries, but in all aspects of our lives.

JESUS CHRIST

Let's begin with Jesus. Set aside for a moment *what he did*, and consider *why he did it*. For what purpose did Jesus come into the world? Was it simply to spread an idea or even several good ideas? Was it to show the Father's power by great miracles? Was it to correct the Law? Jesus came to announce that the kingdom of God was at hand, that in and through him the world was reconciled to God. He proclaimed that salvation not just with words, but by walking with and loving those who were most vulnerable or pushed away to the margins of society. He came to heal those who were wounded and to free those oppressed. He came as Savior, announcing the kingdom.

The ministry of Jesus was not just about preaching a message; it was about offering life-changing, healing love and bringing new life to a broken world. Consider what Jesus said about himself:

- "I came so that they might have life and have it more abundantly" (Jn 10:10).

- "For God so loved the world that he gave his only Son, so that everyone who believes in him might not perish but might have eternal life. For God did not send his Son into the world to condemn the world, but that the world might be saved through him" (Jn 3:16–17).

- "For the Son of Man has come to seek and to save what was lost" (Lk 19:10).

Jesus came into the world so that we might be reconciled to God and so have eternal life. For this he died on the Cross and rose again. It was in that act that he made eternal *life* possible. He did not die and rise again just to prove a point or to make what he preached and taught more believable. He was not hoping for some additional credibility. He died and rose again in order to make what he preached and taught a reality.

Likewise, our goal as evangelizers is not to pass on a good or even great idea through spectacular preaching and flashy teaching. (Although great preaching and teaching are certainly important to our mission.) Our goal, our purpose, is to introduce others to Christ who will for his part bring salvation and new life within them. We offer people new life when they cannot find fulfillment on their own. We offer salvation in Christ for those who feel lost and without hope. We offer more than an advanced belief system; we offer an answer to their hopes and dreams. We offer them a person.

WHO NEEDED SALVATION?

To whom did Jesus go? Who needed him? There were all kinds of different people in the New Testament who encountered Jesus and decided to leave everything and follow him. Jesus, however, did not appeal to everyone in the same way. For some people he provided healing for their wounds or the sicknesses of their friends and family members. To others, he proclaimed a message that they needed to hear and understand before they could willingly make a commitment to follow him. To a smaller group of people (his disciples), he taught a way of life that he modeled himself; he taught them how to love.

Later we will look more closely at stories of particular people and the encounters they had with Jesus in the Bible. First, though, let's take a broad look at some of the people Jesus ministered to. Let's put ourselves in their shoes and try to understand what it was about Jesus that appealed to them the most.

The Sick

In the New Testament, we find story after story of the healing miracles of Jesus. While these people have differing life circumstances, they share something very important: they are outcasts.

The people Jesus heals are in desperate need physically, but also emotionally and socially. He is doing far more than addressing physical needs in these stories. Whether it is because of their illness (leprosy, hemorrhaging), social status (beggars), or nationality (Roman, Samaritan, Canaanite), the people Jesus heals have been rejected by the Jews and, sometimes, by Jesus' disciples.

All of us at one point or another have been injured or fallen ill. Being sick and suffering physical pain can be an awful experience. Sometimes it can be a socially painful experience, too. If you are contagious, people try to avoid contact with you. They do not want to get sick, too. In a similar way, the many people that Jesus heals in the gospels are separated from society and left to fend for themselves either because of their illness or because of their race or social status.

They come to Jesus because they believe he can heal them, and they take the risk that he might reject them just as they have been rejected by others. Jesus disregards the social and religious barriers and helps them. He touches and speaks with those others deem untouchable. He heals them, and perhaps more importantly, he welcomes them into a community that loves and accepts them. It is through these healing encounters and the experience of the love born there that a new Church was formed.

By looking closely at these stories and recognizing the social situation of the people whom Jesus healed, we find similarities with our own lives of faith. Have we ever felt like outcasts? Were we able to find comfort and acceptance in the Church while other groups of people rejected us? Have we ever doubted others' Christian commitment, even rejected them, because we prefer our own expression of the Faith over theirs? Have we ever turned away from someone who is physically sick or mentally ill out of fear or disgust? It may be that those who feel the most unwelcomed by the Church are the ones in the greatest need of what we have to offer.

The Poor

Without a doubt, Jesus came especially to help the poor. In fact, he "became poor" (2 Cor 8:9), showing others that the way to salvation is to care for the poor: "For I was hungry and you gave me food" (Mt 25:35). He references the poor often as premier examples of faith. For instance, Jesus points to the poor widow who offers only a few cents to the Temple compared with the many rich people who put in large amounts (Mk 12:41–44). Unlike the rich, she gives everything she has to the Temple. She puts all of her faith in God and has nothing else to rely on.

Luke tells us that Jesus came to "bring glad tidings to the poor" (Lk 4:18), and in Matthew 5:3, Jesus declares, "Blessed are the poor in spirit, for theirs is the kingdom of heaven." The kingdom, the same kingdom that Jesus proclaims throughout his ministry, belongs to those who have nothing. Jesus holds the poor in high esteem and loves and serves them. He goes so far as to suggest that those who are rich should give away everything they own to follow him (see Mt 19:16–30).

The poor in the gospels are not just people whom Jesus went out to help and serve; they are the people whom Jesus points to as examples of faith. They are in the best positions to turn to God and follow him. They have nothing to hold them back. In a similar way today, we must look inward to see if attachment to material things is holding back our decision to follow Christ. From there, we can turn to those who are able to live detached from material wealth as people who are primed for reception of the Gospel message.

This is a perspective that has been reiterated in recent years by Pope Francis, who challenges us to be a "Church that is poor and for the poor" and to "let ourselves be evangelized" by the poor (*Evangelii Gaudium*, 198). Take a moment to consider Jesus' challenge for us to be poor. What does it feel like to live in financial poverty? We catch a glimpse of this kind of poverty when it results in homelessness, poor education, lack of adequate health care, and perhaps even addiction or criminal activity. These are the life circumstances often directly resulting from poverty. Economic poverty can also bring helplessness and often hopelessness. Why did Jesus turn primarily to the poor? Perhaps because when we are vulnerable, we cannot help but see our lacking, and our emptiness yearns to be filled. The poor, whether materially or spiritually, have few places to turn for help, and perhaps it is easier for them to see God. When we are rich, with material wealth or simply with overinflated self-assurance, we may not sense a need for God at all.

How should we reflect on the poor in the Bible? Apply the principle of poverty to our own lives. Have we developed any attachment to material things so deeply that we place our trust in them rather than in God? Have we chosen financial or career advancement over service to others? Are we so secure in our capabilities and relationships that we see no lack? Are our hearts in a position to want and need God so desperately that we realize we cannot turn anywhere else for fulfillment and salvation? That is the vulnerable self-reflection we must undergo, and it is the situation we must seek to recognize in others if we hope to evangelize the world.

The Crowds

There are many people in the gospels who have not yet given up their attachment to worldly things. These are the people who hear the proclamation of the kingdom of God but do not understand. These people have a different idea of what the kingdom of God should be. They expect a powerful kingdom that will finally place God's people on the pedestal they deserve. Instead, Jesus preaches a different vision for the kingdom, one that praises those who *do not* seek to stand on that pedestal but instead submit to the possibility of being hung in humiliation on a cross.

Those who hear but do not understand the message of Jesus are referred to in the New Testament simply as "the crowds." They are interested in what Jesus has to say, but they are not yet ready to make a commitment to follow him. The parables that Jesus shares and the people who follow him have clearly shown what this commitment looks like, and the crowds are not yet ready to make it. How can they leave everything they know and follow Christ? How can they detach themselves from their goals and life ambitions? How can they place all their trust in Jesus instead?

Imagine yourself as one of the people in the crowds listening to Jesus preach parables about mustard seeds, treasures buried in the field, and lost sheep. These stories challenge the listener to turn away from all attachment to earthly power, money, and glory and turn instead to a path of faith and humility. Isn't this the same challenge we face today? Like the crowds, we hear the message of the kingdom of God proclaimed often. It is a message that always leads to the cross. The question is: will we be able to turn away from our worldly desires and ambitions and turn instead wholeheartedly to follow Christ, even to the cross?

The Sinners

Jesus was known for dining with sinners and tax collectors. Doing so became one of the biggest criticisms of those who would later seek him out in order to kill him. Associating with sinners might lead one to believe that Jesus is a sinner himself. We know, of course, that Jesus was without sin, and it is for this reason that he spends so much of his time and energy helping the greatest sinners. These people are pariahs in the world of the New Testament. They are outcasts, hated for what they do and who they become. Like the many people that Jesus healed of physical ailments, these men and women are not welcome in their own communities.

Why is it so important for Jesus to minister to the sinners? As he says in response to accusations of spending too much time with the sinners of ancient Israel, "Those who are well do not need a physician, but the sick do. . . . I did not come to call the righteous but sinners" (Mt 9:12–13). Imagine being one of the so-called sinners there dining with Jesus as he said these words. For the first time in a long time you feel okay about yourself. Someone actually considers you worthy of company—something you haven't believed until that moment. Hearing those words, you are willing to leave everything to follow Jesus. You want to respond by turning away from sin, because for the first time someone actually believed you could.

The question we might ask ourselves is whether or not we can or will do that. Will we judge others for the wrongs they have done and separate ourselves from them? Or will we forgive and see the goodness in others despite their imperfections? If we look at certain people and judge them for the way they dress or the cars they drive or for things that they have done, we are condemning them to be outcasts. If we truly do want to evangelize, then we have to be able to motivate people to leave behind lives of sin through mercy, not judgment. We must be able to see them for who they really are so that they can see themselves in new ways, too. This is the model that Jesus has shown us. The only other option is to take on the tactics of the Pharisees, who judged them and turned them away from the community out of fear and undue pride.

The Gentiles

For the people of Israel, the most shocking group of people that Jesus reached may not have been the sick or the sinners but the Gentiles, a term used broadly to describe non-Jewish people of the New Testament. Jesus encounters, heals, and makes disciples out of many Gentiles, including Roman soldiers, Canaanites, Syrophoenicians, and Samaritans. The covenant established with Moses in the Old Testament would only apply to the Jews, but Jesus clearly did not heal only those who shared his religion and ethnicity. He served all those who came to him in faithfulness.

While it was not impossible to become Jewish in the ancient world, it certainly was not easy. Outsiders would have looked at Judaism not just as a religion to join but as a family to join. In the gospels, there were many people referred to as "God-fearers" who probably believed in Yahweh but had not become full-fledged Jews. It is clear by Jesus' actions that the covenant would extend beyond ethnic and religious groups as they existed in his day. The letters of Saint Paul and the Acts of the Apostles reveal that it took some years for the early Christians to work out the details of just what this would mean. Still, without a doubt, Jesus had the Gentiles in mind when he carried out his ministry.

Christianity was not exclusive to just one ethnic group. This distinction may have been the key shift that enabled Christianity to spread so far throughout the world. Anyone could follow Christ and still remain a part of his or her own ethnic group. Had we lived at the time of Christ and been born outside of the Jewish people, Jesus could be just as appealing to us as to those who were born as Jews. We could bring to him our deepest pain and most important desires and find hope in his loving response no matter where we were born or what we grew up believing.

There are many people who do not consider themselves Catholic or Christian but who may still want to find God. We cannot let the labels of religious identity stand in the way of people experiencing a loving encounter with Christ. Remember, we do not have to ask someone to adopt our beliefs. Instead, we offer an encounter, an experience of healing and mercy before God. This also means we should seek to serve everyone no matter what religious affiliation they currently have. Whether it be in our Catholic schools, our soup kitchens, our youth groups, or any number of other ministries, we should welcome all those who come to join us and help them find healing for their wounds, answers to their prayers, and inspiration to learn more about their lives and God's will for them in the world.

The Apostles

Put yourself in Jesus' shoes for just a moment. Think about the leaders he might have been expected to call together. You might imagine that he would seek out the first-century version of a religious dream team. They should have been dynamic preachers and influential leaders in the ancient world, right? But in reality, Jesus chose twelve unlikely men to become his inner circle of disciples. These twelve people—the number twelve representing both the twelve tribes of Israel and a new covenant with a new set of twelve representatives—were ordinary men. They were not experts in the Law. They were not priests. They did not have high status within their communities. They were fishermen, tax collectors, and everyday ordinary guys—and they were far from perfect.

In fact, throughout the gospels, the apostles appear to fail more than they show any signs of success. Jesus constantly has to rebuke and correct them for questioning him, doubting him, or answering his questions incorrectly. They constantly show signs of doubt, especially Peter, whom Jesus calls to leadership. Jesus calls Peter out of a boat during a storm to walk on water with him, but his doubt nearly causes him to drown. Peter denies knowing Jesus at the hour of Jesus' greatest need, even after having been warned that he would be put to the test!

What a comforting example these pillars of the Church set for us! We do not have to be perfect, either. In fact, to be a disciple of Christ it almost seems necessary that we should fail before we can truly follow him. Like the apostles, we all struggle to live up to the standards the Gospel has set for us. We so often fall short. We make mistakes, and we make them frequently. Rather than hide from these mistakes, we should embrace them. In terms of evangelization, this actually has a few benefits.

First, the apostles show us what it takes to be a disciple: lots of mistakes. The very idea of "disciple" means we have to perpetually be learning. There is no learning without making mistakes. The apostles made a lot of mistakes, even in Christ's presence, and learned from them. It wasn't just Peter who made mistakes. Take James and John, for instance. In Luke 9, they mistakenly hope (with Peter) to post tents during the Transfiguration; they are rebuked by Jesus for suggesting that they destroy a Samaritan village. They even start a fight among all of the Twelve about which of them would be the greatest in the kingdom of heaven. In order for us to grow and become Jesus' followers, we will make mistakes, too. In fact, we should expect them.

Second, think of the ways in which their mistakes make the apostles so much more approachable and believable. Clearly, they needed Christ's help and salvation, too! Rather than seeing the apostles as perfect people, those interested in becoming followers of Christ found it possible to find holiness, too. They did not feel as though sanctity was out of their reach. Instead, they could follow in the example of the apostles and, despite their own weaknesses, follow Christ, too.

To do ministry today—ministry that calls for new, evangelizing approaches to the way we interact with others—we must be willing to put ourselves on the line and make mistakes. This may mean trying something new in our traditional ministries. Maybe it means asking another person about an issue or life story she is uncomfortable talking about. We might let our passion and conviction for the way something needs to be done in the Church take us too far and end up alienating others. But whatever our fear of making mistakes, we have to be willing to make them. Knowing that the apostles made mistakes, we must be willing to make them, too.

Embracing our mistakes and admitting them—especially to those with whom we seek to share the Gospel—can have a very positive impact. Religious people can seem inauthentic for their perfectionism and as a result lose their credibility with nonbelievers. The tendency of many Christian leaders is to hide mistakes and vulnerabilities and instead project only the good and commendable things about ourselves. Like the apostles, if we show how we continue to need God's grace, we can open a pathway for others to find Christ. The more genuinely open we are about our mistakes, the more hope we offer others.

The Disciples

Jesus, of course, had more than just twelve followers. In the gospels we read about many people who became dedicated followers of Jesus. We know that while Jesus conducted his ministry, he commissioned and sent out seventy (or seventy-two) disciples two by two to prepare the way for him (see Lk 10:1–24). Mary Magdalene is clearly a disciple with an important role, especially in the story of Jesus' resurrection (see Mt 28, Mk 16, Lk 24, Jn 20). The siblings Mary, Martha, and Lazarus are all crucial (Lk 10, Jn 11). We know that many of the people Jesus encountered and healed become disciples, some leaving everything they know and own to follow him.

Imagine that you were there as one of Jesus' disciples in Jerusalem. You would have followed him around, leaving your home and even your family to come follow him. You left everything—all your dreams, your career, your friends, and everything that gave you comfort. Or, if you did not leave your home, you opened it up for Jesus and his ragtag group of disciples to join you despite earning the disdain of your neighbors and friends.

You would have dedicated your life to following Jesus even to his death in Jerusalem. Along the way, you learned what it meant to be a disciple. He taught you what it meant to give up your life to follow him. He showed you what you needed to do when he was gone. Ultimately, your role would be to make other disciples. The only way to do that is to take up your own cross, just like him, and follow in his footsteps.

Today, as disciples of Jesus, we are called to do the same. We are to set aside our own personal dreams and desires and be able to give them up in order to follow Jesus. Being a disciple always comes with a sacrifice of something we think will be better than following him. God has great plans for us if we just let go and accept them. Like the many disciples in the Bible, we, too, must take a leap of faith and respond to his sacrifice of love for us on the Cross by taking up our own crosses so that others may come to find peace, joy, and happiness in their lives through us.

The Pharisees

Maybe the best way to understand what it means to be a disciple is to understand what a disciple is *not* meant to be. In the gospels, the Pharisees provide a detailed description of what not to do. The Pharisees of the New Testament were experts in the Law of Moses. They were the scholars of the Hebrew scriptures who had become the religious leaders of the Jewish people at the time of Jesus. The very name *Pharisee* expresses in its meaning the warning I believe Jesus was trying to make. In Hebrew, the word *pharisaios* means "separatist" or "purist." In other words, the Pharisees intentionally separated themselves and expected other Jews to separate themselves from anyone who did not share in their purity.

Think about this for a moment. Their very identity was based on the idea of separation and superiority over others. They were experts in religious doctrine, and that made them special compared with those around them. Christ and his disciples, on the other hand, intentionally went out to heal anyone who felt marginalized or separated from the community. Christ proclaimed the Good News of a kingdom in which those who are humble and have little will be given more.

The Pharisees, on the other hand, were religious purists and intentional perfectionists. They used beliefs such as the ban of work on the Sabbath to criticize Jesus for healing those who came to him. They did not associate with sinners, Samaritans, or

Gentiles, and they were shocked when Jesus healed and shared meals with any of these groups of people.

But be careful and do not label the Pharisees as simply the bad guys in the Bible. If we put ourselves in their shoes for a moment, we might find that they are more relatable than we first thought. Imagine the motivations they might have had for acting the way they did toward Jesus and the disciples. What were they afraid of? Other than their desire to be seen and praised as perfect people, they had some good intentions. They were passionate about their beliefs in God and the Law and did not want outsiders to threaten or take away from the beauty that was their faith. Their doctrines were so important to them that they felt threatened by those who did not follow them in precisely the same way.

Are we not tempted by these very same kinds of passions and fears today? There are those in the Church today who take a similar, protective approach to Catholicism. Motivated by fear, they hold fast to the doctrines of the Faith and criticize or complain about the people who question them or ignore them. They blame poor catechesis for the problems in the Church today and try their best to express what they think people really should believe. While it may seem to them as though they are protecting the Faith, they sometimes separate themselves from others as overly pious "purists" who exclude those who do not share their beliefs.

We all face the temptations of becoming modern Pharisees and overshooting discipleship. As we take part in a resurgence of evangelization and discipleship, we must be careful not to create a special class of "true disciples" and evangelizers, which we then elevate to an unrealistic status built on the supposition of purity. To try to distinguish between "real" Catholics and the rest of the Church is not the best use of our energy. The Pharisees saw themselves as a special class of people, or "real" keepers of the

Law, and we will likewise be tempted to do the same by comparing ourselves with others who have not yet fully embraced the requirements of discipleship. Instead, though, take on the real identity of a disciple and embrace imperfection and sinfulness as the path to reuniting ourselves with those who feel excluded from the Church. Sure, you should be praised for the incredible sacrifices you have made in the name of God, but that should not be a reason to separate yourself from others.

SAINT PAUL: THE MODEL EVANGELIZER

To talk about evangelization in the New Testament and not mention Saint Paul would be impossible. He is, of course, the patron saint of evangelists. I bring him up in the context of this chapter, though, not because of his great gifts of preaching or writing. Yes, Saint Paul was a gifted preacher as shown clearly through his many travels described in the Acts of the Apostles. Yes, he was a gifted writer responsible for the majority of the books included in the New Testament. He founded many, many churches in all parts of the Mediterranean and trained many people to lead the communities that he founded.

Saint Paul had many gifts, but the one thing that you would think stood in the way of him being accepted by the Church at all actually became his most redeeming gift. People should have hated Saint Paul. Christians never should have accepted what he said or listened to him. Clearly in the Acts of the Apostles and in Saint Paul's own letters, he was known for his many persecutions of Christians before his conversion. Saint Paul killed people for being Christian. He should have been the least qualified to be one of their leaders.

Imagine that you were a part of the early Church that was persecuted by Paul. He was responsible for the imprisonment and death of many of your close friends and heroes. He was even responsible for the death of Stephen, one of the very first deacons appointed by the apostles. How could you ever trust this man and welcome him into your community when he had done so much to hurt you?

That was exactly what the Church did. Saint Paul's story of a 180-degree conversion is an example for all people who do not feel capable of joining the community of Christians. These grave mistakes kept Saint Paul humble and even more motivated to spread the Good News of Christ's redemption. Saint Paul is a model for all of us as evangelizers, not because of his great gifts of preaching and teaching, but because of his powerful and authentic story. Is there anyone who encountered Paul that could say they were not as worthy as him to be a Christian? Is there anyone who met him that could match his story of sinfulness?

New Christians would have been able to relate to Saint Paul as a fellow sinner and find healing for their mistakes as well. They would have looked to him and his story of leaving everything to follow Christ and found motivation to do the same. They would have listened to Saint Paul teach, knowing the authenticity of his message. They would have been excited to learn as much as they could from him before he traveled to the next community. Saint Paul is a model for all evangelizers because he exemplifies the evangelizing ministry that Jesus modeled for us all: to heal, proclaim, and teach no matter who you are or what you have done in the past.

For additional resources on the New Testament roots of evangelization, visit healproclaimteach.com/chapter1.

2

THE STAGES OF EVANGELIZATION

If we are not careful, we can fall into the trap of thinking of evangelization and even of catechesis as a single event—a moment in time in which a person is "converted." Certainly, all disciples have had and continue to have powerful moments of grace and clarity in their lives. We all have encounters with Christ that become powerful memories and motivating factors for conversion. The encounters, though, are steps along a broader journey toward ultimate union with God. As disciples we help others by providing opportunities for these encounters, but we must think in terms of a journey, not of a singular event.

Depending upon where a person is along his or her journey with and toward God, our work of evangelization requires different approaches. The fully committed disciple hungers for nourishment and seeks opportunities to learn more about God and the Christian way of life. People in this group need catechesis (or what we describe in this book as "teaching") in order to be continually formed as committed disciples. They also need to be continually evangelized to be pushed toward continual conversion and to be healed of the pain of sin and selfishness that never really goes away. This group is the equivalent of the disciples in the New Testament.

Who then are the "crowds" in our world today (see chapter 1)? Who are the people who are not yet ready for teaching (catechesis) and need to be healed or to hear the Gospel message proclaimed so that their hearts can be touched and transformed? First is the large group of people who have lukewarm faith in God. They come to Mass occasionally. They bring their children to religious-education classes or Catholic schools. They even profess faith in God and say prayers when they need him most or feel most grateful. However, they often lack life-changing encounters with Christ that might propel them on a journey toward deeper relationship with him. Rather than catechesis, these individuals need to hear the proclamation of Good News to motivate them along the journey of sacrificial love toward God. In the Church, this is the largest and most crucial group of people to activate and engage.

Among the crowds also are the "Christmas-and-Easter Catholics" and those who have essentially left or never really belonged to organized religion. This is the "spiritual but not religious" crowd that does not find value in church or religion. They are not without hope. Through healing encounters with Christ and motivated by a proclamation of the Good News, these lost can be found. But we need to go out and find them.

In this chapter, we will explore what the Church teaches about the process of evangelization. We will look specifically at how the *General Directory for Catechesis* and the *National Directory for Catechesis* address how evangelization and catechesis work together. We will also examine the catechumenate as the model for all evangelization and catechesis, and end with an exploration of how some current Church leaders have begun to describe the process of discipleship. The goal is to get into a *process mindset* so that the evangelizing ministry you form meets the needs of all people wherever they are along their journeys. Knowing what stage a person is in along the process of evangelization helps to determine if healing, proclaiming, or teaching is most needed in a given circumstance.

EVANGELIZATION IS A PROCESS

The *General Directory for Catechesis* describes evangelization as "the process by which the Church, moved by the Spirit, proclaims and spreads the Gospel throughout the entire world" (48). It summarizes the process of evangelization, drawn from the Second Vatican Council document *Ad Gentes* (The Decree on the Mission Activity of the Church), in the following way:

1. Christian witness, dialogue, and presence in charity (*AG*, 11–12);

2. the proclamation of the Gospel and the call to conversion (*AG*, 13);

3. the catechumenate and Christian initiation (*AG*, 14); and

4. the formation of the Christian communities through and by means of the sacraments and their ministers (*AG*, 15–18).

This is the approach Jesus took in his ministry. He **healed** the marginalized who desperately desired that someone talk to them and to feel someone's loving presence in charity. He called the crowds to conversion through parables that **proclaimed** the kingdom of God, which requires self-sacrifice and conversion. He **taught** and formed a community of disciples, selecting some of them to grow that community through the sacraments he instituted.

THE FIVE STAGES OF EVANGELIZATION

The *National Directory for Catechesis* breaks down the process of evangelization even further into five stages (or moments) of evangelization. Each of these stages is directed toward persons at distinct places along the journey toward discipleship and mirrors in some way some aspect of the threefold ministry of Jesus Christ to heal, proclaim, and teach.

1. Pre-evangelization

During this stage, we prepare a person to hear the "first proclamation" of the Gospel. A person at this point is still not ready to hear the Gospel proclaimed in full. Instead, pre-evangelization "builds on basic human needs, such as security, love, or acceptance."[1] This is, in fact, the very same thing that Jesus did in his ministry. He not only healed the sick of their physical ailments but also met their basic human need to feel welcomed and accepted. Pre-evangelization is the "healing" form of evangelizing ministry we talk about in this book.

2. Missionary Preaching

At this stage a person has yet to fully choose to become a believer. This stage especially includes people who follow other religions, people who believe in God but not religion (theists or agnostics), many people who are relatively indifferent to religion but have not completely turned away from it, and occasionally individuals with no belief in God. For us today, missionary preaching is directed also toward the many people who have been baptized into the Church but lack faith in the person of Jesus Christ. To these many groups of people, we extend an invitation to hear and understand the story of Christ's paschal mystery. To these people we offer the "first proclamation" of God's saving love in the world. This stage of evangelization is unpacked in greater detail in this book as the "proclaiming" form of evangelizing ministry.

The next three stages make up what we refer to as "teaching" in this book. Just as Jesus healed the marginalized (pre-evangelization) and proclaimed the kingdom of God to the crowds (missionary preaching), he also taught his disciples how to be one of his followers (initiatory catechesis, mystagogical catechesis, and continuing catechesis). Before catechesis can occur, however, a person must experience at least the beginnings of a conversion of heart. Conversion goes beyond an emotional feeling of God's love. It is the willingness of a person to make the commitment to respond to that love by setting out on a path of discipleship.

3. Initiatory Catechesis

Those who have encountered Christ's healing love and have heard the true Gospel proclaimed can choose to enter fully into the Church through the sacraments of initiation. This stage of evangelization includes introductory catechesis for those just starting out on their intentional path of discipleship. The RCIA is the most common form of initiatory catechesis, but most of traditional religious education is also directed toward this goal in preparation for the sacraments of Eucharist, Reconciliation, and Confirmation.

4. Mystagogical or Postbaptismal Catechesis

Once a person has received the sacraments of initiation, his or her journey is not over. During this very important stage of evangelization, a baptized Christian is led into a deeper understanding of the life of discipleship he has chosen. No longer is the person just introduced to the Christian way of life; she learns to live and participate in it fully. At this stage, one's personal journey of discipleship is fully inserted into the life of the Church community that walks together on the common path toward intimacy with God. Through study and mentorship, he comes to meditate upon and grow in deeper understanding of the experience of the sacraments, prayer, and the life of faith.

5. Permanent or Continuing Catechesis

This form of catechesis extends to all the faithful disciples living the Christian life today. It is a never-ending activity. We are always in need of growing further in our faith. Without a sacramental goal around which to organize a ministry, it can be difficult to develop offerings that contribute to this ongoing form of catechesis. Nevertheless, parishes find ways to nourish committed disciples by providing adult-education series, retreats, small groups, books, and many other opportunities that fit the unique needs and interests of each person.

The challenge we have as a Church is to meet each person at the appropriate stage along the spectrum of these moments of evangelization. We cannot expect, however, that our "Christmas-and-Easter Catholics" will be attracted by ministries designed only for continuing catechesis. We cannot even expect them to participate in the offerings we have for mystagogical catechesis (if we have any), because most of them have not made the 100-percent commitment to give their lives to God. Instead, we have to do the much more difficult work of *missionary preaching* and even *pre-evangelization* to reach them. In other words, we need to make a constant effort to heal those marginalized from the Church and proclaim the saving Gospel of Christ and the message of self-sacrifice that comes with it.

INSPIRED BY THE CATECHUMENATE

While I am technically a "cradle Catholic," I am also the product of the Rite of Christian Initiation of Children (RCIC), which mirrors in many ways the RCIA. I went through the RCIC when I was in fourth grade—long before most parishes had established a catechetical model to accompany the rite itself. Although I was baptized Catholic, I have more memories of attending the

Baptist church with my grandparents on Sundays than I have of going to Mass.

I recall that at some point during my fourth-grade year I felt called to choose something different while attending Mass. I sat in the pew alone while everyone stood up and walked to Communion. Even some of my friends from school walked up, received the bread, and sat down just like the adults. I asked my mom what I could do to participate, too. She turned to her mother and my grandmother (on the Catholic side) for help. Grandma Mary brought me in to meet with our pastor, who said he would just have a few questions to make sure I was ready. He said that he would schedule a special service where he would announce to everyone that I was going to have my First Communion. That was the plan before he started asking the questions. Here is how it went:

> **Father Ed:** How did we come to celebrate the Mass? Where did it come from?
> **Me:** Um, Communion?
> **Father Ed:** It was something in Jesus' life. He talked about the need to learn more about the Passover of the Jews. Where did we get Communion?
> **Me:** ?
> **Father Ed:** But at your age, Jared, I expect you to know all that. Study a little more and then we'll get together and we'll make arrangements for you to receive Communion.

Needless to say, I wasn't ready for my First Communion. I had no idea what he was talking about (they must have skipped the Last Supper in the Baptist services and Sunday-school lessons I had attended with the other side of my family). I did not even know where to start studying. I am so grateful that my grandmother was there taking notes on the conversation to help me get started. Shortly after that I started the weekly Sunday meetings during Mass to prepare for First Communion with a few other children of various ages.

I made a conscious choice to continue in the Catholic faith. Although I did not realize the full weight of that decision at the time, it set me on a path to where I am today. I am sure I learned so much more as a part of the RCIC experience than I might have learned in second grade just going through the motions like so many others. That conscious choice and willingness to be there made all the difference in the long-term impact of the experience.

One of the most practical and valuable outcomes of the Second Vatican Council has been the restoration of the cate-chumenate. "The model for all catechesis is the baptismal cate-chumenate when, by specific formation, an adult converted to belief is brought to explicit profession of baptismal faith during the Paschal Vigil. This catechumenal formation should inspire the other forms of catechesis in both their objectives and in their dynamism" (*GDC*, 59).

In some ways I was blessed to feel as if I was at the edges of the Church because I was able to make the decision to enter more fully into it. I was able to profess our baptismal faith during the Easter Vigil, fully conscious of what I was about to do. That decision, that ownership, was so crucial to my own personal faith journey. This is how the baptismal catechumenate is supposed to work. While I would never say that parents should take a com-pletely hands-off approach and allow their children at every age to decide whether they would like to receive First Communion or Confirmation, I know we must do a better job of helping both children and adults to participate actively in sacramen-tal preparation rather than just holding out hoops and helping them jump through. Just going through the motions, meeting program-attendance requirements and the like, is simply not doing individuals or the Church much good.

How did I get to the point of personal faith commitment? How do countless others arrive there? The goal is built into the very structure of the RCIA and the RCIC. The baptismal catechumenate is articulated in four stages rather than five. Let us briefly examine each one and put them in the context of the evangelizing methods of healing, proclaiming, and teaching.

Precatechumenate

This is the stage in which evangelization leading up to an initial conversion occurs. It is the stage in which a person is welcomed by members of the Church. During this stage the initial proclamation of the Gospel occurs in crystalized presentation, with simplicity not possible if all the rich theological detail of Church doctrine and creed are presented at the same time.

For me, this stage was experienced most fully in the realization that there was something in the Eucharist that I wanted to experience. I did not want to be excluded anymore, and thankfully, I had the full support of my mother, my grandparents, the pastor of our parish, and the many adult Catholics who knew me. I distinctly remember the mother of one my friends telling me how happy she was for me after the Easter Vigil. It made me proud of what I had done. I felt welcomed by a larger community.

Catechumenate

This stage, according to the *General Directory for Catechesis*, begins the process with the "handing on of the gospels" (*GDC*, 88). Here, as catechists, we continue to proclaim the Gospel by unpacking the stories and readings we read and hear in the Bible. The stories give us the context and capability to understand what it takes to be a follower of Christ.

When I started in the RCIC, I knew very little about the Bible or Church teachings. Being excused from Mass and studying the weekly readings with a group of people was an experience I never would have had without the RCIC. Had I been interviewed by our pastor again about the Bible, I would not have offered such confused answers the second time around. I was no biblical scholar, but I had a much better understanding of the basic stories in the gospels even as a fourth-grader.

Purification and Illumination

During this stage a person prepares more intensely, with a profound focus on spiritual readiness, to experience the sacraments of initiation for the first time. This is when catechumens receive the creed and the Lord's Prayer, in special minor rites, because now they are ready to say and believe the words that they contain.

Here the desire for the Eucharist and full unity with the Church becomes much more intense. I remember being so excited finally to receive the Eucharist and no longer to feel like an outsider at my own church. For me, as a baptized Catholic who might have drifted away as an adult, I had the opportunity fully to embrace the creed and repeat the words of the Our Father in union with Christ and his Church. I did not just go through the motions; I made the sacrifices that came with RCIC to embrace my faith and profess it with confidence.

Mystagogy

This is often the most overlooked stage of the catechumenate, but it is also one of the most important. Once a person has received the sacraments, she begins to unpack the experience and strive to understand its meaning more fully through a period known as *mystagogy*, a Greek word that means "leading into the mysteries." During this postbaptismal period, the encounter with God in the sacraments is explored and its meaning made relevant to daily life within the context of the parish community.

This is something I am not sure we ever fully complete. We are always on the path to greater discovery of the mystery of God found within the sacraments. As you will read in the next chapter, I drifted away from my faith as a child. It was not until an incredible experience of healing before the Eucharist that I once again fully embraced the path I stepped into during my experience in the catechumenate.

BECOMING *INTENTIONAL* DISCIPLES

In her book *Forming Intentional Disciples*, Sherry Weddell provides ministers with a common language to talk about the ultimate goal in evangelization and catechesis. While her terminology does not substitute for the way the Church describes the process of evangelization, it is used frequently by ministers today to help put those stages in the context of discipleship. Weddell describes what she calls "intentional" disciples as people who, like Saint Peter, make a "drop the net" decision to follow Christ.[2]

The distinction has helped many people to realize that discipleship is never accidental, unintentional, or cultural. A person has to choose to become a disciple. All too often, though, people who call themselves Catholic or Christian (and especially those who call themselves "spiritual but not religious") lack the essential "drop the net" decision to become a disciple.

Weddell expresses this process of evangelization by categorizing people along a continuum through five thresholds. They are the following:

- **Initial Trust:** A person makes positive associations with Jesus Christ, the Church, or an individual Christian. He may not trust God at this threshold, but he may trust a believer in God.

- **Spiritual Curiosity:** A person is intrigued and interested in learning more about Jesus Christ but not yet ready to make a personal life change.

- **Spiritual Openness:** At this threshold a person is now open to the possibility of personal change but not yet ready to make the commitment. Here a person recognizes and acknowledges that an intimate relationship with Christ is possible.

- **Spiritual Seeking:** Here a person moves from passive to active seeking to know God and seriously wrestles with the beliefs, teachings, and way of life that come with the commitment of discipleship.

- **Intentional Discipleship:** At this final threshold, a person has made the conscious commitment to follow Jesus Christ and reorients his or her life toward a fully Christian way of living that requires selfless love of God and others.[3]

Weddell reiterates the need to think about the work we do as ministers in terms of where people are along their intimate journey with God. Many people simply do not realize that they can even have an intimate relationship with God. Instead, God is abstract and unknowable to them. Even if a person does believe in God and recognizes that an intimate relationship is possible, making the conscience and life-altering decision to reorient oneself toward the Christian way of life is still a necessary part of the process of evangelization.

Everyone at the thresholds of *initial trust* and *spiritual curiosity* are in deep need of the ministry of healing. That is how we build trust with people. We offer to be there for them without asking anything in return and enable them through our friendship and charity to find peace in their suffering.

When we talk about *proclaiming* in evangelizing ministry, we refer to the proclamation of a message that is both reassuring and challenging. God loves us so much that he gave up his life for us. With that gift comes an invitation to share in that self-sacrificing love. It means leaving the old way of life and becoming someone new. This is why people at both the *spiritual openness* and *spiritual seeking* thresholds need to hear constantly the Gospel proclaimed in new and creative ways. That message will compel them to make the commitment required to become intentional disciples.

Finally, those at both the *spiritual seeking* and *intentional discipleship* thresholds need teaching (catechesis) in order to fully understand what it takes to become disciples. As ministers helping people at these thresholds, we can never become complacent. We have to continually convey Catholicism as a faith full of joy, passion, and love. We must convey the mystery inherent in all doctrine and the life of discipleship as a journey of constant discovery and lifelong learning. Since discipleship requires a person to make a personal and free choice, teaching becomes a ministry of guidance, not instruction. A person making this choice needs help and support more than a dictation of doctrines to be memorized and remembered.

What is the result? By helping people to cross these thresholds, we assist them to prepare fully to become intentional disciples—people who are consciously making sacrifices to follow God as a part of his Church. As we think about this stage of the process, we have to be careful not to label people as "intentional disciples" or "disciples" versus "nondisciples." If we do, we fall into the same trap as the Pharisees, who were criticized in the New Testament for being elitist.

Instead, it may be helpful to think of "intentional disciples" not just as special people who have made the commitment to follow Christ but as people who have made the commitment to follow Christ *and* share his love with others. Even Saint Peter had to make another decision after his initial "drop the net" decision not just to follow Jesus but to share the Gospel. That is why in this book I refer to "evangelizing disciples" as people who have not only made the commitment to follow Christ, but who also recognize that along with that commitment to become a follower comes the call to be a leader. A true disciple of Jesus Christ has accepted his call to "make disciples of all nations" (Mt 28:19).

An evangelizing disciple is what Pope Francis calls a "missionary disciple." A missionary disciple is someone who is committed to evangelization—a commitment that should be held by every baptized member of the Church, not just the professional ministers and missionaries.

> All the baptized, whatever their position in the Church or their level of instruction in the faith, are agents of evangelization, and it would be insufficient to envisage a plan of evangelization to be carried out by professionals while the rest of the faithful would simply be passive recipients. The new evangelization calls for personal involvement on the part of each of the baptized. Every Christian is challenged, here and now, to be actively engaged in evangelization; indeed, anyone who has truly experienced God's saving love does not need much time or lengthy training to go out and proclaim that love. (*EG*, 120)

Evangelizing disciples selflessly seek the good of others by healing, proclaiming, and teaching them to experience the love of God. They are not necessarily doctrinal experts. They do not belong to a special class of disciples. Each of us who has made the commitment to follow Christ is called to evangelizing discipleship. With that commitment comes the need to constantly "mature in our work as evangelizers" (*EG*, 121).

Most importantly, an evangelizing disciple works together with other disciples to carry out Christ's missionary mandate. He does this because of his deep love for God, but also because of a love for those who might not be intentional about their discipleship quite yet. Pope Francis points out that "missionary disciples accompany missionary disciples" (*EG*, 173). That is why we have to constantly remind ourselves not to take on that Pharisee mindset. As intentional disciples we never become better than others or more equipped to do the ministry of evangelization than others. We must always seek to accompany and help our fellow disciples in the common evangelizing mission of the Church.

SUPPORT ALONG THE WAY

Recognizing that evangelization is a process, that people are at various stages along the journey toward an intimate relationship with God, should greatly impact the way we think about our ministries. On this journey, people will either move closer toward a more intimate relationship with Christ or they will move further away. Helping people along that journey requires different approaches at different times along the way.

In the next few chapters, we will look at the evangelizing ministry that Jesus modeled in the gospels and consider the ways in which we can incorporate his different methods into the work that we do and the decisions that we make. If we maintain a *process mindset* when we think of evangelization, we can start to employ the methods of healing, proclaiming, and teaching at various points in our relations with others. We can start to think of our ministries—our *evangelizing* ministries—in terms of these three approaches. Understanding each method will help inform the choices you make in providing opportunities for pre-evangelization, initial proclamation, and ongoing catechesis.

For additional resources on the stages of evangelization, visit healproclaimteach.com/chapter2.

PART II

IMITATING JESUS

3

HEAL

If I had to boil evangelization down to just one very simple goal, it would be this: to help people know they are loved. Our most common and essential spiritual desire is to love and be loved. As Saint Paul wrote, "If I have the gift of prophecy and comprehend all mysteries and all knowledge; if I have all faith so as to move mountains but do not have love, I am nothing" (1 Cor 13:2). Love is the reason you and I are here today. It is where we came from and where we seek to go.

While one might think that the reason so many people leave the Church today has to do with disagreement about Church doctrines, it is actually much simpler. The most commonly cited reason for people leaving the Catholic Church is a simple lack of feeling welcome. Tens of thousands of people are leaving the Church because they do not feel accepted or loved and perceive the Church as a source of rejection and hatred.

This has very important implications for ministry. Before we can say anything about what we believe and ask others to assent to those teachings, we need to show them the most fundamental of our beliefs—that God loves them and we do, too. We need to show people our unconditional love regardless of any doctrinal beliefs that we have come to accept as Christian disciples. Without love, none of our personal gifts—gifts of prophecy, knowledge, or administration—matter. If people cannot trust us because of what we do, how can we expect them to believe in what we say?

Jesus knew this. A very large and important part of his ministry was healing the sick, particularly those on the margins of society. Those healing miracles were more than flashy ways to show off his divine power. Jesus healed a particular set of people who not only suffered from physical ailments but also from deep-seated emotional wounds. These people were marginalized and outcast from society. They were the sick and the poor, or the people of other ethnicities and social groups that were not welcomed by the religious elite of his day. The mission of Jesus, first and foremost, was to make sure the people that he met not only felt loved by him but also felt worthy of that love. He made sure that those who felt like outcasts were welcomed into his new community of disciples.

WHAT HEALING MINISTRY REALLY IS

If you are like I was before writing this book, you are very skeptical about the idea of incorporating healing into our parish ministries. It brings to mind all kinds of images and associations that at times make us uncomfortable. You might be thinking of Evangelical revivals with preachers who bring sick and elderly people up onstage to free them from their ailments. The dynamic preacher with microphone in hand strikes down these ailing persons, and they rise up shouting, "It's a miracle! I'm cured!"

In Catholic circles we hear stories of miraculous healings in charismatic renewal gatherings, large and small. I am not discounting these miracles. I do not discount the power of the Holy Spirit to work miracles in our physical bodies. I do not intend to take away from this long tradition of healing in the Catholic Church. At the same time, I want you to believe that no matter what kind of Christian disciple you are or what kinds of gifts you possess, you are capable of bringing healing into the lives of the people you serve. You are because you and I and all of us are called to be Christ's presence in the world. And he brought healing—on many levels.

The kind of healing I focus on in this book is one that anyone can administer. You will not need to obtain some great spiritual gifts or the ability to work miracles. Supreme holiness is not required; in fact, trying too hard to be holy might actually work against you. The kind of healing I describe in this book requires us to be *sinners*, not saints. It requires us to expose our weaknesses so that others can be open about their weaknesses, too.

When I talk about healing in reference to evangelizing ministry, I am talking about inner healing of the wounds that we often cannot see but that hold us prisoner anyway. These wounds often are intensely painful. Many emotional and spiritual wounds are caused by events beyond the injured person's control, but others come because of sin. These sin-spawned wounds separate us from God and other people. They haunt us and tell us we are not good enough, not worthy enough, and not important enough to be loved by others, even God. Often the wounds caused by sin need the most healing and are the most difficult to confront as ministers of Christ's healing love. "Which is easier," Jesus asked, "to say, 'Your sins are forgiven,' or to say, 'Rise and walk'?" (Mt 9:5).

But we are all in need of healing mercy, every one of us. We are born into a world in which we cannot avoid the inner pain of being rejected by others. Again and again we make mistakes and hurt those around us, even those whom we love the most. The pain of separation, isolation, and loneliness, and the frustration of not being good enough, plagues us all, some more than others.

Jesus showed us the way to make disciples. Disciples are people who learn from Christ. They are in an intimate relationship with God and have faith as a response to a loving act that they have experienced and internalized in their hearts. Healing in our evangelizing ministries is all about providing people with the opportunities to have that loving encounter with God today. Tending to those who need healing is step one on the road to making disciples, no matter what ministries we do.

In this chapter we will look at a variety of healing encounters from the New Testament and explore the kind of healing and the transformation that occurred in each. We will see that these stories reveal benefits beyond the physical healings for which they are best known.

Then we will consider ways in which we, like Jesus, can become healers. We will begin by drawing from a concept originally coined by Swiss psychiatrist Carl Jung and explored deeply by Dutch-born priest, professor, and spiritual writer Henri J. M. Nouwen in a book titled *The Wounded Healer*. Nouwen writes about healing ministry truly being fruitful only when it is done by "wounded healers." That is what we are called to do—find in our own wounds the source of healing and from that source reach out to others who are hurting. This identification of ourselves as wounded healers will shed light on the evangelizing ministry of some of the great saints of the Church who show us the way to touch the hearts of others. From their stories, I formulate principles by which we can begin to identify opportunities to help heal those closest to us and to bring healing to our ministries.

JESUS THE HEALER

There are many stories from the ancient world of great figures healing the blind and raising the dead. Jesus was not the only person written about in these terms. So what makes Jesus different from the others?

You will find that the people Jesus heals in the gospels were not necessarily the people suffering from the greatest physical pain. Instead, they were the people who suffered from the deepest emotional pain, caused by rejection and separation from their communities. Jesus healed the marginalized of their physical wounds and helped them to be welcomed by his community of disciples. Those healed were transformed and dedicated themselves to following Christ, and they also found acceptance.

The Cleansing of the Leper
(Mt 8:1–4, Mk 1:40–45, Lk 5:12–16)

Leprosy in the Bible most likely referred to a variety of skin diseases or ailments. In the Old Testament, the book of Leviticus makes it very clear that a person with leprosy is to be excluded from the community. With very detailed descriptions of what constitutes "clean" and "unclean" (Lv 13–14), priests are given instructions on how to inspect those with leprosy in order to determine if they were contagious or not. If they were found to be contagious, they were cast out of the camp. If they recovered, then they could be welcomed back into the community by being shown to a priest who would purify them with a ritual washing.

Imagine what it must have been like to have leprosy in the ancient world as a Jew. Not only would you have had to deal with the physical pain or discomfort, but your family, friends, and religious community would also force you to remove yourself from your village or city. You would have been declared unclean and unable to associate with the healthy people whom you knew and loved.

In the New Testament, when a leper comes to Jesus for healing, people are naturally upset. Yet, in a subtle and powerful gesture, Jesus reaches out his hand and touches the man with leprosy. Imagine this physical embrace. Before this act, no man or woman would dare touch this leper for fear of catching the disease. But Jesus reaches out his hand and touches the man, speaking the words, "Be made clean" (Mt 8:3).

The man is healed and sent by Jesus to a priest so that he can officially be welcomed back into the community. The leprosy is gone, but more importantly, this man is restored as an acceptable member of society. The command to "go show yourself to the priest" (Mt 8:4) is a symbolic one and an important gesture to point out because it illustrates what happens through the healing work of Christ. The leper is welcomed back into the community from which he was cast out. He does not have to feel alone anymore.

And what happens as a result? The man tells everyone, and the reputation of Jesus spreads. Because of this healing encounter with Christ, the man tells the world all about the One who healed him. He becomes a disciple and is eager to share his personal story of encounter with Jesus. Others come to witness Jesus' healing work for themselves, and the crowds gather in increasing numbers wondering what this man is all about.

The Centurion's Servant (Mt 8:5–13, Lk 7:1–10)

Jesus heals many people for their great faith, but for some he heals the ones they love as well. A centurion, who was a soldier in command of one hundred men, came asking Jesus to heal his servant. The fact that the centurion, a Roman soldier and a Gentile (non-Jew), came to Jesus for help is a detail we cannot overlook.

Like Jesus, we must serve those who need help not because of who *they* are but because of who *we* are. We must serve all who come to us in faith, not just the inner circle or the dedicated members of our communities. The Jews who witnessed this healing miracle of a Roman soldier's servant must have been upset. Many of them disdained Roman rule over Israel and wanted nothing to do with the foreigners. Healing a Roman soldier would send the wrong message: it would claim that these Romans were as loved by God as the people of Israel.

It is from this story that we get the prayer said just before receiving the Eucharist at Mass: "Lord, I am not worthy that you should enter under my roof; but only say the word and my soul shall be healed." We all approach Jesus in humble petition and openness to his healing touch. No matter who we are or where we come from, whether we are outcasts or frequent members of God's Church, we come to him with the same humble unworthiness. We are never worthy, yet we come to ask for his healing so that we can be united with him and in communion with others in the Church.

The Samaritan Woman at the Well (Jn 4:4–41)

I am cheating a little bit on this one, but the story of the Samaritan woman at the well is one the best stories of individual conversion from outcast to disciple in the Bible. The Samaritan woman was not physically sick. She did not need to be healed of any disease. She did, however, share in the suffering of the sick individuals that Jesus healed because she, like they, was an outcast. Not only was she a Samaritan, a group mistrusted and disdained by the Jews, but she was also a public sinner, having had five husbands and now living with another man who was not her husband. It was her sin that separated her from the rest of the people in her town.

Jesus approaches the woman, points out her sin, and invites her to drink of the "living water" of which those who drink will never thirst again (Jn 4:14). Jesus is inviting her to be healed of the wounds of her sin and to turn away from all that she has done wrong. Through this conversation, the woman finds acceptance and recognizes Jesus as the Messiah. The conversation leads her to conversion.

The end of the story reveals how evangelization really works. The woman's life is changed, and she testifies to others who in turn believe in him because of her testimony. Specifically, John says, they came to believe because she said, "He told me everything I have done" (Jn 4:39). The woman had more to share than just a physical healing; she found healing through the exposure of her sin. It was a freeing moment in her life. She could now be totally herself and unafraid to turn away from sin. She did not have to try to hide anymore. Instead, she went out to others and brought them into the community of disciples.

Blind Bartimaeus (or the Two Blind Men) (Mt 20:29–34, Mk 10:46–52, Lk 18:35–43)

In the gospels of Matthew, Mark, and Luke, Jesus performs his final healing miracle on his way to Jerusalem while he is passing through Jericho. There he encounters a blind man named Bartimaeus. (Matthew refers to two blind men, and Luke writes of an unnamed blind man, but Mark offers the name Bartimaeus, which means "son of Timaeus.") Bartimaeus is on the roadside begging. People do not like him. When he asks who is passing by, they all tell him to be silent.

Like the other healing stories we have explored, the person in need of healing is an outcast. Bartimaeus is blind and a beggar. People ignore him and expect Jesus will ignore him, too. Bartimaeus needs more than his sight. He needs to be loved.

Despite the scorn of those around him, Bartimaeus calls out all the more, asking for Jesus to have pity on him. Jesus hears him, calls him, and heals him. The man can see, but that is not all. "Your faith has saved you," Jesus tells him (Mk 10:52). The physical infirmity is healed, but he receives salvation as a result of this encounter. Jesus does not say, "Your faith has *healed* you." He says, "Your faith has *saved* you."

What happens at the end of the story? The man follows Jesus on the way. Healed by Christ and shown love for what may be the first time in his life, Bartimaeus follows Jesus into Jerusalem toward the conclusion of his mission. Bartimaeus, many other disciples like him, and the apostles follow Jesus to the Cross.

THE SUFFERING SERVANT

What can we learn about Jesus by *whom* he healed and *how* he healed them? When Matthew first describes the healing ministry of Jesus, he places the miracles within the context of a passage from the prophet Isaiah. This passage is the key to understanding how we, too, can emulate the healing ministry of Jesus Christ. It is from a section of Isaiah that refers frequently to the Suffering Servant: "Yet it was our pain he bore, our sufferings he endured" (Is 53:4).

When we think of Jesus as the Suffering Servant, we think of his passion and Cross. In fact, we hear from that Isaiah passage during the Good Friday liturgy. Jesus, God-made-man, suffered for us to take away our sins. As we read in the first letter of Peter, "He himself bore our sins in his body upon the cross, so that, free from sin, we might live for righteousness. By his wounds you have been healed" (1 Pt 2:24). But Matthew makes it clear that Jesus also bore our suffering during his healing miracles. He took away the infirmities of the men and women he healed, and he *bore their pain*. He entered into their pain with his own heart and shared their burdens. When Jesus heals, he carries our pain and frees us from its burdens.

Let us briefly recall one last miracle story in the Bible. Remember what happened in the story of Jesus raising Lazarus from the dead? Remember what Jesus did when he heard about the death of his friend? John tells us "Jesus wept" (Jn 11:35). It is the shortest verse in the Bible and one of the most powerful ones.

When Jesus performed healing miracles, he bore the pain of those he healed with tender love and mercy. It hurt him to see the people he loved suffering the pain of illness, but even more so the pain of separation and isolation. Jesus was a great healer because he showed compassion and mercy to those most vulnerable, no matter where they came from or what they had done.

HOW JESUS HEALED ME

We all have moments of rejection. Like the people Jesus healed, we experience the excruciating pain of feeling left out. One particular moment in my life, more painful than any other up to that point, occurred during the summer of my freshman year of high school. It was a Friday night and the beginning of a weekend festival in my hometown. Living just a few blocks away from the event, I walked up to join the fun hoping to run into some friends.

When I got there, I saw a group of classmates talking in a circle. You could say they were the "popular" kids in school. I didn't know where to find my close friends that night (this was before cell phones), so I walked up to join the conversation. I tried to ease my way into the circle, but it was as if I didn't exist. No one said hello or invited me into the conversation. They gave me annoyed looks and physically turned away from me.

I was devastated. I immediately walked back home and headed to my room. I was never really an emotional guy, but I cried that night for a long time. I felt as if I was nothing. I felt so bad for myself and the hopelessness of my situation. It felt as though no one loved me, as if I were unlovable.

At that time, I had more or less stopped believing in God. After a year in high school, I had decided that I was smarter than religious people—too smart to believe God was real. I couldn't see any proof that he existed. But I did think that the rules and Commandments made a lot of sense, and the people in the Church were nice enough to trust. If nothing else, they accepted me for who I was. So, when I was invited to join our parish youth group on a retreat at the Franciscan University of Steubenville, I agreed.

It was a completely new experience for me. If you have ever been to a youth conference such as the ones in Steubenville, you know what I mean. The praise and worship time with singing and hand motions seemed so strange and funny to me as an outsider. They all looked ridiculous, but they were clearly having fun. After a few sessions, I joined in, too, telling myself that I was just mocking them anyway. On the second night there was a "holy hour" of eucharistic adoration led by Fr. Dave Pivonka, and in that hour my life was changed.

During adoration that night, I heard all kinds of things that seemed crazy to me—it was, after all, a charismatic conference. There was crying and laughing and speaking in tongues. I did not feel anything myself, but I decided to be open to the experience. I closed my eyes, put my head down, and told God that if he was real, I would really like a sign from him. I will never forget what happened a few moments later. I felt what seemed to be a cool wind blow over me and experienced a peaceful chill down my back. All of a sudden, I recalled that night of the festival and remembered vividly—as if I was back there crying in my bedroom again—how I felt when I was excluded by that circle of popular kids. Then, I felt God say to me, "Jared, when you feel like that, turn to me."

I was healed that night. I had a reason to believe that God was real and, like the blind men Jesus healed in the gospels, I immediately followed him. I was so grateful, so touched, and so inspired that I changed my life from that point on. I became very involved in youth group, started reading the Bible to learn

everything I could about God, and even began watching the
Catholic television channel EWTN so I could immerse myself in
Catholic culture and beliefs. God lit a fire in me, and I responded
by seeking him with passion in every way I could.

WOUNDED HEALERS

I would not have gone on that trip if not for the youth ministers
and fellow teenagers who invited me and made me feel welcome.
I felt comfortable with them and able to open up about what
I had going on in my personal life. If it were not for them, I
never would have experienced that first moment of grace-filled
healing.

As ministers and members of the Church, as Jesus' disciples,
we are called to be healers just like Jesus. We do not heal in the
sense of casting out demons or making the blind see. We heal by
meeting people in their emotional wounds of sin and separation.
This is the first and most essential step in evangelization, even if
it does not at first seem like evangelization at all.

One of the most important books written about evangelization in the twentieth century does not even include the
word *evangelization* within its pages. It is called *The Wounded
Healer* by Henri J. M. Nouwen. Nouwen's thesis in the book
is that the Christian leader and minister of the contemporary
world must become what he refers to as a "wounded healer"
in order to see any success in ministry. As a wounded healer,
a minister is "called to recognize the sufferings of his time in
his own heart and make that recognition the starting point of
his service," which "will not be perceived as authentic unless it
comes from a heart wounded by the suffering about which he
speaks."[1] Remember: How did Jesus heal? He "bore our pain" as
a wounded healer. Likewise, in order for us to heal others, we
have to enter into that pain ourselves.

All too often church leaders spend their time focusing on creating popular programs for people to join, trying to purchase the best curricula and the best educational series, or bringing in the best motivational speakers and retreat leaders to inspire the people they serve. It is much easier to turn to the tools and experts to do the work of evangelization for us than it is to risk doing it ourselves. As Christian leaders, we often forget that it is our personal interaction with others that makes a far more lasting impact than anything or anyone we could bring in from the outside. As wounded healers, Christian leaders are called to focus more on their ability to enter into the pain of another in order to help them find healing. It takes guts, and you never walk away without being changed by entering into that pain with others.

Authenticity is required. Saint Paul is constantly self-effacing and critical about his worthiness as a disciple. Constantly he reminds us that he is "foremost" among sinners (1 Tm 1:15). This is, in fact, his greatest strength. It makes him approachable. He is not some perfect, untouchable celebrity Christian preacher of the Mediterranean; he's Paul, a sinful man who opens himself up to God's will. We should be inspired to do the same.

Remember the key difference between Pharisees and disciples? Pharisees try everything possible to appear perfect. Jesus criticized these "hypocrites" (scribes and Pharisees) who give alms, pray, and fast so that others may see them (Mt 6:1–18). The Pharisees hid behind a facade of perfection and would not let anyone threaten the image of perfection they projected.

Disciples, on the other hand, make mistake after mistake in the Bible. You have to wonder as you read the gospels if they really had the ability to lead the Church after Jesus was gone. Look closely at the Gospel of Mark, and you will be hard-pressed to find any redeeming qualities in the apostles! How can this be? Mistakes and wounds are what give them strength. They are not perfect, unreachable saints who are blessed with special powers. They are just ordinary men who responded to God's calling to them.

As disciples and ministers, we are not called to be perfect. In fact, we are called to be just who we are—imperfect witnesses to the Gospel. Others will approach us with trust because of our wounds. Rather than push them away with guilt and unworthiness, our mistakes and missteps show that we are human just like everyone else. Any attempts to cover up our mistakes and weaknesses will be exposed and discredit us as true disciples.

OBSTACLES TO HEALING

Wounded healers have wounds. They have made mistakes and suffer from them. They have been hurt by others and carry that pain or at least a memory of that pain. This suffering might be seen as a curse since it is certainly difficult to bear, but the suffering is also a gift that enables us to walk with others on a common journey to joy. The problem is we have a hard time embracing this fact.

Alleviating the Pain: Denial

When people are in extreme physical pain, doctors prescribe painkillers. The hope is that the pain will go away, at least for a little while. People can become so used to the numbing of their pain that an addiction forms and they continue to take the painkillers long after their pain is gone. They have become numb.

Many people turn to extended use of prescription drugs to numb not only physical but also emotional pain; others turn to alcohol, food, sex, money, overconsumption of material goods, social media, video gaming, or power. These can all provide addictive relief to various kinds of emotional suffering.

Sometimes it takes years to realize that these things do not provide perpetual relief to the pain. But at some point, most people hit rock bottom. They get in so deep with the addiction that they have nowhere to go but up, and in the excruciating pain of humiliation and desperation, many reach for God.

Jesus is not a painkiller. He does not numb our suffering. Instead, he draws near and suffers with us. Through his passion and death on the Cross, he was ridiculed and rejected. He was mocked and beaten. He knows what it is like to experience physical pain and to feel utterly abandoned. He was given the opportunity to numb his pain while on the Cross, but he declined. Jesus heals our pain because he bore pain in his human body upon a cross and so became the model for all evangelizing ministry today.

Like Jesus, we have to be authentic and brave enough to feel pain in order to let Jesus heal us and free us to help others heal. It is much easier to ignore our pain and the suffering of others or say things like, "Everything is going to be all right," or, "Things happen for a reason." It is a natural reaction to want to comfort people by telling them things will be fine if they just suffer through it. So we say things to try to get them to think about something else.

Instead, in order to help others find healing, we need first to be willing to feel their pain and walk with them, or simply to sit with them through it. We cannot rush the resurrection. Often what we and others who are wounded need most is simply company through our own Good Fridays. We have to be willing to be wounded healers. Changing the subject or hiding the painfulness does not help anyone feel better but ourselves.

Avoiding the Pain: Deceit

As mystic monk Thomas Merton put it: "For me to be saint means to be myself. Therefore the problem of sanctity and salvation is in fact the problem of finding out who I am and of discovering my true self."[2]

Very often we try to be something we are not because it fits into the mold of who we think we should be, particularly who we should be as Christian leaders. We do our best to hide sins and mistakes and even incidental imperfections. We work hard to appear sublime and saintly. We gloss over the truth and portray ourselves as having everything all figured out; we seek to convey that we are immune to bad choices and repeated destructive behaviors. When fleeing from the opportunity to enter into another person's suffering, we may be tempted to deny our own sinfulness and other human weaknesses.

For years I strove to appear perfect to my students in Catholic schools and in parish religious-education classes. I pretended to be perfect and extra-holy, while in my personal life I struggled with sin and poor prayer habits. In class I did everything I could to be professional and to be an example for the kids, but in real life I often made mistakes and failed to practice what I preached and taught.

A few years ago as an eighth-grade catechist, I realized that I had gone the entire year without really teaching with testimony. I offered activities and lessons but not my own personal stories of struggle with faith. My eighth-graders knew their stuff. They were prepared for the bishop's pop quiz during their Confirmation Mass, but I couldn't say for sure if they knew why it was all important. This is the reason I believe so many young people struggle to find God in religious-education classes in parishes and Catholic schools. The students do not have enough teachers and catechists acting as witnesses to show them the way to encounter God despite all the difficulties in doing so. As I wrote in the introduction to this book, I am as guilty as anyone for this shortcoming in evangelizing children.

The more we try to conceal our weaknesses, the more distant other people will remain. The more we admit our weaknesses to others, the easier it will be for them to relate to us. In short, we need not to deceive but to be transparent, honest, open—ready to connect with others in our common woundedness. Without our willingness to be vulnerable, God's strength cannot be known.

UNITY IN BROKENNESS

Many people have a hard time relating to the Church. They don't feel comfortable. They don't feel worthy enough or "holy" enough to be there. Going to church makes them feel uncomfortable because they have a hard time relating to the people there. It seems to them that the Church is for the very pious, not for people who are struggling through life just trying to make ends meet. The saints on stained-glass windows and depicted in statues seem extra-holy, like superhuman people whom ordinary people could never ever become themselves.

All saints were sinners at some point. In fact, even while they lived saintly lives they recognized their own imperfections. Take Saint Thérèse of Lisieux, for example, who wanted so desperately to be a nun at a very young age that she even dared personally to request special permission directly from the pope to join the convent earlier than prescription allowed. She seems entirely unrelatable, right? Actually, if you read her autobiography, *The Story of a Soul*, you find page after page of her inner struggle with sin. Saint Augustine's autobiography, *The Confessions*, shares his story of struggle with sin. All saints were at one time sinners and remained sinners even in moments of holiness. They were never perfect. In fact, it was often in their weakness that God was able to work through them in most striking ways.

When it comes to religion, we find unity in our brokenness before we find unity in our holiness. The more we try to display our perfections above our brokenness, the less likely people are to connect with us. We are all sinners—all of us, even the most holy ones among us. This should give everyone hope for acceptance into the Church. And it should shift the way we see others who want to be welcomed into our community as newcomers and outsiders.

The healing that we can offer others through the Church starts on the common ground of brokenness. Through the recognition of our common brokenness we realize we do not have to feel alone. We can find healing from the pain of sin and separation through communion with others. In this way, the Church heals the world—not through physical miracles, but through the imperfect outreach by the members of the Body of Christ, each one of us, laying bare our own unique stories of suffering.

FIND YOUR OWN CALCUTTA

At this point in the book, you might be thinking that you should leave your ministry and do something that is more healing-focused, such as prison ministry or helping the homeless. If that truly is your calling, then by all means pursue it; but just make sure that the fear of healing the people in your care right now is not the real motivation for jumping ship. You might be called to do something else, but there is no reason why you cannot start where you are now, even if you are working in teaching ministries such as children's catechesis or adult faith formation.

I can think of no better example of someone who shifted from teaching-focused ministry to healing-focused ministry than the beloved Blessed Teresa of Calcutta—Mother Teresa. We have all heard of her and know of her great deeds in the world, serving the poor and founding the Missionaries of Charity, but you may not know her full story and what led her to her remarkable work in the slums of Calcutta, India.

When eighteen-year-old Agnes Bojaxhiu moved from Albania to India to join the religious Sisters of Loretto, she felt called to be a teacher. She worked in a school for twenty years, eventually becoming the principal and an influential leader in Catholic education. Then, on the way to an annual spiritual retreat, something changed. She described later that she felt a call within the call to leave teaching and serve the poorest of the poor. While she worked in education, the poverty of those around her took a toll on her heart. When she felt the call to leave teaching and instead serve the poor and sick, she took action.

Leaving the comforts of her home and school, Sister Teresa went into the streets to be present to the poor and sick in Calcutta. She took basic-training courses in medicine and began to serve those in greatest need. She started with nothing and even had to beg for her own food and shelter, having separated from her religious order. Soon, though, she gained a following and with a group of women founded the Missionaries of Charity who, in addition to the customary vows of chastity, poverty, and obedience, vowed to serve explicitly the "poorest of the poor."

The mission of her order is about more than service to the poor and treatment for the sick. When accepting the Nobel Peace Prize, she received it in the name of "the hungry, the naked, the homeless, the crippled, the blind, the lepers, *all those people who feel unwanted, unloved, uncared for throughout society, people that have become a burden to society and are shunned by everybody*."[3]

Think back to the healing stories of Jesus we reviewed at the beginning of this chapter. Remember that Jesus healed those particular people not only because they felt physical pain but also because they were outcasts. Mother Teresa did not create a healing ministry only to alleviate physical suffering (she was even criticized for not providing more medicine to ease physical pain), but to heal the pain of isolation and loneliness that poverty and illness create.

Before you buy your ticket to Calcutta, however, heed the words of Mother Teresa. When someone asked her if he should come to Calcutta to serve the poor, she reportedly wrote back: "Stay where you are. Find your own Calcutta. Find the sick, the suffering and the lonely right where you are—in your homes and your own families, in your workplaces and in your schools."[4]

I believe she was talking to you and me. We do not have to travel the world or go on a mission trip to do missionary work. There are people in your own home, at work, in your neighborhood, in your parish, and in your youth group, class, or Bible study who need to find healing from the deep wounds of loneliness. Start with them and—to use another one of my favorite quotes attributed to Mother Teresa—"never worry about the numbers. Help one person at a time and always start with the person nearest you."

To me, "find your own Calcutta" means starting where we are and seeing how we can heal those under our care right where we are. Who are the people in your ministry who feel unwanted, unloved, and uncared for? How can we develop a relationship with them in order to help them find healing for their wounds? If you really want to emulate Mother Teresa and the Christ she emulated, then start where you are and help heal the pain of the people right in front of you.

HEAL WITH HUMILITY AND HELP

Helping people find healing for their deepest wounds is a lot to ask of us. The very idea seems impossible and even stressful to consider. Rest assured, it is not you who does the healing. Instead, we constantly turn to God and the saints for help. With humility we recognize that it is Christ who heals those around us. With Christ's help, we can humbly lead our brothers and sisters to the healing miracles they need the most. This is a lesson we can learn from one of the most famous North American healers: the Miracle Man of Montreal.

A young, uneducated, and sickly man arrived at Notre Dame College in Montreal to join the Congregation of Holy Cross novitiate in 1870. Initially, he was turned away. His health was so poor that he was not expected to make it through formation. Besides, he could hardly read or write at all. The young man, with the help of his mentor, Father André Provençal, appealed to the local bishop and was eventually accepted into the congregation. He took the name André—André Bessette—after the priest who guided him there. While they did not know it at the time, they had just accepted into their community the first Congregation of Holy Cross saint.

Brother André was assigned menial tasks and responsibilities, including the duties of porter (the gatekeeper), a post that he held for forty years. In his later years, thinking back to his initial rejection and subsequent duties, he said, "When I first came to the college, I was shown to the door . . . and I remained there for forty years!"[5] He never quite earned the respect of his fellow religious brothers and priests, even after miraculous events began to happen around him.

In addition to serving as porter, Brother André served in the hospital. It was there that miracles started to occur. On one occasion he called a sick young boy "lazy" and told him to get up and go play with the other boys. The boy got up and went to play, leaving no trace of the illness that brought him there. It was this kind of unwavering confidence that a person was or would later be healed that characterized many other stories of Brother André's healing encounters. He would tell people matter-of-factly that they were healed, or he would rub oil or medals on their wounds and encourage them to pray to Saint Joseph.

Just as Jesus was criticized and rejected for his healing work, Brother André was rejected by his colleagues at the college. The local doctor in particular lashed out against him. He called Brother André "Old Greaser" and "Old Smear," referring to the oil he used to heal the sick. This all changed, however, when the doctor's wife, who had become ill, asked him to bring Brother André to heal her. At first he refused, but eventually, for the love of his wife, he relented. Brother André visited her, and miraculously she was healed. The doctor never criticized him again.

Brother André lived an exemplary life that transformed the lives of others. It is clear that the miraculous work attributed to him is due to his deep humility and faith in God. He never took credit for the miracles. In fact, he thought the very idea that he was able to cure anyone was absurd. He was even known to come to tears of sadness when people attributed the miracles to him: "How can people be so foolish? How could anyone believe that I, Brother André, poor and ignorant as I am, might heal them, or perform miracles? Well, I don't. The Good Lord is the only author of all these miracles."[6]

As you set out on this journey to heal the wounds of those who feel left out and unloved, remember that it isn't really us who does the healing. We have to be humble in order for this to work. Like André Bessette—who was beatified in 2010—we cannot expect to do any kind of healing work—even emotional healing—through our hard work alone. It is always God who does the healing, not us. We are simply humble servants bringing people to the Lord for help. The moment we think of ourselves as the ones doing the good work is the moment we lose our ability to be healers.

HAVE THE COURAGE TO HAVE COMPASSION

When an outbreak of leprosy hit the Kingdom of Hawaii in the mid-1800s, the reaction was not unlike the response of the people of Israel in the Old Testament. Thinking that leprosy (Hansen's disease) was highly contagious, the kingdom passed a law that banished anyone with the disease to the island of Molokai. More than eight thousand people were banished to the island, isolated from their families and friends.

With so many people in the colony, the local bishop realized he needed to send a priest to minister to the people. Father Damien de Veuster (known to us as Saint Damien of Molokai) was the first among four priests to volunteer. While there, he did more than the typical work of a priest. He dressed wounds, cared for the sick, and started building homes, orphanages, and a church. Many of the people in the colony, realizing their hopelessness, turned to alcohol, partying, and apathetic inactivity in response to their fear of death. On one occasion, Father Damien was said to have gone into a remote place on the island called "the crazy pin" to break up the drinking and dancing of the people there.

Saint Damien was a welcoming and compassionate man. He provided hope for the people in the colony, and his work became known worldwide. The secret to his success, though, could be characterized by how he described his ministry to his brother in a letter: "I make myself a leper with the lepers to gain all for Jesus Christ."[7] Likewise, we are called to do the same. We are all called to become like those we serve—to recognize that we are no better or worse than anyone else. As Pope Francis wrote, "Evangelizers thus take on the 'smell of the sheep'" (*EG*, 24).

Saint Damien was a courageous, wounded healer. He did not let disease and the fear of getting sick stop him from serving those suffering from isolation in Hawaii. He became one of them, was accepted by the people there, and walked with them through the darkness. After ten years working in Molokai, he contracted the disease. His sharing in the emotional wounds of the people there was now matched with sharing their physical pain. Saint Damien died in 1889, the "apostle to the lepers" and a "martyr of charity."

Can you imagine volunteering to serve on an island full of people with a contagious disease that is surely going to be your death sentence? I cannot even imagine the fear I would have experienced arriving there for the first time. Saint Damien approached them with love. He had courage to make himself vulnerable so that others would see the power of God. May we all have the courage to put ourselves at the risk of pain by trying to heal the pain of others.

MIRACULOUS HEALING TODAY

We looked at miracles in the New Testament and miracles at the hands of great saints in the Church's history to show a deeper purpose behind those miracles. Miracles of physical healing are precious gifts, signs of God's mercy and love. But it is dangerous to rely on these kinds of miracles as the only evidence of God's healing mercy. The majority of disciples today experience a different sort of healing.

Powerful moments of conversion often involve an experience best described as healing. Many people return from a retreat, for example, sharing an experience of "being healed" of emotional wounds, conflicts, or challenges that they had never dealt with properly. Many of these individuals had been avoiding the pain, but during the retreat they could not avoid it any longer. God brought it to the forefront of their experience and offered his healing touch. This was my experience of healing and the same experience of so many others who have encountered God in a real, personal way.

HEALING IS NOT ENOUGH

In order to lead a person to a true conversion, the loving touch of Christ is essential. Without that experience of healing, without an experience of God's love, it is almost impossible to have faith in him. Faith is always a response to God's loving work in our lives.

After that moment or series of small moments of healing, people often fall back into old habits. Year after year of chaperoning teenagers on trips to summer Steubenville conferences made this obvious to me. The kids had overwhelming life-changing experiences, but for many of them it was not enough to get them to turn their lives around. Any time you return home from a retreat, there is an adjustment. Life may be changed, but life at home will still be the same unless a person is committed to leaving behind the ways of the past.

Not everyone whom Jesus healed immediately became disciples. In the Gospel of Luke, we find a story of Jesus healing ten lepers while traveling through Samaria and Galilee (Lk 17:11–19). He healed ten, but only one man came back to thank Jesus and glorify God. The man happened to be a Samaritan, a foreigner who would have been marginalized by the Jews. We never find out what happened to the others.

The powerful experiences of God's grace need a context. That context is provided by the message Jesus proclaimed to the crowds in parables and stories. It is a message of hope for a kingdom very different from this world. In fact, for many people the kingdom Jesus preached about did not make sense at all. What kind of kingdom puts the last people first? Kingdoms conquer others through power and riches, but the kingdom of God that

Jesus proclaimed was nothing of the sort. The kingdom Jesus proclaimed requires us to leave everything and follow him.

This proclamation will be the focus of the following chapter. Everybody has hopes and dreams. Everybody wants a life just a little bit better than the one he has. It is a persistent desire and hope for something better. The proclamation that we share will harness that hope and lay plain the path to true happiness, true peace, and true joy in this world and the next.

For additional resources on how to heal, visit healproclaimteach.com/ chapter3.

4

PROCLAIM

We are all born with an innate desire to grow. This desire reveals itself in the way we strive for personal and professional success. We seek out degrees, titles, and promotions. Some of us strive for fame and fortune. In these cases we are not suffering so much from the effects of separation and isolation, but striving to rise above others to obtain status, recognition, and rewards. These pursuits often stand in the way of our ability to be self-giving and loving toward others. They push others away and even deprive us of the love we are really seeking (whether we realize it or not).

The desire for growth, though, is not a bad thing. It motivates us to improve the way we relate to one another. It inspires Christian leaders, for example, to give of our time to help grow our parishes, to help the poor, to support nonprofit organizations, or to improve our skills at work and in our hobbies. It inspires parents to seek what is best for their kids even when they may not embrace changes for themselves. When we seek to give glory to God and others, we find peace and joy in our lives. When we seek to give glory only to ourselves, however, we are always disappointed.

This is where preaching and proclamation come in. A great preacher ("proclaimer" might be a better term here since most of us do not actually preach from a pulpit) is able to connect his or her message with the dreams and goals of a particular audience. People listen and relate, recognizing themselves in the message they hear. These great preachers also challenge the audience with something new and different. They surprise with a different perspective and convince their audience to make changes to their lives in ways they may not have felt they could do before.

Jesus did just that. In his parables and preaching about the kingdom of God, he provided a vision that was not what people thought it would be. Personal glory was replaced with humility. According to Jesus, the greatest in the kingdom are those who put others before themselves. In order to enter into the kingdom, one has to live a life of sacrificial service of others no matter how unfair it might seem.

A critical moment in every disciple's journey is the decision to leave behind what one has, often including plans and dreams for our futures, and instead surrender to God's plan. This is a story repeated over and over again from Genesis to Revelation and continuing today. It is the model of faith followed by the Patriarchs, the prophets, the kings, and the apostles. God calls, and people must leave behind their old way of life and pursue something new.

This chapter is about the way in which we can help convince people through our evangelizing ministries to make the decision to transform their lives. To "proclaim" is to show people a path toward the kingdom of God that they cannot find on their own. Proclaiming the Gospel is not just about being an especially articulate preacher or sharing Jesus' story in a certain strategic way; it is about showing with your way of life and with your words that discipleship requires self-sacrifice and love.

In this chapter, we will look at what most people consider to be the proper form of evangelization: proclaiming the kingdom of God. This is truly where a person is convinced and converted toward embracing God's will and accepting the love of God by responding in love for others. What most people in our churches need today is not more teaching or better catechesis but more and better proclamation of the Gospel. They need to be shocked out of their seats and set on a path of change and self-sacrifice that is required of Jesus' disciples.

> Woe to me if I do not preach [the Gospel]. (1 Cor 9:16)

PROCLAIMING IN PARABLES

If you have one nearby, flip through a Bible that has Jesus' words highlighted in a different color. You know the ones I'm talking about, right? The orange or red ink stands out compared with the narrative in black. Look closely, and you will find that in most instances of Jesus' speaking, he is sharing a type of story we call a parable. At the time, these stories actually came as a surprise to the people who heard them. They certainly can be confusing to us, but rest assured they were confusing to those who first heard the stories, too. Immediately after the first time Jesus preaches in parables in the gospels, his confused disciples ask him why he spoke in such coded language. Look at the way Matthew describes this event, and keep in mind the audience of people Jesus is trying to reach: "The disciples approached him and said, 'Why do you speak to them in parables?'" (Mt 13:10).

Matthew makes it clear that the parables, at least in this case, are meant for the *people who have not yet become disciples*. At the beginning of chapter 13, it is clear that Jesus "sat down by the sea" and spoke to "large crowds" (Mt 13:1–2). The crowds, we can assume, are not yet committed disciples but are still very interested in what Jesus has to say. The crowds, as we said in chapter 1, are like the "spiritual but not religious" people we encounter today.

So, why does Jesus preach in parables? He answers, "Because knowledge of the mysteries of the kingdom of heaven has been granted to you, but to them it has not been granted" (Mt 13:11).

Jesus didn't teach in parables; he proclaimed salvation in parables. Each parable conveys something essential about the kingdom of God, which Matthew connects to the act of proclaiming. Teaching, you will recall, is something Jesus does in the synagogue or privately in homes or on journeys with his disciples. His *disciples* receive teaching about the mysteries of the kingdom, but the *crowds*—those in need of evangelization—are taught in parables because presently they "look but do not see and hear but do not listen or understand" (Mt 13:13).

In other words, we do not *teach* the unevangelized. We cannot expect them to understand the mysteries of God's kingdom, because they are not yet ready. They have not accepted these mysteries for themselves yet. Matthew drives this point home by again invoking the prophet Isaiah: "They will hardly hear with their ears, they have closed their eyes, lest they see with their eyes and hear with their ears and understand with their heart and be converted, and I heal them" (Mt 13:15; see also Is 6:10).

To be converted, we must encounter the healing touch of Christ in our hearts. Without recognition of the love God has specifically for us, we have no motivation to follow him. But what is next? To teach them all there is to know so they understand what we believe? Not yet. For the lost—those who cannot see or hear yet—need something different. They need the *first proclamation*. They need to understand what the kingdom of God is really all about; otherwise all that religious stuff will just seem like crazy talk. Even if a heart has been touched by the amazing love of Christ, the requirements for full-fledged discipleship call for a way of life that is often very different from the one being lived now.

THE PURPOSE OF PARABLES

There are a lot of different parables in the gospels. The content of the stories relate to a number of familiar settings in the lives of the crowds to whom Jesus preached. He shared stories about farmers, shepherds, workers, landowners, servants, kings, rich men, moneylenders, widows, judges, families, virgins, bridegrooms, and even a Samaritan. These were all familiar roles, images, and experiences, but they were placed within stories that challenged conventional wisdom of the time. Why would a shepherd risk ninety-nine sheep to save just one (see Mt 18:12–14, Lk 15:1–7)? Why would a man who finds a treasure bury it in a field and then go sell everything just so he could own the field where he buried the treasure (see Mt 13:44)? Why would a father forgive a son who squandered away half of all that he had and throw him a party, but then completely shortchange his loyal son who had been with him all the time (see Lk 15:11–32)? Why does such a small mustard seed grow into such a large tree, and why is the kingdom of God like that seed (see Mt 13:31–32, Mk 4:30–34, Lk 13:18–19)? Why would a landowner pay the same wage to all of his workers no matter how long they actually worked (see Mt 20:1–16)? How could a Samaritan care for a Jew with so much kindness (see Lk 10:29–37)? The list goes on and on.

The point is that in each one of these stories there is a surprise. Jesus takes a commonly understood aspect of the lives of the people who hear him, compares it to the kingdom of God or God himself, and shifts to a new way of thinking about things. Here is the exciting thing about this strategy. Jesus knows that the crowds are not ready to make the commitment to discipleship yet. They experience the world with human understanding and expectations rather than with trust in the loving work of God. The parables start where his listeners are and end where

Jesus wants them to be. They catch attention with familiar things but stretch the hearer to think differently about them, just as they need to think differently about God in order to follow him. They start with what *is* and show people what *could* and *should* be.

This is the same approach that we are challenged to take. We need to help many people come to a different understanding about God and discipleship than what they remember from childhood. Many of these people are not anti-Christian or anti-God by any means. Many of them were even baptized or raised going to church on Sundays. Even still, offering them complex explanations about Church teaching will not work quite yet. Much of Church teaching will likely come across more like legal impositions than invitations to a happier life. Why? Because they have not yet accepted the call to discipleship and the sacrifices that will bring.

KERYGMA AND DIDACHE

From the very beginning of the Church, we can distinguish between the work of preaching and teaching. The two Greek words used throughout history to express the difference between these two modes of the evangelization process are *kerygma* and *didache*. These are the very same two words that Matthew uses to describe the work of Jesus, who taught in the synagogues and proclaimed the kingdom of God (Mt 4:23, 9:35). They are the same words that the early Church used to describe two separate and distinct forms of ministry.

Kerygma is the *first* proclamation, or as Pope Francis described it in *Evangelii Gaudium*, it is the *primary* proclamation. It expresses the essentials of our Faith to those who have yet to fully accept it in their lives. According to Pope Francis, the essential message of the kerygma is: "Jesus Christ loves you; he gave his life for you; and now he is living at your side every day to enlighten, strengthen, and free you" (*EG*, 164). The kerygma, then, is a message of reassurance broken down into three parts:

- Jesus Christ loves you.
- He died for you.
- He is with you today.

This information is not just something for us to understand; it is something that requires a response. That response is the critical step in evangelization. If we accept this death as a gift and welcome Christ's presence here with us today, then we have to change our lives. Knowing and accepting that God loves us unconditionally leads us into gratitude, and eventually we respond by loving him back—and others, too—in an unconditional way. Essentially, we respond by taking up our own crosses and following in his footsteps.

In some ways, maybe kerygma is just a fancy way of saying that we need to proclaim the essential truth that we can have an intimate relationship with God. Christ died for *me*, for *us*. It was more than just a noble act or commendable story. It was an act of love for me, his beloved. That calls for a response. We have to choose to accept that gift or ignore it.

Didache, on the other hand, is the deposit of faith passed down through the Church from Jesus himself. The term means "teaching," and it is also the short name of a Christian manual compiled before AD 300, also known as *The Teaching of the Twelve Apostles*. Through Church teaching, we come to a deeper understanding of how we can know, love, and serve Jesus Christ as a response to his love for us. Essentially, didache offers us the tools we need to grow more fully into an appreciation and embrace of the creed and the Lord's Prayer. The beliefs contained in these gifts can be transformative when pursued as ideals that we strive to live out after we have made a commitment to respond to God's love by leaving everything and following him. Didache simply cannot come before kerygma. It has always been for the disciples, not the crowds.

WHAT ARE WE PROCLAIMING?

Let's bring the concept of proclamation to a more practical level. What is this proclaiming really all about? What do we actually do when we proclaim the kingdom of God today? We know Jesus preached about the kingdom of God in parables. We also know why he taught in parables. Those who were not yet disciples could not fully understand the meaning of his teachings without first making the commitment to live a different kind of life and accept a different perspective on the kingdom of God.

From a practical standpoint, what does this mean for us? Should we spend our time brainstorming and thinking of parables and stories that have hidden meanings? I used to think that. I used to try to come up with modern equivalents of vineyards and landowners, sheep and shepherds, and seeds being sown. The fact is, though, Jesus' use of parables was unique in the New Testament. Look at the Acts of the Apostles, and try to find one of the apostles preaching in parables. Read Saint Paul's letters, and try to find a parable that he used to preach about the kingdom of God. Check out the early Christian writers. How many parables did they make up themselves? Sure, they use analogies to describe God, but you won't find many new parables.

The apostles and other early Christians had a different story to tell. They constantly shared the same story over and over again: Jesus suffered, died, was buried, and rose again. That was how they proclaimed the kingdom of God. Paul himself points out this essential fact about preaching: "We proclaim Christ crucified, a stumbling block to Jews and foolishness to Gentiles" (1 Cor 1:23). Like the parables that Jesus told, his crucifixion is impossible to understand unless you are willing to accept that the Christian life requires self-sacrifice and unselfishness. It requires love.

To proclaim the kingdom of God today is to proclaim Christ crucified. The paschal mystery is just that: a mystery. The only way to understand that mystery is to experience the love of Christ and be willing to live that love on a daily basis.

To put it in more practical terms, here are some of the ways in which we can preach Christ crucified:

- **Share the Paschal Mystery.** Share "The Greatest Story Ever Told," but not just the facts. Explain what is going on behind the events of Christ's death and resurrection with a special emphasis on why he died and whom he died for.

- **Personal Testimony.** Share your story of an encounter with God that led you to experience a change and conversion in your life. Share your own dying and rising and what it's like to wait long for new life.

- **Saint Stories.** Discuss the stories of Christian martyrs, saints, courageous people in the news, or stories from books that exemplify sacrificial love. Share the stories of saints such as Saint Francis of Assisi, who gave up everything for the love of God.

- **Preach with the Way You Live.** Don't just say it; live it. Make personal sacrifices that people can see in the way you volunteer, serve others, and live a life of simplicity.

No matter what you say or do, remember that the goal is not sacrifice for the sake of sacrifice. Jesus did not die on the Cross to give us an example of his great commitment to a cause. He died on the Cross because he loves us. Similarly, we do not sacrifice our time and energy in loving service to others because we are simply good people. We do not give things up during Lent because of some sense of duty. We make difficult sacrifices always as a response to God's love for us and our unconditional, no-strings-attached love for our neighbors.

FREEDOM THROUGH SIMPLICITY

The *kerygma*, the primary proclamation, is a message that people are hungry to hear. We have to believe that; otherwise, we will be afraid to share it. You must accept that people are desperate for this message of God's love. Look closely at the reasons given in the New Testament for Jesus' coming into the world. The people who followed and believed in him were waiting for him. They were waiting for the Messiah who would "bind up the broken-hearted, to proclaim liberty to the captives" (Is 61:1).

Most of us have been catechized enough to know the context of Isaiah's prophecies and the history of the Jewish people. They suffered from years of captivity and separation from their homeland. Even at the time of Jesus' birth, people were looking for the Messiah because they did not like Herod, their Roman-appointed king, or the overall Roman rule. As we know, though, Jesus did not come to free the Jews from worldly captivity. That does not mean, however, that he will not heal or free us today.

We proclaim the Good News of Christ's love that frees us not just from captivity of worldly powers, but from the captivity of sin. Sin is something that imprisons us, and we need someone to free us from its oppression. Thankfully, Jesus' death and resurrection frees us from sin. This is the great message of freedom and liberty that we offer to those who are not yet ready to make the jump to full discipleship. This is the healing message we have to offer. Christ frees you from the captivity of sin, and he heals you of the wounds that the captivity causes.

Until someone experiences the healing power of God's love, the best thing we can do as evangelizing disciples living by the law of the spirit is to live a life that shows what being free from sin can actually be like. Now, until we are saints, we can never fully find freedom from the effects of sin. We can, however, live a life of "evangelical simplicity." This is a term I heard Msgr. Charles Murphy use in a webinar I did with him. He used it in reference to both Saint Francis of Assisi and Pope Francis in his book *Reclaiming Francis*.

Saint Francis of Assisi is a prime example of evangelical simplicity, though he embraced it to an extreme level. Francis, a charismatic and rich young man, had everything he wanted in life. He was a popular guy, a war hero, and he managed a business with his father that would have kept him rich and happy for the rest of his life—or so he thought. Saint Francis never found much comfort or joy in the constant pursuit of fame or money. Instead, he was pulled out by God toward a different path. Francis, a wealthy man, realized the joys of poverty and living a simple life while on a pilgrimage to Rome. He joined a beggar in Saint Peter's Square and in compassion returned home to spread the message of a better way of life. Praying before the Cross of San Damiano, he heard the call from Christ to "rebuild my Church," and he set out on a mission to proclaim a message of simplicity in pursuit of the Gospel way of life.

His life of sacrifice was not just a commendable thing to do. His passion for the love of God above all else inspired thousands to follow in his example, too. With the love of Christ, these followers responded to the Spirit and made sacrifices. They assumed a simple way of life in order to make space for the love of God. Through his example, people saw the hopeless pursuit of material possessions and wealth in their own lives and turned instead toward God.

This is a theme played out again and again among the great leaders in the Church. Saint Anthony, for example, left the city and went out into the desert inspiring an entire movement within the Church that sought out the monastic way of life. The Desert Fathers, in their detachment from worldly desires, offered a path of freedom that put on display the suffering caused by pursuit of material things. It laid plain the captivity of sin, and many people left the city in pursuit of a better life in the desert.

Many of you reading this are like me. We have families and employers that need us. We are probably not called to leave everything and live a life of vowed poverty. Many men and women are showing us this example through entering into the religious life. They should be held in high regard and respect so that the joys of their way of life can be seen as an example of the peace that comes in simplicity. For the rest of us, though, we have different challenges. We are tasked with living a simple way of life that pursues unity with God above the attachment to things of this world. It is a life in pursuit of balance. Each of us must discern the level of simplicity we create in our lives individually or as a family. It would be foolish to offer or seek a numerical limit or guidelines for a certain income level, type of car, or any details like that. Instead, choosing to live a life of evangelical simplicity means showing others by the way we live that we are not attached to the material things of this world.

SEEK THE GREATER GLORY OF GOD

At various points in our lives we all have pursued different career aspirations, financial goals, or other achievements. For example, I always wanted to be a writer and a speaker. I loved the idea of getting up onstage, sharing a message, and getting praise for my outstanding books with life-changing ideas. But as I have written books and gone out on the road, I realized that not a lot of good comes from my own personal glory. With the kind of books I write, I do not accomplish much if someone becomes a "Jared Dees fan" but not a bigger "Jesus Christ fan." All those dreams of being a writer and speaker mean nothing anymore unless God gets the credit. Balancing that dream and desire is a challenge still today, but one I use to help guide me.

The great Saint Ignatius of Loyola had a similar realization in his own journey of faith, and I have turned to his life as an example to follow. From an outsider's perspective, the conversion of Saint Ignatius might not seem to be a conversion at all. As the youngest of thirteen children, Ignatius's father raised him to be a cleric as an adult. However, with much convincing from his eager son, the father allowed him to follow his brothers into service as a knight. This did not mean a life completely devoid of religious fervor. As one story goes, Ignatius challenged a Muslim warrior to a duel for not professing the divinity of Christ.

When Ignatius was injured in battle, however, his true conversion took place. A canon ball injured one leg and broke the other. Through many surgeries his leg became functional, but due to a protruding bone, Ignatius could not properly wear the armor of a courtier, a piece of armor worn over the shin. Despite continued medical procedures that he convinced the doctors to perform, they were never able to fix his leg completely. For the rest of his life, he would walk with a limp. He would never be able to fight as a knight again. His childhood dream was crushed.

That did not stop Ignatius from dreaming. While he recovered he often thought of saving a damsel in distress and winning her heart with the chivalrous bravery every knight dreamed of possessing. Looking for something to do during his recovery, he asked for medieval romance novels to pass the time, but there were none in the hospital. Instead, he was given a book of reflections on the saints and the gospels called *De Vita Christi* (Life of

Christ). Being bedridden and with nothing else to do, he read the book many times. He realized that by contemplating the gospels and the lives of the saints, he felt at peace—a peace he did not feel when dreaming of great acts of chivalry.

Reading this book along with the realization of the loss of his future as a knight led him to take a different path in life. Once released, he dedicated himself to a life of prayer, developing what would become his great *Spiritual Exercises*. He laid down his armor before the Virgin Mary following the traditional rituals of chivalry reserved for knights and ladies. He had dedicated his life to service of God instead of fame and glory. His motto became the motto of the Society of Jesus (the Jesuits) he would found: *ad majorem dei gloriam* ("for the greater glory of God!").

Prior to his conversion experience, Ignatius sought his own glory and the glory of his homeland. Afterward, though, he sought only the glory of God. This conversion is the experience of recognizing the true Gospel message of the kingdom of God. Instead of seeking worldly gain, Ignatius sought to gain hearts for God. He humbled himself and left behind all previous notions about his life. He was able to understand and live the message that Jesus proclaimed in the parables.

We also have dreams and desires that seek our own glory rather than God's. The people we hope will be touched by God's love also have these same kinds of aspirations. Through the proclamation of the Cross and sharing stories of the sacrificial love of saints, we can help others seek the greater glory of God and the glory of the people around us.

PREACH A SIMPLE MESSAGE

This will come as no shock to you, but Southern Baptists are excellent preachers. I come from a family of Southern Baptists and, in fact, my uncle was a Baptist minister in Mississippi. I loved listening to him preach. He had an incredible way of lowering his voice or slowing his speech at exactly the right time to create an effect that kept everyone who listened to him absolutely mesmerized. It almost didn't matter what he was talking about. When he told a story, you listened. Usually, though, he had a very simple message or spoke about just one small section of a scripture passage and talked about it much longer than you could ever think was possible. It is no surprise, then, that the leaders of Baptist communities are often referred to simply as "preachers" rather than ministers or pastors.

These gifts have allowed many pastors of large megachurches to attract thousands of new people to their communities—many of them former Catholics. Can we blame them? I love listening to the pastor of North Point Community Church in Atlanta, Andy Stanley, preach. I have listened to his podcast, and I have read some of his books. He is dynamic in speech but not overly energetic as we think of with Martin Luther King Jr. or other great preachers. Stanley's message is always simple and memorable. In fact, he is often criticized for offering such simple messages when he preaches.

One day I was driving my car listening to him preach about Peter, and he made a comment that forced me to stop and think. He said, "Now this is Peter, and if you are Catholic, that is huge." Stanley knows his audience. Many of them were baptized Catholics who have joined his community. I knew this was true statistically, but to hear him state that publicly really got to me. It got me thinking about how Catholics can become better preachers—not just the priests and deacons among us, but the catechists, youth ministers, and adult-faith-formation leaders, too. What lessons can we learn from the great preachers of today? Or maybe instead of looking around today, we can look back into our Church's history and consider how one of the greatest preachers of all time shared his homilies.

In the late fourth and early fifth century, the bishop of Constantinople grew in fame for his excellent preaching. He was so well-known for his preaching that people referred to his mouth as if it were made of gold. His name, Saint John Chrysostom, means "golden-mouthed"—a nickname that stuck with him for centuries.

What did Saint John Chrysostom do so differently from everyone else that he could receive such fame as this? He was, reportedly, a very energetic and passionate speaker. We can all learn from that, of course. We cannot really preach the kingdom of God if it does not inspire and compel our hearts to feel some excitement. What we might consider instead, however, are the topics on which he preached.

John Chrysostom liked to preach most of all using scripture and moral teaching. He liked to give homilies about practical topics that people could apply to their daily lives. Rather than give long-winded exegeses about the scripture passage, making allegorical connections, as did his contemporaries at the time, he offered more practical interpretations of scripture that related to real-life issues such as poverty and the need for reform in the Church. If something was happening publicly in his community, he addressed it. At one point, the people of Constantinople destroyed many statues of the emperor, and John Chrysostom preached a series of homilies to denounce their behavior. He did not focus on the abstract; he gave straightforward advice to his congregation. As a result, many people converted to Christianity.

Is Saint John Chrysostom any different in style from the popular megachurch preachers we know today? Like Chrysostom, they focus on highly practical advice and simple, memorable messages. They avoid long theological arguments about the underlying meaning of a passage and instead focus on straight-forward interpretations that are anchored in real-life situations. They are speaking directly to the experiences of the people who hear them.

I am no expert on preaching, and I wish I had an ounce of my uncle's ability to captivate an audience through storytelling. I do know, however, that focusing on a very simple and practical message when I speak to larger groups always has a much more lasting impact. When I speak at conferences or at parish events, I have found that the more practical the message, the more meaningful it is, because people know immediately what to do with the information I offer. When we preach, let's grab our listeners' attention with simple, practical messages instead of long-winded theological explanations.

STRIVE FOR PERFECTION WITHOUT BEING PERFECT

It is very easy to fall into the trap of proclaiming a perfect way of life that is attainable through personal improvement. Yes, we have to preach against the things in our lives that drive us away from God and others. The kingdom of God calls for great sacrifice. We just have to be careful not to be angry with sinners who have become attached to such things. We also must be very careful not to blame the things that lead to sin. On their own, money, work, food, alcohol, and sex are not evil things. All can be used and directed toward good. It is the way we use them that leads us to sin. It is the sin that is bad, not the things themselves.

This was a critical realization for one of the most important evangelists in the Church's history. Saint Dominic founded an "Order of Preachers" because of an encounter he had with a religious sect in the south of France who called themselves "the pure." These "purists" (known as the Albigensians) saw the world as divided into the good spiritual realm and the evil earthly or material world. They preached a way of life that required complete separation from all evil in the world. As a result, they held to an overly sacrificial and ascetic way of life. Saint Dominic, on the other hand, set out on a mission to preach the true Gospel in opposition to the Albigensian message of guilt and sin.

Many Christian preachers at the time had lost almost all credibility in the south of France, and people turned to the Albigensians as the only true authentic Christians. Many popular preachers lived lavishly, staying at the best inns and having many servants. The Dominicans, on the other hand, lived what they preached. They became sort of monastic evangelizers by adhering to the Rule of Saint Augustine and living a life of poverty, prayer, and obedience.

If we truly want our messages to be heard and believed, we have to live what we preach. If we expect people to turn away from an excessive attachment to the stuff in their lives, then we need to be acutely aware of our own attachments, too. It is always a balance. On the one hand, we don't want to separate ourselves completely from the world as if it were evil and the source of all sin. We can have healthy relationships with food, drink, TV, technology, and entertainment because in themselves they are not evil. We just need to be aware of where our attachments might take away our authenticity. We can do this by following the example of Saint Dominic and appreciating the goodness in the things of the world by not letting them direct our lives.

It is our own struggles with these attachments that make us human. Unlike the purists whom Saint Dominic opposed, we appreciate the fact that we can't be perfect through our own hard work and commitment to self-sacrifice. We need God's help to be free from sin. The more we struggle, the more authentic our witness will be to those who go through the same challenges we do. Make mistakes and learn from them, but don't hold other people to a standard higher than we can reach on our own.

TRANSITIONING FROM PREACHING TO TEACHING

If we have proclaimed the Gospel well, then the people who hear us will have a decision to make. They will need to decide if becoming a disciple is worth leaving their old life behind. They must decide if they will turn to God as the source of strength, peace, and love rather than turn to the things they turned to in the past.

Proclamation leads to a decision to seek conversion. Usually, this isn't something that happens immediately, and it is arrived at only following often-intense struggle with questions that arise as an early response to hearing the first proclamation or kerygma. Individuals on the road to conversion ask questions that are no longer antagonistic or doubtful but curious and hopeful. They want to know more about the Catholic faith because there is something in it that is pulling them away from the comforts of their lives and into a new way of living. They are curious and realize they need help.

This is where the third mode of evangelizing ministry comes in. Remember, Jesus taught in the synagogues, addressing people who had already made a commitment to love and serve God. In our ministries, those who have heard and accepted the proclamation of the kingdom of God, of Christ crucified, are now ready to receive the teachings of the Church. This is where we are able to shift from evangelization into modes of catechesis and development of the Christian disciple. Jesus gave us a model for this, too.

For additional resources on how to proclaim, visit healproclaimteach. com/chapter4.

5

TEACH

Have you ever noticed how converts are especially fervent about their faith? Converts have a passion about their beliefs that leads them to be constantly learning. After they first make the decision to dedicate their lives to God, they read and learn everything they can. Everything is so new and exciting. They have question after question about the Faith. At some point during their conversion they set out on a journey to uncover the reasons why Catholics do what they do. Their excitement drove them to learn so much so fast that they quickly knew the answers to questions that even those with twelve years or more of Catholic education may not be able to answer. These passionate converts tend to share a lot of similar behaviors. They ask a lot of questions and do not accept simple answers. They spend time on their own searching for answers to the most difficult theological questions. They continue to seek understanding even after they learn new answers. They do more than just believe in new ideas; they change the way they live.

Longtime believers, on the other hand, often lack that same passion and optimism. The excitement can be almost nonexistent. Years of attending Catholic schools and religious education have for many taken the excitement out of learning about the Faith. Instead, they feel as though they know everything already. Nothing is new. Nothing is interesting. The term "cradle Catholic" has in some cases become synonymous with the person born into the Faith who does not know much about it, or at least does not much appreciate it.

When I talk about teaching in this book, I'm highlighting activities meant to inspire a passion for learning about the Faith for all people, whether we are recent converts or cradle Catholics. Teaching the Faith is about discovering and uncovering a mystery that, as disciples, we never tire of experiencing in deeper ways. It is not about imparting all the answers and teachings to be memorized and accepted. We teach in order to inspire and ignite a passion for learning something new and drawing closer to Christ. We invite people into an experience with the truths of faith, which are transformative and life-changing. In other words, we make people lifelong learners; we make disciples.

JESUS THE TEACHER

Jesus was called "teacher" or "rabbi" many times in the New Testament. It was certainly a crucial part of his identity. "You call me 'teacher' and 'master,' and rightly so, for indeed I am" (Jn 13:13). Yet, when he spoke of himself as a teacher, he did it with humility, always crediting the source of his teaching: "My teaching is not my own but is from the One who sent me" (Jn 7:16). We also are called to teach the lessons of the One who sends us. Only then can we begin to focus less on ourselves and our understanding of specific ideas and more on the people we teach and the ways in which we can motivate them to want to learn more. When I work with catechists and teachers, one of the most common challenges I hear about is the effort it takes to get kids and adults engaged and excited about learning the Faith. Jesus provides a model to help us make that engagement a reality.

The key phrase to understanding the method Jesus used to teach his disciples is from chapter 5 of Matthew: "You have heard that it was said . . . but I say to you . . ." He repeats this phrase over and over again in this chapter, not to discredit what people already know, but to challenge them to go a little further and a little deeper. With this series of lessons, Jesus doesn't just list a group of doctrines to be accepted and memorized; he takes an idea that is generally understood and challenges his disciples not just to follow it but to live it wholeheartedly. He challenges his disciples to think differently. The doctrines require a change in the way they live. To live what Jesus teaches is uncomfortable and nearly impossible without a solid relationship with God. To accept these teachings, the disciples had to abandon what they already understood and motivate themselves to approach things differently.

Take a look at what Jesus did to challenge his disciples to go beyond what they already understood:

YOU'VE HEARD IT SAID . . .	BUT I SAY TO YOU . . .
You shall not kill (Mt 5:21).	Whoever is angry [will be] liable to fiery Gehenna (Mt 5:22).
You shall not commit adultery (Mt 5:27).	Everyone who looks at a woman with lust has already committed adultery with her in his heart (Mt 5:28).
Whoever divorces his wife must give her a bill of divorce (Mt 5:31).	Whoever divorces his wife (unless the marriage is unlawful) causes her to commit adultery, and whoever marries a divorced woman commits adultery (Mt 5:32).

Do not take a false oath, but make good to the Lord all that you vow (Mt 5:33).	Do not swear at all (Mt 5:34).
An eye for an eye and a tooth for a tooth (Mt 5:38).	Offer no resistance to one who is evil. When someone strikes you on (your) right cheek, turn the other one to him as well (Mt 5:39).
You shall love your neighbor and hate your enemy (Mt 5:43).	Love your enemies, and pray for those who perse-cute you (Mt 5:44).

We know these laws as precepts of the Ten Commandments. These laws would have been ingrained in everything Jesus' Jewish-born disciples believed about morality and daily life. The disciples would have been raised memorizing each of the laws and following them for fear of punishment.

Notice what Jesus does as a teacher. He takes what his disciples already know so well and introduces a new and challenging way of seeing things. Instead of asking them to abandon completely what they believe and know, he challenges them to go deeper in order to gain a greater appreciation of these truths.

This is the same model that we should follow when teaching about Church doctrine, especially within the context of the new evangelization. Today, many people in the pews of Catholic parishes are bored. The kids in Catholic high schools and parish religious-education programs are bored, too. They have heard the stories and teachings so many times that nothing seems new anymore. So many are not motivated or even invited to ask questions. As a result, they never embark on that journey of discovery in faith that is so important for disciples.

In order for us to be truly remarkable teachers and catechists, whether it is in religious education of children, youth ministry, marriage preparation, RCIA, or adult faith formation, we have to think of ways to present our beliefs in ways that challenge conventional thinking about the world. We have to offer new and creative insights into the stories and teachings Catholics have heard for years or even decades. Or, at the very least, we need to make sure that we do not strip all sense of wonder and awe out of the process.

THE GOAL OF CATECHESIS

What we are talking about in this chapter, of course, is what the Church calls *catechesis*. Catechesis is part of evangelization, not separate from it (see chapter 2). We cannot separate healing and proclaiming and focus solely on teaching (catechesis) if we truly desire that our ministries be evangelical. That, I hope, has become clear by reading this book. What, then, is the goal and purpose of catechesis in the Church today?

In his apostolic exhortation *Catechesi Tradendae*, Saint John Paul II clearly defined the meaning and purpose of catechesis. In my experience, the most commonly quoted passage of the text comes from paragraph 5: "The definitive aim of catechesis is to put people not only in touch but in communion, in intimacy, with Jesus Christ."

If that is the goal of catechesis, however, how does one get there? In the same paragraph, the pope wrote something we cannot overlook: "The primary and essential object of catechesis is, to use an expression dear to Saint Paul and also to contemporary theology, 'the mystery of Christ.' Catechizing is a way to lead a person to study this mystery and all its dimensions . . . to understand the meaning of Christ's actions and words and of the signs worked by him, for they simultaneously hide and reveal his mystery" (*CT*, 5).

Do you see how catechesis is different from learning the alphabet or memorizing math facts? For one, we do not just learn facts and doctrines; we encounter and study a *person*. No simple biographical study will do. We seek to understand a mystery—a mystery that is simultaneously hidden and revealed with every new step along the catechetical journey. In catechesis, the mystery always remains new, fresh, and worth discovering, because that is how one person relates to another person. Because of its newness, we constantly seek to learn more and do more to come to know, love, and serve God in deeper ways.

The primary goal of catechesis, then, is to instill in believers the desire to continually discover the mystery of Christ. It is to motivate people to want to learn more for themselves. We can never instill this desire in those whom we teach if we believe we have all the answers. Remember, our teaching is not our own; it comes from Christ. The best way to teach is to introduce people to the mystery and then get out of the way. The best way to teach is by *coaching*, not *lecturing*.

THE LOSS OF LEISURE IN EDUCATION

One reason why we have such a hard time engaging people in our educational and catechetical ministries has to do with a much broader cultural situation, which we may or may not realize influences the way we think about learning. Our educational system today places such strong emphasis on grades, test scores, standards, and compartmentalized subject areas that we have lost touch with the most essential ingredient for learning: *leisure*.

Believe it or not, the word *school* is derived from the Greek word *skole*, which means "leisure." The original idea of "school" was to be a place where people would come to do philosophy. They would come and listen to great thinkers share ideas and engage in dialogue. The discussions they had were an end in themselves. There were no philosophy degrees to be earned (in sharp contrast to today, when a PhD is the mark of highest academic achievement). People came to learn, share, and reconsider what they believed and understood about the world.

Today, schools tend to be less focused on ideas and more focused on quantifiable results. Leisure is the furthest thing from the culture of our schools. We have an overemphasis on the *results* of learning and not on the *art* of learning. Learning is no longer seen as an end in itself but as the means to some other self-serving end.

We are starting to see the pendulum shift away from the results-only educational focus. Among all of the popular online TED talks, the most viewed video is by Sir Ken Robinson, titled "Do Schools Kill Creativity?" In that video, Robinson makes the argument that "we don't grow into creativity; we grow out of it. We get educated out of it."[1] Instead of fostering creativity in our schools, Robinson suggests, we tell children everything they need to know to become valuable, hardworking contributors to society. It is a model based on the nineteenth-century need for industrialism. With such a strong focus on the factory, we created a national educational system focused on mass production of a labor force rather than the unique formation of individuals as whole persons.

Let's be very clear. Education and catechesis are not the same thing. Education has specific goals in mind that focus on developing the whole person, but with a particular emphasis on the intellect. Catechesis, too, has the goal of developing the whole person, but its primary purpose is to form that person in the image of our God.

Think for a moment about the faith-formation and sacramental-preparation ministries you have been a part of over the years as participant or as minister. Were these ministries based on the results-focused educational system of the nineteenth and twentieth centuries? Was the emphasis placed on the experience itself or on the outcome of the experience? I am not just talking about religious education in classrooms; I am also thinking of RCIA and marriage-preparation programs that are designed to quickly and efficiently impart everything there is to know about certain doctrines before their time is up and sacraments are scheduled to be received.

I am sad to admit that I have made many of the ministries I have run to be focused more on education than on catechesis. I have attended and planned high-school retreats and marriage-preparation retreats in hope of changing hearts, but became so wrapped up in changing opinions about issues such as premarital sex or cohabitation that I lost sight of the people I was there to serve. I went on a mission trip in college hoping to change the world, but I returned home frustrated that we did not have time to build more buildings or teach more Bible lessons to the kids. I have designed lesson plan after lesson plan focused on achieving learning objectives that often completely ignore what was actually going on in the hearts of the students I taught.

All of these frustrations and misconceived notions about catechesis come from a fear I know every minister shares: what if we are not doing *enough*? What if we are unable to convince people of the beliefs we share? What if they do not understand properly? What if we run out of time? Faced with these fears, it is easy to rely on models of education that focus on producing neatly measurable results. Are we so afraid of failure that we keep returning to classroom models of catechesis rather than delving into the obviously more risky, life-altering evangelizing ministry to which Christ calls us?

Let me be very clear about what I am fighting for. I envision a different kind of approach to catechesis in our Church today—one based on the broad history of the Church, not just the recent history of our Western industrialized society. We must provide catechetical opportunities that form disciples in love with Christ, not primitive theologians with certificates of completion. The Church calls us to make disciples, not theologians. Our goal must always be to provide opportunities for encounter with Christ and to help those who have experienced such encounters to understand and integrate those experiences into their everyday lives. This starts with something we all try to create in our ministries: *engagement*.

ENTERTAINMENT VERSUS ENGAGEMENT

One way of looking toward a new vision for catechesis is to think in terms of *engagement* rather than *entertainment*. Faced with the need to attract more people to attend our ministry offerings and remain interested while they are there, parish leaders and volunteers tend to turn to entertainment models to increase participant engagement. We search and search for the best YouTube videos or DVDs to show at catechetical gatherings. We hire dynamic public speakers to come share a message with people in our parishes and schools, hoping that the smiles on the faces of the listeners is also an indication of transforming hearts. We look for the best icebreakers and games to get young people happy and having fun while they are with us. And, of course, we feed them with the best food we can offer (on a reasonable budget, of course).

But entertainment is not the answer. Entertainment, unlike engagement, has a short-term gain. When we are entertained, whether by a book, a TV show, a movie, a play, or a sporting event, we enjoy it for just a limited time. These are all fun and enjoyable, but they remain self-contained for the most part. Activities that are entertaining usually require only passive participation. We sit back and let others share their creative work with us and never really get involved in the work ourselves.

I like the way Henri Nouwen put it: "Radio, television, newspapers, books, films, but also hard work and a busy social life all can be ways to run away from ourselves and turn life into a long entertainment. The word *entertainment* is important here. It means literally 'to keep (*tain* from the Latin *tenere*) someone in between (*enter*)'. Entertainment is everything that gets and keeps our mind away from things that are hard to face. Entertainment keeps us distracted, excited, or in suspense."[2]

Engagement is unlike entertainment in that we are required to participate. When we are engaged participants, we do the creating. We cannot be passive observers; we have to be actively taking part in the event. Engagement is not easy; it is challenging. We have to work hard to accomplish a common goal with others. When we are engaged, we are focused on solving a problem and working with others. Instead of *reading* about theological ideas, we *write* them. Instead of *listening*, we *talk*. Instead of expecting someone to provide all the *answers*, we ask good *questions*.

Think back to the way Jesus taught. He shared what people already knew and understood but challenged them to go deeper. Instead of passively accepting that we should not kill, we let our hearts be transformed so that we will not even become angry with people. We do not just avoid adulterous acts; we let our hearts be transformed so that we no longer have adulterous thoughts. Jesus takes a passive acceptance of an idea and challenges us to be engaged in the transformation of our hearts in order to follow him. Catechesis, therefore, is not just the acceptance or even the understanding of an idea; it is the process by which we let ourselves be conformed into what the idea calls us to be.

MYSTAGOGICAL CATECHESIS

In the last chapter we looked at the difference between two important words in the Church's understanding of evangelization: *kerygma* and *didache*. A third very important word for understanding how the Church understands both evangelization and catechesis is the process known as *mystagogy*. Mystagogy (a leading or training into the mystery) is the final period in the evangelization process you read about in chapter 2. In the ancient Church, newly initiated members of the Church would continue their formation beyond the reception of the sacraments during a period of mystagogy.

In mystagogy, newly initiated Catholics (neophytes) are drawn into a deeper understanding of the mysteries of the Faith experienced in the liturgy. In the ancient Church, Cyril of Jerusalem, for example, would preach to the newly baptized about the sacraments in which they just partook. He would preach about the symbols and the meaning of their actions and words in order to help them understand why they did what they did.

The goal of this work, however, was more than just deeper understanding. The goal was for the new members of the Church to realize the spiritual and moral transformation that was taking place within them. Unpacking the mystery of Christ experienced in the sacraments offers more than an appreciation of symbolism; it beckons us to be transformed through efficacious (change-producing) participation in the symbols themselves. The mysteries do not just express meaning; they transform us.

This, unfortunately, is a model we have a difficult time attaching to our faith-formation ministries today. In too many places the reception of Confirmation marks catechetical "graduation." No matter how hard we try, getting kids to extend their religious-education experience into a high-school youth-group experience is a very difficult task. First Communion, which is usually done at the end of the spring semester, typically occurs after the catechetical program year is over. Parents attend a baptismal preparation class just once before the day of their infant's Baptism and are rarely invited to reflect on the experience once it has taken place. Marriage preparation occurs during the many weeks leading up to the wedding, but rarely does a couple meet again with the priest or sponsor couple in the early months or years of marriage to explore the mystery further.

Mystagogy must be a part of all ongoing, permanent catechesis. It must be a part of everything we do in adult faith formation, in adult continuing education, and in our children's programs as well. Why? Not because we as Catholics need a better appreciation for the rich symbolism of the Mass (though this is certainly important). Mystagogy helps us appreciate the transformation, the change that God is working in our lives through the mysteries encountered in the Church's liturgy. I know this sounds far-fetched, but it happens whether we realize it or not. The Eucharist does not just remind us of the unity of the Church; *it creates that unity for those who participate in it.* Immersion in the waters of Baptism does more than remind us of Christ's salvation won through his dying and rising; it makes that salvation a reality in our lives. We die and rise with Christ!

These are more than just concepts to understand; they are sacred realities to experience.

I like the way Father Andrew Gawrych, a Holy Cross parish priest, does mystagogy with his RCIA participants. First, he asks them to share their raw experiences, recounting every detail of their initiation. Then, he starts to take notes on a board in three columns: What Happened, Thoughts and Feelings, and Meaning/Theology. The "theology and meaning" always comes after the neophytes have recounted their experience of the Sacraments of Initiation.[3] It is the opposite approach that we often take as teachers and catechists.

This mystagogical method of catechesis can be applied beyond just the Sacraments of Initiation and the liturgy. We can do this very same thing with the way we teach the doctrines of the Faith. Pope Francis wrote this about our profession of faith, the creed: "The creed does not only involve giving one's assent to a body of abstract truths; rather, when it is recited the whole of life is drawn into a journey toward full communion with the living God. We can say that in the creed believers are invited to enter into the mystery that they profess and to be transformed by it" (*Lumen Fidei*, 45).

If we teach our doctrines as abstract truths, they will remain just that: abstract. If, however, we take a mystagogical approach to catechesis, then we can help those we catechize to find the ways in which their lives can be transformed by the doctrines of the Faith. This means we have to provide an experience of the creed before we can fully explain the meaning. Understanding how and when Jesus "was crucified by Pontius Pilate" is one thing, but to know that he had us in mind while dying on the Cross should trigger within us a change in the way we look at Jesus. That God is the "creator of heaven and earth" is a nice thing to recognize, but knowing it should force us to see the world in a different way—as a total gift of overflowing love from God.

THE INDUCTIVE AND DEDUCTIVE METHODS OF CATECHESIS

Very often, when we are placed in a position to teach something about our Faith, we come in with a considerable amount of knowledge, or at least more knowledge than the people we are asked to teach. A priest or deacon has years of seminary classes to draw from. Lay ecclesial ministers have some kind of theological training or considerable reading, or have at least attended, watched, or listened to a workshop on a particular topic. It is natural, then, to try to cram in everything we have learned about a certain topic within the time limit we are given. In other words, it is natural to present a laundry list of abstract truths for people to recognize and memorize as the teachings of the Church.

I am asking you to forget, just for a moment, that you know anything about the topics you are teaching. Put yourself in the position of someone who does not know a thing. Put yourself in the position of the people you will be teaching. I know it is hard. I have a bachelor's and a master's degree in theology. I love teaching and talking about what I know. Get me going, and you will have a hard time shutting me up. The problem is, spewing out information does not evangelize or lead to conversion. It does not take into account any kind of methodology for communicating the Faith to others.

The *National Directory for Catechesis* highlights two processes that take into account the real-life situations of the people we catechize. I urge you to choose one or both approaches when you are planning your lessons. You can communicate the Faith using either an inductive approach or a deductive approach.

Both methods present the truths of faith but do it within the context of human experience. If we do not engage with the experiences of the people we catechize, then all we are doing is presenting information, hoping that someone is hearing it. We must do more than that. We must show how that information, the truths of the Faith, transforms us.

FAITH ➝ EXPERIENCE

Let's start with the *deductive method*, which is a much more common way of sharing the Faith. In the deductive method we begin "with the general principles or truths of the faith and [apply] them to the concrete experiences of those to whom the catechesis is addressed."[4] The word *deductive* comes from the Latin word *deducere*, which literally means "to lead out." We do not present the truths of faith and stop there. We present the truths and bring out their deeper meanings for us today and for our present situation as human beings.

Let's consider an example in ministry. Imagine you are about to give a talk during an upcoming marriage-preparation retreat for your parish. You and your spouse are asked to talk about intimacy and the Church's teaching on sexuality and contraception. You have read the encyclicals and attended a "theology of the body" workshop. You remember being in the couples' shoes when you got married, knowing almost nothing about natural family planning (NFP) and the problems with contraception. You might be inclined to give the CliffsNotes version of the Church's teaching since it may be the only opportunity these couples will ever have to learn it. There are only forty-five minutes set aside for your talk, so you better drive those points home, right?

Instead of cramming as many facts into your presentation as possible, you decide to present the teachings using the deductive method. You offer a very simple truth of our Faith: the Church considers contraception and birth control to be morally wrong even for married couples. Rather than offering the bullet-point list of reasons why the Church teaches this, you appeal to your own experience as a Catholic couple. First, you state the Church's teaching; then you share what life is like putting that teaching into practice. If you can do it with authenticity and honesty, the couples will be intrigued rather than angered. They may have more questions about the details of the Church's reasoning after your talk, and that is when you pull out that long list of bullet points you originally thought were so important. We want people to ask questions. We want to make sure they are motivated to ask *why* rather than simply rejecting or accepting a teaching automatically based on what they already know or think they know. If we give them all the answers, they won't have any reason to ask questions.

EXPERIENCE ⟶ FAITH

Now, let's consider the *inductive method* of catechesis. "The inductive approach proceeds from the sensible, visible, tangible experiences of the person, and leads, with the help of the Holy Spirit, to more general conclusions and principles."[5] While the Latin word *deducere* means "to lead out," the Latin word *inducere* means "to lead in." Using the inductive method, we focus on human experiences and encounters with God and, through the reflection on those experiences, come to conclusions that line up with the principles and teachings of the Faith.

Here is another example. Imagine that you are asked to give a one-hour talk on the New Testament to catechumens and candidates in the RCIA. You only have an hour. That is a lot to cover in just one hour. The natural tendency is to want to squeeze in to that short amount of time every possible fact about the stories, the people, the types of books, the origin and development of the canon, and so on. The time limit impels you to want to speed through the facts and hope they stick.

Instead, though, you decide you want to take an inductive approach to teaching the New Testament. You start by appealing to your audience's human experiences. You ask them to imagine they were living just a generation after Jesus died and rose again. You ask them to share the kinds of questions they might ask the disciples and the other people who might have known Jesus. After listening to these questions, you help them make connections between these questions and the content of the New Testament, particularly the gospels.

Then, you ask them to shift gears and instead consider what they would do if they had to write a book about the life of their grandparents. Where would they go to find information about them? How would they organize the information into a book? Using these questions and considerations, you can start to explain how the evangelists wrote the gospels by making connections to the way we would write about the lives of our grandparents.

Do you see the difference? Rather than dictating all of the information you can with the limited amount of time you were given, you asked questions. You engaged with the audience's experiences and led them into a reflection on those experiences (real or imagined) in order to reach a conclusion that lines up with the lesson in faith you were trying to communicate. You can hand them plenty of reading material or links to explore what you were not able to cover. With so much information available online and in books, it is much better to motivate people to go and want to learn more than to tell them all they need to know in less than an hour.

Ultimately, it does not matter how much or how little you know about the topics you are going to teach. What really matters is how much you know about the experiences of the people who are learning. Pope Francis gave some very valuable advice to priests preparing homilies that applies to all those engaged in catechesis: "We need to develop a broad and profound sensitivity to what really affects other people's lives. Let us also keep in mind that we should never respond to questions that nobody asks" (*EG*, 155).

ASK AND ENCOURAGE MORE QUESTIONS

One of my favorite stories about Jesus' early life is the story of his parents finding him in the Temple. If you look at this story very closely, you might notice something odd in the description of the scene. Luke writes that Jesus was "sitting in the midst of the teachers, listening to them and asking them questions" (Lk 2:46). The next passage, though, says "all who heard him were astounded at his understanding and his answers" (Lk 2:47). That seems odd, doesn't it? Jesus asked *questions*, and the people there were amazed by his *answers*? Maybe the teachers were asking him questions, too, or maybe Jesus was answering his own questions, but the text does not say that. All it says is that Jesus asked *them* questions.

Questions are the key to effective catechesis. Ask any question about theology, and you invariably find yourself asking another question. It is an endless journey of discovery pushed ahead by a buildup of questions. When we stop asking questions, we stop learning. When we stop learning, we cease to be disciples. Therefore, it is essential that we teach more with questions than with answers.

If we present Church doctrine as simple statements of fact without discussion, then our learners never embark on that journey of discovery. In fact, if we force-feed the answers to questions nobody is asking, then we really cannot expect them to remember what we said.

Don't get me wrong. I am not suggesting we present Church doctrine by instilling what I have heard some bishops call a "hermeneutic of doubt." A hermeneutic of doubt approaches Church doctrine from the perspective of doubt first. It is a false-until-proven-true mentality. That is not what we are getting at with our focus on questions. We are trying to teach and model faith, not doubt, for those we teach. What I am suggesting is that we present doctrine in such a way that it connects with human experience and opens a door to deeper discovery. This is, again, where the inductive and deductive methods come in handy. We want people to ask questions to clarify and understand concepts more deeply so that they can come to grateful appreciation and deeper love of God.

Using a questions approach to catechesis is precisely the approach taken by one of the greatest teachers in our history. Have you ever read parts of Saint Thomas Aquinas's *Summa Theologiae*? It is a very long book. The reason why it is so long is not because Aquinas was too long-winded in his writings. In fact, he tended to be very succinct and particular about the words he used. The *Summa* is long because of the format, which begins each article of faith with a series of questions that explore every possible perspective and question one might ask about a given doctrine. He presents excellent questions (that likely came from debates he had in his mind and in real life or from his many students) and then challenges himself to respond to those questions. His format is simple:

1. Ask a question.
2. State the objections.

3. State the truth of faith with arguments for it.

4. Respond to the objections.

Thomas Aquinas wrote his *Summa* with the beginner theologian in mind, starting each article of faith by introducing a question as a gateway into deeper understanding. The lesson for us is clear: start with a question. Consider the possibilities, and then introduce the article of faith by responding to the questions. We may not always have the answers, and that's okay. The point is to *ask* questions, not just answer them. The more we ask questions, the more we can model the process by which every person discovers the meaning of our Faith.

EVANGELIZING APOLOGETICS: DEFEND WITHOUT BEING DEFENSIVE

While our focus may be on asking questions, we do not hide the truth. As ministers and disciples, we often find ourselves defending the Faith from the misconceptions and misunderstandings of outsiders and seekers. This can lead into a debate either one-on-one or in a group setting. Even in places of traditional catechesis and religious instruction (children's religious education, Catholic high schools, teenage youth groups, marriage preparation, RCIA meetings, etc.), we can find ourselves engaged in a debate about Church teachings. We often refer to these debates as one aspect of apologetics.

Whenever you find yourself engaged in apologetics, remember that when we *defend* our Faith we are *sharing* it, too. When you find yourself in a debate, it is tempting to become defensive and even antagonistic toward the person or group of people with whom you are speaking. So how do we defend without becoming defensive?

When asked a direct question about the doctrines of the Faith, we cannot avoid a direct answer. Ultimately, our goal will be to direct people into activities where they can experience a healing encounter with Christ and listen to a proclamation of the Gospel in preparation for an explanation of what we believe. Recognizing that, without that initial proclamation, true catechesis simply is not possible, we must still find ways to motivate people toward learning more about what we believe.

Saint Catherine of Alexandria, patron saint of both preachers and teachers, might offer some inspiration here. She defended Christians and their opposition to worshiping idols at the end of the third century. Catherine, who was a convert and the daughter of a pagan king in Alexandria, traveled to Rome to present herself to the Roman Emperor Maxentius, who was responsible for many Christian persecutions. The emperor received her and arranged for the best pagan philosophers to engage in a moral debate with her. As the legend goes, Catherine not only won the debate but also inspired many of her opponents to convert to Christianity despite their being under threat of execution.

The circumstances under which Catherine defended the Faith threatened certain death. She took courage anyway. She was tortured and imprisoned and ultimately put to death, but not before she was able to convert many other people who visited her, including the Roman empress and wife of Maxentius. I have to believe that it was not just her eloquent words that convinced others to change heart and mind. The very act of showing up must have impressed her opponents. Her courage must have inspired them to see beyond only her words. She did not let the fear of death influence her perspective. She was able to defend the Faith without being defensive and combative.

Like Catherine, we need to respond to emotional objections and attacks with courage. We cannot hide what we believe, and if we are not careful, our fear of rejection may gloss over the truth. We must stand firm in the truths of our Faith even if it means rejection and persecution. The more we show others how passionately we believe in God, the more they will begin to see that our Faith is something worth exploring.

"COME AND SEE"

When we are in "teaching mode," many of us have a tendency to get so caught up in the lessons to share and doctrines to explain that we forget what really inspired us to be Christian disciples in the first place. Our stories very much mirror the experience of the first disciples to follow Jesus in the Gospel of John (see Jn 1:35–51).

The first two disciples in the gospel, Andrew and (traditionally) John, son of Zebedee, first appear as disciples of John the Baptist (see Jn 1:36). When they heard their master call Jesus the "Lamb of God," they immediately followed Jesus instead. Why? Well, this is what Jesus wanted to know, too. He asked them, "What are you looking for?" They responded, "Where are you staying?" There is, of course, an answer to that question. If I am ever traveling and someone were to ask me where I am staying, I would tell them the name of a hotel. But Jesus extends an invitation, "Come, and you will see" (Jn 1:39). He doesn't give them a direct answer; instead, he invites them into a more intimate relationship. That relationship is what Andrew and John are really seeking.

Andrew, now a disciple of Jesus, goes to share his testimony with his brother Peter (see Jn 1:40–41). He brings him to Jesus, to the place where he was staying, and Jesus gives him his name Peter, or Cephas, as the rock upon which he will build his Church

(Mt 16:13–20). Notice a pattern here? John the Baptist testifies, and Andrew becomes a disciple. Andrew bears witness before Peter, and he becomes a disciple, too. This is an important lesson for us to remember as teachers. We are more than educators; we are witnesses. We share our relationship with God by inviting others to join us in that intimate place with him. We bring others to Jesus, inviting them to "come and see."

This pattern is again repeated with Philip and Nathanael. Jesus and his disciples head to Galilee where they meet Philip. Jesus says to Phillip, "Follow me," and of course he does. What does Philip do next? He finds Nathanael and bears witness to Jesus, whom he identifies as Jesus of Nazareth. Nathanael asks a very direct question that would pretty much insult Philip. He asks doubtfully, "Can anything good come from Nazareth?" Think about this for a moment. Has anyone ever asked you a question that puts you in a defensive position like this? You know the questions I mean: questions that seem to insult the very beliefs that we hold. Rather than getting upset or defensive, rather than giving a pointed defense of the testimony he just shared or trying to "win" over Nathanael through an eloquent response, Philip simply says, "Come and see" (Jn 1:46).

That is our task as teachers: not to give well-crafted lessons and explanations but to extend invitations over and over to "come and see." In other words, we are to be witnesses more than teachers. As Pope Paul VI wrote, "Modern man listens more willingly to witnesses than to teachers, and if he does listen to teachers, it is because they are witnesses" (*Evangelii Nuntiandi*, 41). The more we are able to motivate the people we teach to come and see for themselves the truth about what we teach, the more effective we will be in our evangelizing ministries.

At the same time, we also need continuously to come and see for ourselves. How else can we invite people into relationship with God unless we continually strengthen our relationships with him? That is where we begin the next section of this book. Now that we have explored the threefold evangelizing ministry of Jesus Christ, we are going to discover how to apply it in our lives and ministries.

For additional resources on how to teach, visit healproclaimteach.com/ chapter5.

PART III

EVANGELIZATION TODAY

6

BE EVANGELIZED

Before we can go out and evangelize others, we have to be evangelized ourselves. Before we can make disciples, we must continually grow as disciples, whether we are newly initiated or veteran ministers. This chapter goes beyond cliché advice such as "pray more" or "read an inspirational book." Letting yourself be evangelized is an ongoing journey of sacrificial abandonment to God's will. So before you skip this chapter, thinking that you have already been evangelized or that your prayer life is good enough as it is, consider going through some of the exercises I offer here.

This chapter may, in fact, be the most difficult one to read and is at the same time probably the most important. We cannot find success in evangelization unless we continually seek to be evangelized ourselves. I am going to ask you to get out of your comfort zone and do things that may scare you a little. Why? Because God's grace is especially active when we get out of our own way. God works through us when we are uncomfortable and a little bit afraid. When we think we have it all figured out, he is no longer welcome to work through us.

This chapter is about getting comfortable with being uncomfortable. We are called to continual conversion, allowing ourselves to be always transformed into the image and likeness of God in ways we least expect. There is no way around it: evangelization is uncomfortable and hard. We have to be vulnerable, and we have to operate under the fear that we will be rejected. Healing others with compassionate care requires us to be open and authentic and to risk rejection. Proclaiming the Gospel calls for ongoing conversion. Teaching with a focus on real-life experience forces people to be willing to ask difficult questions about life. In all three cases, we risk rejection. Therefore, the religious and spiritual lives that we live must give us the ability to do our ministry amid uncertainty. We must prepare our hearts to rely on God rather than the warm reception of others.

"Blessed are they who are persecuted for the sake of righteousness, for theirs is the kingdom of heaven" (Mt 5:10). We might read this and think Jesus is just talking about the early Christians who were quite literally persecuted and killed for their belief in God. There is a lot, though, that we can take from this *persecution mindset.* Sharing our faith is personal and difficult. It makes us vulnerable to attack. When we recognize that these words from Jesus apply to us today, we should find a little comfort in that uncomfortableness. Rejection is just a part of what it means to evangelize. In reality, most of the time we won't be rejected or persecuted by others. Most of the time the response that people offer to our healing, proclaiming, and teaching will be some form of gratitude or, at worst, simple apathy. Nevertheless, we have to expect and be willing to get hurt, because not everyone is going to have intense love for God as we do, no matter how hard we try to evangelize.

In this chapter we are going to explore the ways in which we can let ourselves experience the healing love of Christ and let go of the things or habits in our lives that we turn to for a false sense of strength. We will look at ways we can consistently embrace our identities as disciples, always interested in learning something new, so that we can become better teachers and disciple-makers.

We will, of course, talk about the good habits and ways in which we can develop a strong spiritual life, but beware: this chapter does not provide a list of surefire ways to prepare ourselves to do evangelizing ministry. There are no surefire tactics because we must look into our hearts and break down the barriers we unknowingly put between God and us. Knowing what those barriers and bad habits are is only the first step. To choose to let go is still incredibly difficult. Let's begin.

CHALLENGE 1: I LOVE ME

My most memorable experience with the Sacrament of Penance may have been the most difficult thing I have ever done in my life—or at least it was at the time.

I was on a retreat in college. I met with the priest during confession time, told him my sins, and waited for his penance. I expected the usual assignment of a prayer or two, but he did not have a Hail Mary or Our Father to give me. Instead, he asked me to go find a mirror, look at myself, and say, "I love you." I laughed and said, "Are you serious?" He nodded and gave me absolution.

I went outside and made my way to the bathroom, which was the only place with a mirror I could think of on the retreat grounds. I checked to make sure no one else was in there. I was alone. I walked up to the sink, looked at myself in the mirror, and stared. Why couldn't I just say it? What was holding me back? It was just a few silly words, right?

Finally, I looked at myself and said, "I love you." It didn't work. I didn't mean it. I wasn't satisfied. So, I took a deep breath, looked into my eyes again, and this time I meant it. "I—love—you." The tears started coming. Keeping my gaze focused on my own teary eyes, I said again, "I love you." I said again with a smile, "I love you. I love you." There I was, looking at myself in the mirror of a public restroom, bawling my eyes out. It was one of the simplest, most amazing spiritual experiences of my life.

There is a scene in the 1997 movie *Good Will Hunting* where Robin Williams's character says to Matt Damon's character, "It's not your fault." He repeats those words again and again until finally Damon breaks down in tears and believes it. That was what it was like for me in that moment in front of that mirror. Although I could not describe it this way at the time, I felt in a very real way the power of being free from sin. You see, sin is not just a bunch of things we have done wrong. Sin has an effect on us. It separates us from God and others, and it makes us believe we deserve to be isolated from them. We blame ourselves so deeply that we believe we are no longer worthy of love.

If there is anything that unites us as human beings, it is this underlying core desire to feel loved. As we grow older, we try to compensate for this fear and act, dress, and do things in a way that we think will make us feel better about ourselves. But nothing ever seems to satisfy.

Here is your first challenge for getting comfortable with uncomfortableness. Go find a mirror, look at the person you see reflected before you, and tell that person, "I love you." Don't just think it; say it. Say out loud, "I love you." It will feel awkward at first, I know, but you have to say it out loud and mean it. This is the first step. Remember, all of evangelization can boil down to this core human desire to be loved. We have to start with ourselves and believe in our hearts that we are worthy of love in order to accept God's unconditional offer of his love for us.

CHALLENGE 2: OUR PERSONAL ENCOUNTERS OF THE THIRD KIND

Unfortunately for us, many people today are as likely to believe in having a personal encounter with aliens as they are in having a personal encounter with God—in some cases, they might even find the aliens to be more likely! We live in a society that sees God as a distant and inactive being who does not interact with the world. Many people profess, at least, to believing in some spiritual being, even though they may not have experienced that being as a reality. They think God is outside of the world and completely impersonal.

As disciples and ministers, we know differently. We have had personal, intimate encounters with the Lord Jesus Christ. We know beyond any doubt that not only is God real, but also he loves us. We know he loves us because we have witnessed him working in our lives through a series of unique encounters with him.

Pope Benedict XVI and subsequently Pope Francis have stressed the central role of an intimate encounter with Christ in our experience as Christians. It is central to the idea of evangelization. Here is Pope Francis quoting his predecessor: "I never tire of repeating those words of Benedict XVI, which take us to the very heart of the Gospel: 'Being a Christian is not the result of an ethical choice or a lofty idea, but the encounter with an event, a person, which gives life a new horizon and a decisive direction'" (*EG*, 7).

Jesus' parting words to his apostles before his Ascension into heaven included these reassuring words, "You will receive power when the Holy Spirit comes upon you, and you will be my witnesses . . . to the ends of the earth" (Acts 1:8). Indeed, we are witnesses to our own personal encounters with Christ and the tough choices we have made to incorporate the Gospel into our lives. For many people, the very idea of these stories is completely foreign, which is why we must be compelled to share them as often as we can.

You and I and all Christian disciples have many stories of Christ working in our lives. These personal encounters helped us to experience the reality of God's loving care for us as his children. I am guessing that amid the busyness of your life, work, and ministry you do not take the time to remember these stories often enough. As you prepare yourself to go heal, proclaim, and teach, taking the time to recall these personal encounters is crucial to your effectiveness as an evangelizer.

Take out your journal or grab a piece of paper and just start jotting down all the different stories in your life when you experienced a personal encounter with the living God. Label this list your "Encounter Stories." It may be a profound moment of grace that initiated a conversion in your life. Or, it could be something small that happened as recently as this week, such as a divine coincidence that showed God at work in your life. It may even be about a person who influenced you or introduced you to Christ. Whatever the stories may be that come to mind, jot them down to help jog your memory. If you want, spend some time thinking and reflecting on these stories and how they shaped you and still apply to you today.

Take a look at your list of encounter stories. These stories are the building blocks for almost everything you do from this point forward in your evangelizing ministry. You might even decide to keep this list handy and continue to add to it as time goes on. Continue to recall the words of Benedict XVI echoed by Pope Francis: "Being a Christian is not the result of an ethical choice or a lofty idea, but [an] encounter." The more we can share our encounter stories with others, the more they will be willing to open up their minds and hearts to their own personal encounters with the living God.

CHALLENGE 3: REMOVE THE ARMOR

In some way, shape, or form, we are all hiding. We are trying to protect ourselves. Just like Adam and Eve, who after their sin tried to hide themselves from God, we try to hide our shame and our brokenness. Each of us has an innate fear of being exposed as an imposter. Sometimes we try to escape by hiding parts of ourselves that we fear will be rejected. Other times we hide those parts of our lives by magnifying other parts of our personalities that we think people will like instead. We fear the pains of separation and rejection and try to protect ourselves from them. But in the process, we shut out Christ and do not seek for him to be there to heal the pain.

The Gospel that we proclaim calls us to leave everything and follow Jesus. Often what we hold on to the tightest are the habits we turn to in order to find comfort and safety. We do everything we can to disguise who we really are inside. We fear if someone were to find out who we really are and expose it to others, we would be devastated. So, we build up strong armor to protect ourselves. This is the very same armor that the Gospel of Christ will dismantle.

Our armor takes many different forms. On one extreme we can try to conjure up an image of ourselves for others that makes us seem perfect. While we may not realize it at the time, our words sound like bragging. When we do this, we offer details or stories about our lives that are unprompted and often irrelevant to a particular conversation. We talk about past achievements that may seem to be relevant context to a given statement but sound more like bragging to others.

The other extreme is probably more common among ministers. As a defense against the possibility of being exposed as impostors, we become self-effacing and overly humble. The low opinion of ourselves may become so extreme that our personal anecdotes or comments about our work or personal life seem to be fishing for compliments. It seems as though behind those comments is a hidden hope that the apparent negative self-image will be met with affirmation and praise that would counter it.

Beyond the words that we say about ourselves, we also look to material things to help protect us from vulnerability. This comes in the form of clothing, cars, houses, and devices, among other things. We hope that others will direct their attention and praise toward the material things in our lives so that we can divert attention away from exposing who we truly are.

As a Christian disciple and evangelizing minister, you probably have a stronger detachment from the material things, actions, and words than many other people, but it is a struggle that never goes away. Until we are united with Christ in heaven, sin will always lead us into a state of protection from pain. We all experience the pain and fear of self-doubt as we create armor to protect ourselves. Thankfully, when most of us are with our close friends and family, we do not have to hide. We feel comfortable and able to be ourselves in front of them. We do not worry about what they think of us, because we know they love us. There is no reason to doubt their love or to question our lovability while we are in their presence.

There are others, though, who make us feel as though we should be someone else, someone who we are not. It may be a boss or a colleague. It could be the local car mechanic or a random person you met at the gym. The point is, we often act in a way that is inconsistent with who we really are because we fear we might be rejected because of that truth.

Just the other day, I was meeting with a theology professor. We were talking about various things related to the Church, theology, and evangelization. I'm no PhD in theology, and I tried to compensate for the obvious gap between us by using big words to make myself seem smarter than I really was. Then I started to second-guess myself. An internal dialogue started to play out in my head: "No, that's not the right meaning of that word. What were you thinking?" There was no reason, really, for me to be afraid. He was not going to judge me for my level of articulation, and the conversation ended very well. I was afraid of my lack of theological education (despite the fact that I have a couple of theology degrees) and tried to protect myself by overcompensating with big words I didn't really know how to use.

Here is your next challenge. Think back to a recent conversation or experience in which you felt defensive and guarded. Whom were you trying to impress, and what did you do to try to protect your vulnerability? What did you say? What were you afraid of exposing about yourself?

Now, the next time you encounter these same feelings of self-doubt and defensiveness, release them. Give yourself permission to be yourself. Smile. Allow people to see who you really are because, as you told yourself in the mirror during our first challenge, you are worth loving. God loves you and created you just the way you are, and for a very good reason.

What does this have to do with evangelization? If you cannot be comfortable with yourself, you will not be able to encounter others at a level of vulnerability that is needed for God to enter in.

CHALLENGE 4: SEE OTHERS FOR WHO THEY REALLY ARE

It is a knee-jerk reaction. We cannot really control it. Very often we react to an encounter with another person feeling threatened by their presence or put off by their personality. We don't like them, and we don't know why.

Throughout my life, God has consistently shown me the failure of operating in this way. In my freshman English class in college, for example, I couldn't stand one of my classmates. He talked all the time and always seemed as if he was trying to be smarter than he really was. I never liked him and never got to know him during that semester. Much to my chagrin, the next year he became one of my roommate's best friends. A year later, he started getting involved in our campus-ministry retreats and events. That's when I finally got to know him and heard his stories of struggles in college and in high school.

Mike, the guy I despised in my freshman English class, became one of the most inspirational people I have ever met in my life. I invited him to join the retreat team with me and got to know him well during our weekly meetings preparing all of the retreats at Miami University. Mike had a pretty hard life. He started college with an awful roommate situation as a freshman, rooming with a guy who was verbally abusive and downright mean to him. Throughout his life Mike battled Crohn's disease, and then later during his college years he suffered from an acute form of stomach cancer. During our senior year, he took a full load of classes even while undergoing chemo and literally carrying a makeshift stomach in a backpack. His senior year culminated in an inspirational event where he spoke to hundreds of students on the stage of Miami's performing-arts center. Mike inspired so many of the people he met. This little, scrawny young man had big dreams and a big impact on the people around him, and his legacy lives on today. The year after we graduated, my friend Mike lost his battle with cancer.

I wish I could say my story with Mike changed the way I see people, but I still suffer from poor judgment of other souls. If I could have just set aside my personal opinions and gotten to know Mike during freshman and sophomore years, I could have experienced two additional years of close friendship with him. I should have learned my lesson, but I still react in fear and judgment and even dislike people I meet sometimes. That kind of reaction is always deceiving. You never know how a person might be able to touch your life if you but get to know him.

Think for a moment about the last time someone who was poor or homeless came up to you on the street and asked you for money. What did you say or do in response? Even more importantly, though, what did you *feel*? Did you feel compassion and love or annoyance and fear? It is the feeling inside that really matters more than what we say or do. It is the feeling that matters to us as evangelizing disciples seeking to heal those on the margins, proclaim the Good News to the crowds, and teach other disciples.

Often, the people we like the least are also the people we know the least. I disliked Mike for the first two years I knew him. Even after I got to know him socially, I didn't like him. Our campus minister had asked me to invite him on the retreat team long before I did it. It wasn't until after I heard him share his testimony that I finally saw him for who he really was. When he opened up his heart by sharing his story, my heart and mind were opened, too. Mike became a friend.

This is not a challenge about giving money to the poor or doing nice things for people you dislike. There is a very good chance that those things will happen, but that is not the goal. The goal is to get to know people we may dislike so we can see them for who they really are. The next time you encounter someone who puts you off somehow, instead make the effort to get to know him. The challenge I'm proposing to you is to ask questions. Ask deep questions about a person's life and life story. Ask uncomfortable questions.

If the person doesn't feel like answering, that's okay. The point is to open up the possibility of a deeper, more personal relationship with someone whom we may be misjudging. Asking questions is the best place to start. Ask about a person's family or about memories she has of growing up as a kid. Ask him how he is doing and what kinds of things he likes to do. We need to focus on our hearts before our actions. Our actions should be an extension of what we believe and feel in our hearts. It should be a result of an openness we have to the love of God working in our lives, even in people we at first don't like.

CHALLENGE 5: MAKE PRAYER A HABIT

In addition to asking questions and getting to know people for who they really are, how do we transform our hearts to receive others with charity (unconditional love)? First, let's recap what we have done so far. The first challenge asked you to admit to yourself that you love yourself—that you are worth loving. Then I asked you to spend some time remembering the moments in your life when God made it clear that he loves you. Now, I hope, you understand the reason we went through those exercises. We are letting our hearts be transformed by God's loving work in our lives so that we can share it with others.

The next challenge is an ongoing one, but it starts today. The only logical way we can become more loving like the saints and see as God sees and love as God loves is to spend more time with him in prayer. Prayer is hard. It does not always lead us into a wishy-washy love feeling. That is not the kind of love that God cultivates within us in prayer. Rather, the true benefit of a consistent prayer life is the ongoing transformation of our hearts. This is why establishing a habitual prayer life is so important.

Do you have a designated time and place in which you pray? Have you made the commitment to pray in a special way every single day whether you feel like it or not? As I was writing this book, I started to read the daily readings each morning right when I woke up. Every single day (and I mean every day), I feel tempted to skip prayer and get right back into this book or another pressing project. It is the commitment along with a consistent time and place that makes it much easier to stick with this daily habit. I do not allow myself to make exceptions; I just do it. But the temptation to skip never goes away.

I started thinking about prayer habits a few years ago. I came to the realization that, while I did pray daily with my family before meals and before bed, I didn't really have a consistent personal prayer life. I started by adding a morning prayer habit to my day and then later added additional times and places for prayer throughout my day. Here is how you can create a consistent prayer life for yourself:

1. Make a list of your daily routines: morning, lunch, evening, and so on.

2. Pick a time when you can add a daily, uninterrupted few minutes for prayer.

3. Write down step-by-step everything you do at that time. For example, when I wake up in the morning, I get out of bed, drink a glass of water, make coffee, and head to the computer at my desk.

4. Pick one specific trigger, or cue, that you will use to remind you to pray. For me, that was making coffee and sitting at my desk. As soon as I sit down, I pull up the USCCB website and read the readings for the day. This trigger is the most essential part of my process. When the trigger is gone, I often forget to pray. When I am traveling, for instance, I frequently forget about prayer or have to force myself to remember to pray because of the different

routine and place. Without my coffee maker and desk at home, I lack that same trigger to pray.

You can repeat this process throughout your day. I now pray the Rosary every day, beginning with the first decade with my daughter on the way to dropping her off at school and continuing on with the other decades during the rest of the way to work. On days when we do not drive to work or school, I have to force myself to remember to pray. The trigger is the car ride. I have also added a daily Angelus prayer, triggered by an alarm and an app reminder that pops up on my phone. The phone also reminds me to say a prayer before work with a setting that is triggered geographically. Whenever I am in a half-mile radius of our office building, the prayer reminder pops up. Recently an update on my phone removed that reminder, and now the act of arriving at my desk triggers a mental reminder.

I cannot say every one of these daily prayer moments has been an existential experience for me. The transformation of the heart is a process that is slow but definitely evident. Individually, the moments of prayer can be transformative experiences during my day, but usually they are not. Usually, I have to force myself to concentrate and focus. I have to mentally set aside the many things on my mind for the day. Yet, put together, the consistent turns to prayer have transformed me in many ways. These brief times of prayer have helped me to add perspective to the struggles in my life, and to approach life united with the will of God rather than with a heart separated from him and his grace. I am able to look back on encounters with other people in the context of the life of Christ and prepare myself to see others as he sees me and the rest of the world. Prayer has enabled me to grow closer to God so that I can allow myself to grow closer to others.

CHALLENGE 6: LOVE YOUR ENEMIES

This is a tough one. The challenge comes directly from Jesus himself: "Love your enemies, and pray for those who persecute you" (Mt 5:44). Now, think about this one for a moment in the context of evangelization. Remember, our number-one priority is to make sure people feel loved. That is what healing and proclaiming are really all about. We can heal by showing people we will be there for them if they need us. We proclaim by showing people that God loves them and that he is there for them when they need him.

To show anything other than love toward our enemies is a failure in evangelization; it is a failure in discipleship. God wants to draw all people to himself, and the only way for us to be united with him is to be able to be united with his people, too. When we hate our enemies, we separate ourselves from them. In this way, we divide ourselves from God as well. God loves every person and wants us all to be united together. At the same time, we may be sending a message to our enemies that we do not love them or even that they are not worthy of love. This is the antithesis of evangelization. It is a rejection of God's command.

Who are our enemies? You might think you do not have any enemies and ignore this challenge. Many people would laugh if I told them I had enemies. When I think of enemies, though, I am thinking of anyone we hold anger or resentment toward in some way. It could be a coworker, a friend, an acquaintance, a family member, or even a group of people we hear about in the news. They do not have to be sworn enemies for life. They can be business competitors or just people whose personalities cause us to act differently toward them. There may be very good reasons to be angry or hold grudges. They might be awful toward us. They might even persecute us. The challenge, though, is clear: respond in love and pray for them instead.

We cannot limit the scope of our work in ministry and evangelization to the people we like. It is our interaction with the people whom we do not like or can barely relate to that offers an even greater opportunity. For them to experience love from us when they least expect it is a sign of true commitment to evangelizing ministry. The challenge to love our enemies is about responding to people with patience. To love our enemies is to seek understanding about the deeper motives behind their actions. Loving our enemies means resisting the urge to be angry or hold a grudge and instead forgiving constantly the wrongdoing that hurts us. To love our enemies means praying for forgiveness for ourselves and praying for the good fortune of those we strongly dislike.

CHALLENGE 7: TWO BY TWO

It would be great if we could do all of this on our own, but that is impossible. There is no amount of grace that will propel us forward as super-evangelizers who change the world without any help from others. According to the Gospel of Mark, Jesus called together the twelve apostles and sent them out "two by two" on a journey to the surrounding towns and villages (Mk 6:7). In the Gospel of Luke, Jesus calls together seventy-two disciples and sends them out in pairs ahead of him "to every town and place he intended to visit" (Lk 10:1).

Whom has God paired with you? Think about it for a moment. Who is the first person that pops into your head when you think of people with whom your friendship is based on a relationship with Jesus Christ? This is a person who holds you accountable. He or she prays for you and cares for you. When something goes wrong in your life, this is the first person who comes to help and listen to your troubles. When you slip away from doing what you know you should or need to do in life, this person is there to put you back on the right path. You share interests and passions and are eager to deepen your relationship with God together.

It does not have to be just one person. As a dedicated Christian, you are likely to have many people like this in your life. These are the people you turn to when things are not going so well. You are able to open up to them, in some cases more easily than with your family or even close friends. You are close with a lot of other people, people whom you love and care for, but this group of people connects with you on a different level. The critical thing that you share together is a common faith and a reliance on God. This propels you and inclines you to support one another in prayer and compassion, even if you have not known each other for very long.

Make a list of the people whom God has matched with you to go out two by two. Can you think of anyone? It may be individuals, married couples, friends, or mentors. Make a list, and think of your relationship with these people. What is the basis of the connection you have? Where did you meet, and what kinds of goals do you share?

Now, here is where the challenge comes in. It is one thing to recognize the people in your life whom God has matched with you in a spiritual friendship. It is another thing to embrace the fact that you are friends who, like Jesus' disciples in the gospels, are called to go out to the people whom Christ intends to visit. Are you ready to take your spiritual friends to the next level? Instead of just asking them for prayers, ask them for a little bit more.

The first thing you can do is ask them to serve with you in an evangelizing ministry. Whether you are a parish worker or a volunteer, these spiritual friends are the people your parish needs to help and volunteer. Have you ever thought to invite these people to serve? At some point someone asked you to help out, too. If someone had not asked, you probably would not be doing what you are doing for the Church today. There is a lot of power in the act of invitation. Make the suggestion and see what happens. They may thank you later.

You can also ask for their help in other ways. Now, do not fall into old habits of thinking about evangelization as proselytism, as if you were going to ask someone to start knocking on doors or ganging up on people you are worried about. When you approach a spiritual friend to ask her to help you with evangelization, you do not have to say the "e" word at all. Instead, you might turn to her to

- help a new friend feel welcomed in your community (heal)
- pray for someone who is hurting either physically or emotionally (heal)
- ask her to share her testimony and conversion story with you or others (proclaim)
- join or welcome someone to a Bible study or small group (teach)

CHALLENGE 8: THE ROLE OF THE SPIRIT

Thankfully, Jesus has given us more than spiritual companions to help us in our mission of evangelization. It is very clear both in the gospels and also at the beginning of the Acts of the Apostles that Jesus does not send his disciples out on their own. They are sent with the power of the Holy Spirit.

The Holy Spirit plays a crucial role in inspiring Jesus and his apostles throughout the Gospel of Luke and then in the Acts of the Apostles. As a boy, for instance, Jesus was led by the Spirit into the Temple where his parents later found him (see Lk 2:41–52). All the gospels agree that Jesus was led by the Spirit into the desert after his baptism (see Lk 4:1). We are also led by that Spirit because we were baptized in the Spirit. Saint Paul wrote, "For those who are led by the Spirit of God are children of God" (Rom 8:14).

In the first public act of leadership after Jesus' death and resurrection, the apostles experienced the outpouring of the Holy Spirit on Pentecost. They were seen speaking in many different languages and appealing to all kinds of people, yet they were rejected by others. Peter took the lead and gave a speech recounting the history of salvation. Those events immediately led to the conversions of three thousand people (see Acts 2:14–41). So, what does the Holy Spirit do for us in our evangelizing mission today?

First, the Holy Spirit will teach you the words to say. I still get nervous before every religious-education session I teach. I am not sure why this happens, but I often get more nervous preparing a lesson in front of a group of kids than I do giving a workshop or a keynote presentation at an adult conference! It may be because there are just so many questions to ask and answer with the students that I worry I won't be able to provide the right answers. This is a fear I hear often from volunteer catechists and ministers. They are afraid they will not have the right words to say. It is a fear of failing the kids and their futures.

Thankfully, Jesus assured his disciples—and assures us today—that "the Holy Spirit will teach [us] at that moment what [we] should say" (Lk 12:12). We have to trust in this. It is okay if our answers are not perfect. In fact, we have to trust that the answers we were given to share by the Holy Spirit were the right ones for a particular time. Remember, we are just one link in a chain of people who will help whomever we are evangelizing in their lifelong journey toward God.

Second, the Spirit inspires us not only to be able to teach, but also to be able to provide personal testimony of our connection with Christ. Just tell your story. At his Ascension, Jesus said to his apostles, "But you will receive power when the Holy Spirit comes upon you, and you will be my witnesses in Jerusalem, throughout Judea and Samaria, and to the ends of the earth" (Acts 1:8). Likewise, we are able to proclaim the Gospel not only as teachers but also as personal witnesses to the effects of Christ's presence in our lives and in the world. This proclamation, emboldened by the Spirit, will touch the lives of the people we meet. We must have confidence in the Spirit's ability to touch people with our stories, even if we doubt our ability to do it ourselves.

Finally, the Spirit enables us to heal those suffering from the pain of sin and separation. Rather than looking to the healing miracles, expecting to see the Spirit's inspiration in the physical transformations, look to the examples and explanations of what the Holy Spirit really does in the Church. At Pentecost, the apostles immediately began to speak in many different languages and were heard and understood by a diversity of people (see Acts 2:4–6). Saint Paul is adamant about the baptism into the one and the same Spirit of God (see 1 Cor 12:13). The Holy Spirit unites us together as one people, as one Church. That is why the Holy Spirit is so critical to evangelization. The Spirit heals the wounds of division and separation among God's people and empowers us to find reconciliation with one another. It inspires us to heal in the way Jesus actually healed, even if a physical transformation never takes place.

Here is your challenge. It comes from Father Theodore Hesburgh, the legendary president emeritus of the University of Notre Dame. I had the pleasure to be present at a few Masses where he presided or preached before he died. In his old age, his homily was always the same. It included simple advice that he had used often throughout his remarkable life. He asked us all to say a prayer with him: "Come, Holy Spirit."

It is a simple yet powerful prayer to offer. For us truly to live out our calling as disciples and evangelizers, we need the Spirit. We need the help and guidance of the Spirit to go out and spread the love of God. Set down this book. Close your eyes, and pray these words, "Come, Holy Spirit." The next time you are about to do any kind of evangelizing activity, whether it be healing, proclaiming, or teaching, one-on-one with others or in groups, pause and seek God's help by praying, "Come, Holy Spirit."

CHALLENGE 9: BREAD FOR THE JOURNEY

Jesus gives us more than his Spirit to help us along the way; he gives us his very self. His true presence in the Eucharist is more than just a reminder or a comforting experience of his memory; it is an efficacious presence of his very life. As a result, Jesus acts through us along our journey, propelling us forward and guiding us by uniting us with him and with our fellow Christians.

As Saint John Paul II wrote, "Let all pastoral activity be nourished by [the Eucharist]" (*Dominicae Cenae*, 4). Without the Eucharist, without an ever-deepening unity with Christ, it becomes very difficult to do Catholic evangelization. How could we share what we do not have? How could we share Christ when we do not take the opportunity to find unity with him and the Church?

By participating in the Eucharist, we deepen our personal connection with Christ and we are united with his Body, the Church. Through the liturgy, we are united with our brothers and sisters in Christ. Is there any other purpose or goal in evangelization than to seek unity and peace? We go out to help others find God, but also to help them find comfort and hope in a community of fellow disciples.

As I have talked to people about their stories of conversion or reversion to the Catholic Church, the Eucharist almost always plays a central role. For the people who felt separated or outcast because of sin and selfishness, the Eucharist provided the ability for them to find the healing they needed to be united back into the community. For us as Catholics, the Eucharist must be the driving force and inspiration for all that we do as evangelizing disciples. By uniting ourselves with Christ and the Church, our venial sins are forgiven and we find strength against the mortal sins that would divide us from God and others. The Eucharist heals because it unites.

According to the *Catechism of the Catholic Church*, one of the other effects of the Eucharist is that it "commits us to the poor" (1397). That always seemed to be an odd effect to me, but it actually makes perfect sense. Through the greater unity with God and others, we find greater compassion for those in the greatest need. Think of all those parables about the kingdom of God. In each one, Jesus proclaimed a God who loves us deeply and a kingdom of people who put others before themselves. How could we become a part of that kingdom without a commitment to those in greatest need?

The powerful effects of Christ's presence in the Eucharist are so great, yet so difficult to comprehend. How can our God possibly be present in bread and wine? Ask a well-catechized Catholic to answer a question like this, and he will tell you, "It is a mystery!" Indeed it is, but not a kind of unsolvable mystery we should give up trying to understand. It is a mystery we never stop ceasing to understand more clearly and believe more sincerely. The Eucharist drives us into deeper understanding as we try to comprehend the incomprehensible. That is why we continue to grow as Christian disciples with the power of the Eucharist.

For this final challenge before moving on to the next chapter on one-on-one evangelization, consider the Eucharist in the context of the Mass. The word *Mass* comes from the Latin *missa*, which means "go forth." This is why at the end of the liturgy the priest or deacon makes one of the following proclamations at dismissal:

- "Go forth, the Mass is ended."
- "Go and announce the Gospel of the Lord."
- "Go in peace, glorifying the Lord by your life."
- "Go in peace."

Each one quite obviously begins the same way: *go*. This echoes the words of Jesus at the end of the Gospel of Matthew: "*Go*, therefore, and make disciples of all nations" (Mt 28:19). This challenge is an ongoing one. Every time you attend Mass from this point forward, listen for this final dismissal and take the words to heart. They are a call to arms. You are being sent, but you are not alone. Having received Christ's presence in the Eucharist and finding unity with his Church, we go forth in peace to glorify God by the way we live and to proclaim the Gospel to those we meet.

We are always being sent and never asked to keep Christ to ourselves. Take this to heart every time you go to Mass. Remember, you are being sent. Go!

Where are you going? To find others with whom you can share the Gospel, of course! In the next two chapters we will explore the ways in which you can evangelize through personal relationships as an evangelizing disciple and then in both small and large groups in your evangelizing ministries.

For supplemental resources and support in carrying out these challenges, visit healproclaimteach.com/chapter6.

7

ONE-ON-ONE EVANGELIZATION

When I give talks to leaders in Catholic parishes about evangelization, I like to invite the audience to recall a specific moment or a series of moments when they encountered Christ (just like your list of encounter stories in chapter 6). It always amazes me to see such joyful smiles on the faces of the participants as they share their stories. For many of them, this is the first opportunity they have been given to share their conversion stories with the people they work with. The conversations are always heartfelt and sometimes even bring tears of joy.

At a recent event, a participant made an incredible observation that I did not foresee when planning the discussion. She noted that in almost every story she heard from her table, there was a person who in some way enabled these encounters with Christ to happen. Think about that for a moment. In order to meet Jesus, someone has to introduce you to him. Our encounters with Christ almost never occur in a vacuum; they almost always involve some person—maybe a friend, a family member, a mentor, a teacher, an author—who inspires us first to see God and then to take a chance on God. In many ways, our stories of encounters with Christ are really stories about our relationships with others.

You are or will be in someone else's encounter story. Someone someday is going to share the story about how they met

Jesus and experienced a transformation in life thanks in part to a relationship with you. Follow in the footsteps of the saints and leaders in this book, and there are likely to be many people who will include you in their stories. You and I have the power and responsibility to guide people on a path toward an intimate and ongoing encounter with Christ. He has called us to be his witnesses, and we answer by simply entering into a relationship with others and sharing our relationship with God.

This chapter is focused on our ability to minister to individual people and develop an authentic relationship with them that is anchored in a love of Christ. We can have no ulterior motives. This is not a chapter about how to make friends strategically with people so you can convert them into active members of the Church. No, the goal is to develop authentic, lasting, and intimate relationships with the people around you with no strings attached.

Throughout the chapter we will look at the ways you can incorporate the heal, proclaim, and teach aspects of evangelizing ministry without falling into the trap of trying to categorize people along their journeys of discipleship. There is no if/then prescription for healing, proclaiming, and teaching. The more you view what you do in one-on-one interactions as a part of a systematic *strategy* of evangelization, the less authentic you will be and the less likely others will be to call you when they need help. Getting better at one-on-one evangelization is simply about developing our ability to love.

NO GOALS

When you are trying to intentionally "evangelize" someone, the inclination is to want to direct the person's progress toward some kind of predetermined goal. Probably the most unnatural part of the heal, proclaim, and teach approach to ministry is that we have to separate ourselves from the tendency to set goals. Whether or not a person will be transformed by God through your relationship with him or her is totally up to the Spirit.

Why is this so important? Because if our ultimate goal while developing a relationship with a person is to get him to do something *we* think will help him (go to church, for instance), then this ulterior motive is going to be perceived as the real reason for our interest in that person. Think of the stereotypical used-car salesman who puts on a smile and listens to your car troubles. Ultimately you know he just wants to get you to buy a car before you leave the lot. It's hard to trust anything he says because you know he's working on commission and he cares more about the sale than what's best for you. (Now, I've met many honest car salesmen. We're talking about the stereotype here, not necessarily the real thing.) The point is, as we develop relationships with people, we have to make them authentic with no ulterior motives.

The foundation of anything we do in one-on-one evangelization is simply to be there for someone when she needs us. This is what "healing" means. When someone is in need, we are there for her. In Henri Nouwen's *The Wounded Healer* we read an imaginary story of an MDiv student ministering to a man about to enter into surgery. Nouwen creates a mock conversation between them in which what the man says actually reveals a hidden fear that he's not willing to admit. Behind the entire episode is a very real need and desire: that someone will be there waiting for the man when he wakes up.[1]

Instead, the ministry student tries to respond to his comments and concerns with surface-level anecdotes about Church teaching. He does not engage more deeply in the conversation to get beyond the words the man actually says. He remains at the level of impersonal ideas and is, therefore, unable to truly meet the man in the place of his greatest need. He is unable to really connect the man's situation with the Gospel, because the Gospel is put in an abstract and barely relevant context.

How is this moment an opportunity for evangelization? It is not because it offers the opportunity to share the Church's wonderful teachings about death and dying. It is not even a good opportunity to proclaim the story of Christ's death and resurrection. It is an evangelizing moment because of this man's coded cry for help, and the desire to be loved and accepted for who he is and what he has done with his life. It is an opportunity for healing.

When we engage in one-on-one evangelizing ministry of any kind, the first and maybe only rule is simply this: be there for the person. Be present and willing to listen to what is going on in his or her life. Maybe not only listen, but also seek to understand what is really going on in the hearts and minds of the people we meet. Don't worry about sharing the Gospel or Church teachings. Resist the temptation to share your anecdotal stories. Instead, ask questions and offer your compassionate presence in the moment without any intention to fix the person's problems. Look at the person, see him or her, and love.

THE ART OF ACCOMPANIMENT

In modern times, people crave human connection, and they often find outlets for that desire through distant, technological means. Many youth send hundreds of texts each day but falter in direct conversation. They build relationships with other young people via social media or video gaming yet struggle to connect in person. Adults are not much better. We check social media frequently to see the latest updates from family and friends, yet often we can't find time to see one another face-to-face. From young to old, we use technology as a way to connect with other people, often to the detriment of creating lasting friendships.

The importance of a face-to-face, long-lasting relationship has never been clearer. This is even more the case in terms of the need to be effective evangelizers. Pope Francis, seeing the need for this approach, observed that "the Church will have to initiate everyone—priests, religious, and laity—into this 'art of accompaniment,' which teaches us to remove our sandals before the sacred ground of the other (cf. Ex 3:5)" (*EG*, 169). What does the Holy Father mean by the "art of accompaniment"?

Essentially, the art of accompaniment is about listening with openness. Rather than just listening to someone during a conversation, we ask questions about what our friend is saying and seek to find out what is really behind the words he says. In response, we open up our hearts and allow ourselves to experience a compassionate closeness that is required for a genuine spiritual encounter.

The goal of the art of accompaniment is to open up and be a person whom someone can confide in rather than seeking to find a solution to someone's problem. Ultimately, as Pope Francis pointed out, "each person's situation before God and their life in grace are mysteries that no one can fully know from without" (*EG*, 172). We have to resist the temptation to know in good counsel what should be done. Instead, we simply invite our friends into an experience of being healed in Christ. We might not actually use the word *healing*, but we can certainly extend invitations to prayer or participation in the sacraments. From there we can accompany them on a new stage in their journey of embracing the cross and leaving all behind for the sake of the Gospel.

When is the art of accompaniment most important? We have in place official capacities in which we are called to carry out the art of accompaniment. It can be especially appropriate for godparents, or RCIA and Confirmation sponsors. They are asked to walk the journey toward the sacraments. The temptation when serving in these roles is simply to complete the book or the program that the parish has provided or just to attend the required meetings along the way. Sponsors are called to do more than this. They should seek to go deeper and get beyond the teaching alone and also provide some healing and proclaiming whenever possible.

Likewise, godparents should accompany the parents of their godchildren along the journey of parenthood. They vow to "help the parents of [the] child in their duty as Christian parents" during the Rite of Baptism. Godparents should practice the art of accompaniment with their godchildren's parents as the children get older. As they grow, they can also begin to accompany their adult godchildren as faithful companions.

Mentor couples who assist engaged couples on their way to matrimony can also practice the art of accompaniment. They meet with the engaged to do more than just complete a program or read through a book. While taking part in a marriage-preparation program, they also go deeper and listen to the real questions and struggles of the couples they mentor. They listen and provide support along the way. Whenever possible, they proclaim the love of God and bear witness to a marriage that is strengthened by Christ, but always with authenticity and openness about the real challenges they have experienced along the way.

We also accompany other ministers along their journey. "Missionary disciples accompany missionary disciples," as Pope Francis pointed out (*EG*, 173). Jesus sent the disciples out two by two. Saint Paul writes to and talks about many of the other disciples such as Barnabas, Timothy, and Titus whom he accompanied along the way. Likewise, we should be present for our colleagues and coworkers and fellow volunteers in our ministries. We should support pastors and priests as well. In each case, we need to go beyond a professional relationship no matter how uncomfortable this might be at first. If we recognize that we walk together on a journey of discipleship, then we can help each other continue to encounter Christ and seek to realize more deeply his kingdom.

PROMISE TO PRAY

How can we truly practice the art of accompaniment? The rest of this chapter includes more practical applications for living out the art of accompaniment in your life as an evangelizing disciple and minister.

One of the best things we can do as evangelizing disciples is to assure people that we care about them and are there for them if they need us. We can easily say this, but how do we actually live it? One critical way to practice love and charity toward others is to keep them specifically in our prayers. Prayer and intercession on another person's behalf is incredibly powerful. Would Saint Augustine have had his conversion if it were not for his mother Saint Monica's constant prayers for him? Would you be interested in reading this book right now if it were not for the prayers of friends, family, and ministers who helped you along the way?

The trouble is that it is hard to remember to pray for others. We tell people all the time, "I'll pray for you," but how often do we follow through with this promise? The commitment to pray is almost always a spiritual battle against forces that want to keep us from prayer. That is why it is so important to set up habits that enable us to keep these promises. We cannot expect ourselves to remember every prayer commitment we have ever made, which is why we often include an intercession such as, "and for all those whom we have promised to pray for . . ." I do this too, but I think we can do more.

Lately, I have gotten into the habit of carrying around a notepad everywhere I go. In it I record my most important tasks of the day to help prioritize my work. On that page of paper, I also take notes of the people I need or want to pray for on that day. I pray for them when I first write down their names and the intention just in case I don't get the chance to pray for them again that day. At the end of the day, as a part of a daily practice, I come back to that paper and offer intentions for each of the people I wrote down.

By praying for others, we certainly help make an impact on their lives, and we strengthen our own bonds of trust and charity toward others. When we ask them to share a little bit about themselves or ask if there is anything we can pray for in their lives, the barriers of defensiveness often come down and we share vulnerability. This opens the way to a relationship of trust that can be a true source of healing. It can lead into sincere conversation about God and give us the opportunity to proclaim the Good News, or it might never develop that way. But we will have loved.

WHEN EVERYBODY KNOWS YOUR NAME

Remembering names is one of the most important skills to learn in ministry and evangelization. I remember the shock my wife and I experienced a few years ago when we joined our very large parish and the pastor, having only met us once before, remembered our names. It was a small but incredibly powerful gesture. It turns out many, many other people in the parish had the same experience when they first joined or started to get involved in the parish. It is a wonderful skill that our pastor, Father Bill, has worked hard to cultivate. It seems as if it's such a small thing, but it makes a huge difference.

It is so crucial to learn names. Many times we are given name tags at parish or school events to help people learn our names. It is easy to forget names in large groups of people, but eventually we stop referencing the name tags of the regulars and begin to use the names of people we have come to know. So, how do you get better at remembering names? Don't rely on name tags. Try one of these strategies next time you meet someone new, because it might be the first step in a friendship that could blossom into an evangelizing encounter:

1. **Repeat the name after you hear it.** One of the best ways to make sure you remember a person's name correctly is to repeat his name back to him. This is especially helpful when you are not quite sure if you heard it correctly the first time. Always repeat the name back to the person. "John, great to meet you. My name is Jared."

2. **Use the name in conversation, frequently.** You can't expect that saying the name just once is going to keep it fresh in your memory. Immediately begin asking questions, addressing a person by name to practice and train your brain to remember it. "John, where are you from?" [Response.] "That's awesome, John; what do like about living there?" It might seem forced from your perspective, but in reality people love hearing their names. It makes them feel interesting and worthy of being remembered. When someone calls us by name, we are not just another person in the crowd; we are a person with a name and a unique story to tell.

3. **Visualize the name.** When asking for clarification or restating a name, many people like to use visualization techniques to remember it. Imagine the name written out on a piece of

paper, or picture a scene in which a person's name is connected to something you can remember, such as an animal, famous person, or place. When meeting a Stephen for the first time, you might imagine the word *Stephen* spelled out in stones, making a connection to Saint Stephen the martyr.

4. **Use mnemonic devices.** Other people like to use verbal cues to remember names. You might think of alliterative descriptions such as "Juggling Joe" or "Jammin' Jane" to set someone apart from the crowd. These phrases don't have to be shared. They are just simple ways to remember names. It is easier to remember a "juggling Joe" than just a person named Joe.

5. **Write the name down on paper.** Later, after meeting someone new, write the name down on a piece of paper or in a computer file with one or two details about that person. When I am at conferences meeting multiple new people each day, I either write down a few details about our conversation on the back of their business cards or I keep track of the conversations on a separate sheet of paper. It really helps me to remember to follow up later and to remember conversations when someone e-mails me later.

6. **Pray for the person by name.** We are talking about evangelization, remember, not just any chance meeting or some kind of business opportunity. One of the best ways to remember the name of a person who has shared something about herself is to pray for her. Praying for people by name is a powerful experience both for you as the pray-er and for the person for whom you pray.

HOW TO LISTEN TO PEOPLE'S PROBLEMS

We often get the opportunity to evangelize in regular everyday conversation. Sometimes people confide in us. They have rough days, fights with their spouses, hard times at work, personal fears, and so on. What do we do in response? How do we have those conversations in such a way that others are led to the healing touch of Christ?

Remember, as Christians we are *wounded healers.* We do not claim to have all the answers. In fact, we may have no idea how to help. People often come to us not for advice but for comfort. They want to get things off their chests and vent. These stories can be difficult to hear, and it is often difficult not to try to help fix the problem.

I cannot be alone in finding it very difficult simply to be present and experience the pain someone describes without trying to fix it. We might try to change the subject or lighten the mood with a joke. Sometimes this is helpful in cheering someone up, but if it avoids the pain, it may be misleading the conversation. We can also be tempted to brush it off and tell the person that it is really "no big deal." This discredits the pain they are feeling and is often more motivated by our own fear of intimacy than what is best in the situation. Likewise, communicating the "fix" of saying things such as "It's God's will . . ." can also discredit another's pain, despite our best intentions to help the person see the troubles from a wider perspective. In these tender moments of human encounter racked with pain, we have the wonderful opportunity to evangelize because such vulnerability can open the door to a healing encounter with Christ.

So, how do we become wounded healers in these kinds of situations? Unless you are specifically asked by a hurting person for help in solving a problem, offer only your ears and compassionate heart. When people share their sorrows, they first want

someone to listen; they may not want to come up with strategies to solve the problem quite yet. Instead, ask questions to go
deeper and get to the level of our shared human condition. Ask
those questions that you are afraid to ask—the ones that tug on
your heart. These kinds of questions, which get people talking
about tough times, offer the opportunity for someone to talk
to you about something he might not get to talk about with
anyone else. Ask questions, listen, and share stories of shared
challenges, but never try to "one up" what you have heard or
try to make someone feel that his situation is not quite as bad as
yours. Trust me, asking the questions that tug at your heart gets
easier as you learn to ask them and grow accustomed to hearing
others respond.

At the end of these conversations, make two commitments.
First, promise to pray for the person. Do not say anything else.
Just let her know you are there for her and that you are going to
offer her struggles to God in prayer. Then, of course, pray! This
is crucial. Do not skip this step. It is essential for evangelization.
Pray for the person. Second, commit yourself to checking in with
that person again. When you see her, ask about the situation.
She will certainly remember having shared her pain, so ask for
an update and continue to ask questions. Then repeat again and
again. Eventually, you may get the opportunity to do what feels
more like traditional evangelization by talking about God and
the paschal mystery, but sharing this too soon may push people
away. Let's explore this opportunity a little further so we can
proclaim the Gospel in one-on-one conversation without being
preachy.

HOW TO PROCLAIM IN CASUAL CONVERSATIONS

Sometimes during these conversations, people will ask for advice about resolving a problem. At other times we see what we believe to be a good suggestion, and the desire to help weighs on our hearts. How do we know if we have enough wisdom to be able to help?

If we are encountering the person at a level of deep personal struggle, then we should be able to put ourselves in his or her shoes. That is critical, because doing so enables you to see things as they are rather than how you might see them as an outsider. We must guard against being judgmental and certain about a course of action when it is someone else's life. Temptations toward these attitudes need to be tamed so we can clearly see how to help in a more loving way.

If we are genuinely wounded healers, then we should be able to see ourselves in the same situations others are in. We will not claim to know all the answers; we only claim to know many of the problems. Therefore, when people come to us for advice, we should seek answers in our own personal experiences and not respond with things we think we should say. We want to be authentic in our responses. It is okay to admit we do not have the answers and to trust in the Spirit to inspire us or lead our friend in the right direction.

At the same time, these encounters are opportunities not just to help heal our wounded friend but to proclaim the Gospel. We have to stay grounded in our own authenticity, our own story of struggle and strife. If in that story we can find God's work in our lives, then we have something to share. Most of the time, when people ask tough questions or ask for help in a given situation, they do not want the textbook Church-teaching answer; they want reassurance that they are not alone. As a friend and companion, we have already met that need in one way. Now we need to reassure people that while we are there for them, God is there for them in an even greater and deeper way.

Remember, when we proclaim the Gospel we do not share a story of some abstract idea. We share an intimate encounter that is set within the context of Christ's saving mission and his death and resurrection. When we talk about what Jesus did in the context of our own personal struggles, there is hope that we don't come off as "preachy" or simply too religious to be believable. Start from the point of shared pain, and then talk about the healing encounter in the context of that pain. If your story doesn't include that level of shared pain, then it probably isn't appropriate to share it. Instead, it will likely come off as preachy and out of place.

Jesus loves us; he died for us; and he is with us today. Remember, these are the points that we want to make through telling stories of the Gospel, intertwined with our encounter stories of bumping into Christ. All we can do is tell the stories. We cannot control what is heard or how someone will react. But we can trust in the Holy Spirit, saying our simple prayer of petition, "Come, Holy Spirit."

WHEN QUESTIONS COME UP IN CONVERSATION

Sometimes, though, people do not come to share their personal struggles or ask for help. They just want to know why the Church teaches what it does. Keep in mind that after a person feels welcomed by you and trusts you, one of the biggest roadblocks between that person and his willingness to give God or the Church a try are his misunderstandings of Church teaching. To outsiders, the Church can seem out of touch with reality. They may perceive an organization that seems to condemn more than it offers help with suffering. They may perceive an institution that preaches subordination with oppressive laws and commandments rather than offering freedom and salvation. When asked, of course, we need to provide responses to questions about Church doctrine as best we can. Once again, we must trust in the Holy Spirit that our answers will be appropriate in that particular moment, recognizing that the other person's journey will continue on from here.

Keep in mind what a good thing it is that he or she is asking the questions. That means there is some interest. Often, when people feel they already have the answers, they close themselves off to God's grace. Even still, sometimes a question is phrased with hostility. We should answer as best we can, all the while seeking to understand the motivation behind the questions. When a person is angry about the Church's teaching on divorce and questioning it bluntly, for example, recognize that behind that question may well be intensely felt pain either from his own divorce or that of a loved one. The very same kind of woundedness often resides behind questions about gay marriage, contraception, cohabitation, confession to a priest, praying to saints, and doubts about the Virgin Mary.

Often people who ask questions about doctrine are not disciples; they are from the group of people that the Gospels call the crowd. Remember how Jesus communicated with them? He spoke in parables because knowledge of the kingdom of God was granted to the disciples, but not yet to them. If you think back to the chapter on proclamation (chapter 4), we said that we do not need to come up with creative, modern parables to proclaim the Gospel. We have the greatest story—the story of Christ's death and resurrection—to share with people. That is why, when we work with a person who is at a curiosity-and-seeking stage in her evangelization journey, we must do everything we can to direct the questions and our responses to the saving mission of Jesus Christ.

It is never easy to answer tough questions, but our responses always need to do two things. First, we must surface the deeper meaning behind a doctrine of the Church and connect it in some way to God's infinite love expressed most clearly in his saving death on the Cross. Is this immediately going to resolve the hurt people feel because of the Church's teachings? Probably not, but it is a start. Regarding divorce, for example, it can be messy. The annulment process is a challenge and often draws into question any kind of beauty we might have proclaimed in our conversations. That should not stop us, though, from sharing the truth as it relates to Christ's saving mission while we continue to accept our calling as wounded healers.

Second, we need to relate the doctrine being explored to the experiences, emotions, and dreams of the person who is trying to understand and accept it. We have to get past a "because the Church says so" mentality and discover a deeper meaning that helps both us and the persons we encounter as sinners. Sometimes this requires us to go deeper, read more, and understand something more deeply with the person who has asked the questions. This can be a wonderfully fulfilling process as we discover what the Church teaches in the context of a life situation that puts it to the test. Knowing textbook articulation of Church teachings is one thing, but integrating it into the lived experience of a particular person in a particular time and place can be an eye-opening process for both you and that person.

THE MENTORSHIP MODEL

When I was a freshman in college, a young, super-cool guy used to come into our dorm to meet with some of us. He was a singer in a Christian rock band and a dedicated member of Campus

Crusade for Christ. It was not long before he had a core group of guys whom he invited to join a Bible study in the dorm's basement. I'm sure all of this went into his training as a representative of Campus Crusade for Christ, but everything he did was perceived with complete authenticity. All of us truly felt that we could trust Scott with anything, and he never let us down.

With a few of the guys, he started setting up regular one-on-one meetings. In a lot of ways, he was an informal mentor helping answer questions or just lending a listening ear when it was needed. I was always so impressed by how likable he was and how many of the guys in my dorm got to know him so well. To me, Scott remains an exemplary evangelizing disciple. He was an incredible example of one-on-one ministry that is often referred to as the mentorship model of evangelization.

At certain points in our evangelizing ministry, opportunities arise where we can work more closely with an individual in a semiofficial capacity as mentor. In this kind of relationship, we make the commitment to check in regularly, tackle questions, offer advice, and provide a level of accountability that enables a person really to break through in his or her journey of discipleship. This doesn't have to be a clear-cut mentorship program. We can do this informally or formally, whichever works best for us.

As I got more involved with the Catholic campus ministry as a college student and no longer attended the Campus Crusade for Christ, I lost personal touch with Scott. As the year went on, though, I continued to see some of the great things happening with the other guys in my dorm. Taking a few lessons from his one-on-one approach to ministry, I gained the following insights about Christian mentorship:

- **Be yourself.** Most of us thought Scott was a cool guy. He was in a band and he was very outgoing, but not everyone liked him. He was totally himself even if it meant some of the other guys in the dorm were turned away by his personality.

- **Make the time.** Scott showed up often just to check in. He was a busy guy, but he still made time for the guys he was connecting with in our dorm by showing up as much as possible.

- **Ask questions.** Scott asked about our lives and wanted to know more about us. That's probably the reason we saw this minicelebrity to be so authentic. He showed us he really cared and told us he was praying for us.

- **Make a person feel welcome.** When we ran into Scott at larger Campus Crusade events or gatherings, he would introduce us to his upperclassmen friends. He always made us feel welcome even though he was so much older and more connected than we were.

- **Extend invitations.** Without any strings attached, Scott invited us to the Wednesday night gatherings, overnight retreats, and Bible studies. He always had something to invite us to throughout the year.

These are all just building blocks for developing a long-lasting relationship. There are many opportunities for people to become mentors: adults and youth-group members, sponsors and catechumens or candidates for full communion, married couples and the engaged, spiritual directors and those they guide. The goal is to work closely with people who have encountered Christ's healing love, who have made sacrifices to live for God's kingdom, and who have become disciples of Christ. As mentors, we help a person who has chosen to follow Christ continue on in her path of discipleship so she can grow deeper in the Faith.

The mentorship model for evangelization and catechesis is often called "discipleship" in the Church today. Jim Schuster, a youth minister in Virginia, described to me the role of a discipleship mentor as providing "a source of guidance, discernment, and accountability."[2] Whether it is meeting at a McDonalds or a Starbucks, or in the youth room at the parish, Schuster finds ways to reach out to kids who are ready to go further spirituality or who really need someone to talk to. "Ideally," Schuster told me, "[mentors] are helping keep their mentee focused on the goal of their discipleship, intimacy with Jesus, celebrating new victories and breakthroughs with them, and coaching them through difficulties that arise."[3] This very same relationship can be cultivated not only between adults and kids but also from student to student and adult to adult. Age does not make a person a mentor. Maturity in discipleship does.

EVANGELIZING THE PEOPLE WE LOVE

As good Christians, we know we are supposed to share our faith with others in our daily lives at home, at work, in our neighborhoods, and with our friends and family. But it just seems so awkward. It makes us feel uneasy and pushy. We want to share our faith, but we do not want to give the impression that we are judging people we love for not being religious like we are. We do not want to become proselytizers.

The great thing about the heal, proclaim, and teach approach to evangelization is that you do not have to feel any of those things. Evangelization, in this sense, is seeking what is best for others. We are not trying to take away someone's freedom; we are trying to help him find a freedom he so very much deserves— freedom from isolation and alienation, freedom from guilt, freedom from sin, freedom to become who he is really meant to be in life. We can do this through the evangelizing, healing ministry that Jesus showed us.

Many people whom I have talked to about evangelization share something I struggle with daily: it is easier to share my faith with strangers or acquaintances than it is to share my faith verbally with my close friends and family. When I am Jared the Catechist or Jared the Writer or even Jared the Parishioner, I find it easier to be in evangelization mode than I do when I am with the people I know and love in my personal life. I can think of a couple of reasons for this.

First, I think we fear intimacy. I can physically feel my heart shake when a conversation descends from surface-level topics into something deeper and more heartfelt. Some people crave this kind of human connection, but I tend to feel uncomfortable. I often have to retrain my mind and heart with some of the exercises in the previous chapter in order to commit myself to being willing to stay in those kinds of conversations. There, in our discomfort and nakedness, we open ourselves up to experience and share our pain. That is a hard thing to do willingly.

Second, I think we fear rejection and loss. We fear losing touch with the people we love dearly who are closest to us. Talking about religion can be worse than talking about politics because it is such a personal subject. The threat of being rejected or getting into an argument makes it difficult to bring up the beliefs that are such a central part of our lives. We do not want to offend anyone, because then they might separate themselves from us or, worse, stop loving us.

How, then, do we have a conversation about faith? How do we invite those closest to us to enter into a personal relationship with Christ? First, we have to be willing to open up and allow others to open up to us. We have to get in touch with the parts of their lives that are hidden, protected, and not easily shared. We will not be able to introduce someone to Jesus through intellect alone; we have to connect Christ to those vulnerable recesses of their lives.

This is a process that can take a very long time. It requires commitment and patience. Keep in mind our no-goals mentality. Instead of focusing on results, focus on a heart open to healing. We don't need to begin with trying to get the person to go to church even if we think that is the best thing for him. Our only hope is to tear down our own armored protection from vulnerability and the tendency to judge. We simply need to be present. We have to set aside trying to control outcomes and let God do the work.

Whether we are given the opportunity to have these conversations or not, we must live a way of life that shows our commitment to the kingdom of God. To our close friends, family, and coworkers, we have to show this commitment to self-sacrifice, service, and dedication to our faith in God. They should be able to see in us a life of prayer and evangelical simplicity. We make obvious our participation in a parish community that is welcoming and feeds us spiritually in significant ways. We are a part of something worth inviting people into. When the opportunity arises, we extend the invitation without any expectations or judgment. Then, we let the Spirit do the work.

Sometimes our friends and family may be interested in talking, listening, or even joining us in church. Sometimes, while they are with us in that welcoming community dedicated to encountering Christ, they experience something worth exploring further. From there, we maintain our selfless love for them, our selfless way of life, and continue to be present on the journey, helping to answer questions about new concepts that they may never have considered before.

It is never easy to evangelize our friends and family, because we often take the wrong approach, trying to win them over as if we were having a debate. But Jesus taught us to "evangelize" with no motive other than love. That's it. We love them and extend invitations.

EXTENDING AN INVITATION

We have been touching on an essential moment in the process of evangelization without going into enough detail: at some point, we will have the opportunity to offer a simple, no-strings-attached invitation to join us on our faith journey, to come and see who God is. When those opportunities arrive, we try to make connections between what we know to be going on in a person's life and an activity, resource, book, ministry, event, or group that relates to that individual's circumstances.

For example, if someone is struggling with a big life decision, we can do our best to counsel that person through it, but we could also share a spiritual book or prayer practice that we have found to be valuable. I've seen many younger people share music with others that has helped them through tough times. Again, the invitation to prayer is a great way to help others. If someone is dealing with the pain of loss or fear of sickness, we can invite her to pray with us right there on the spot.

At some point we will feel pulled to extend our relationship beyond the one-on-one connection and into the larger community of the Church. Our hope should be that our relationship with individuals also bears fruit in growing small and large groups in the context of a parish community. That is why I believe that having at least one "inviteable" event is critical to the success of our evangelizing ministries.

An inviteable event is an offering of your ministry that constantly welcomes newcomers with very few barriers that might prevent someone from coming. Retreats such as Kairos, Search, Christ Renews His Parish, and so on are common inviteable events. Diocesan conferences and youth rallies are also common inviteable events. Youth ministries usually have a weekly youth night that enables them to grow their memberships week by week. Sunday Mass itself ought to be the ultimate inviteable event, but it needs to be celebrated in such a way that newcomers know they are welcome and that focuses on the first two priorities of evangelization, healing and proclaiming. (For more on the Mass as *the* inviteable event, read chapter 6 of the popular book *Rebuilt* by Michael White and Tom Corcoran.) As we shall see in the next chapter, it is so important that we always have something to invite people to.

Inviteable events are opportunities for healing and proclamation. We are not primarily aiming to teach participants to be disciples. That will come later. First we make connections between what is going on in their lives and the Gospel message, which beckons them toward intimate relationship with Christ.

As we develop a relationship with someone in the context of faith in Christ, we also stay anchored in our own community of disciples—our parish. Our invitations must always connect our personal relationships to a broader relationship with Christ's Body, the Church. Eventually, we are going to have the opportunity to share a community with the individuals with whom we have built relationships. This leads from a one-on-one approach to a group approach to evangelizing ministry.

For additional resources on one-on-one evangelization, visit healproclaimteach.com/chapter7.

8

GROUP EVANGELIZATION

Connection to a community gives us a sense of belonging. We feel welcome for who we are (or maybe even in spite of who we are), becoming members of something larger than ourselves. We share common goals and mutual support that push us through difficult times and provide comfort when we need it. In groups, we learn habits and take on values that become a part of us and strengthen us.

I am forever blessed, for example, to have been a part of my high-school football team growing up in the small town of Huron, Ohio. Friday-night football was everything to that town and still is. As kids we grew up idolizing our players and counting the days until we would get to wear the crimson and gray uniforms. Despite my mediocre football skills, I felt welcomed into a brotherhood as a high-school football player. We fought together, sweat together, bled together, and continue to remain friends today. I learned so many important habits that have enabled me to succeed today: perseverance, integrity, work ethic, internal motivation, teamwork, and leading by example. I would not be doing what I do today if it were not for the friendships I made and the lessons we learned together.

I have also been blessed to be a part of many communities and groups that have helped me to grow in my faith. I am forever indebted to the small and large groups in high school, college, and graduate school and as an adult in a parish that have pushed me to develop as a disciple. Just as I was welcomed on the football team and encouraged to grow in mind and body, I have been a part of many communities that have welcomed me and encouraged me to grow spiritually. All of the small- and large-group ministries in our parishes should provide meaningful and intimate support to their members, which will enable them to grow as disciples.

This is a chapter about groups that are small (such as Bible studies and prayer groups) and groups that are large (such as retreats, game nights, speaker series, and prayer services). We will look at some very practical ways in which you can create experiences that will welcome newcomers and support, sustain, and inspire dedicated members. We will look at various approaches in a general way, and in part IV we will look closely at things we can do to provide healing, proclaiming, and teaching experiences specifically designed for various age groups.

FROM ONE-ON-ONE TO GROUP EVANGELIZATION

Bestselling author and marketing expert Michael Port shared a key strategy in his popular book *Book Yourself Solid* that all of us can apply to evangelizing ministry. He calls it the "always-have-something-to-invite-people-to offer"[1]—a long name, yes, but a revealing one. Port writes, "People generally hate to be sold, but they love to be invited."[2] The same sentiment applies to religion. People don't like to be "sold" on what they should believe, but they do like to be invited to join communities and events that offer fun and interesting experiences. This invitation is often the first step toward not only knowing Christ but also knowing his Church.

In a one-on-one relationship, you develop a level of trust that makes you believable when you talk about the impact that your faith in God and your Church community has had on your life. It has to come from somewhere, right? In order to evangelize, we must let ourselves *be* evangelized within a community of people who are on the same journey we are. We do so by participating in events, communities, and programs that support us, strengthen us, and inspire us to change. Participating in these groups not only improves our own lives; it gives us something we can share with others.

In the Catholic Church today, some of the most popular "always-have-something-to-invite-people-to offers," or as we are calling them, "inviteable events," include these:

- Retreats (Kairos, Search, Christ Renews His Parish, Cursillo, etc.)
- Conferences (World Youth Day, Steubenville conferences, National Catholic Youth Conference, etc.)
- Theology on Tap
- Youth nights
- Small groups and Bible studies
- Married-couples date nights
- Lenten dinners
- Parish picnics

If you have participated in any of these events, you know their power. We will examine many of these in detail in later chapters as we address various age levels, but let's list a few essential elements that make them universally successful.

1. Small groups make sure newcomers do not get lost in the crowd.

It is a scary thing to join a new, large community for the first time. The size and number of people you do not know can be intimidating. This is why small groups are so essential. Maybe the simplest way to give a large-group event a small-group feel is with icebreakers. At teen events they are more common, but icebreakers are effective at every level. Sure, people may not like the idea of playing ridiculous games, but they do "break the ice." They allow people to open up to a small group of people with whom they were joined in the games. This increases the level of comfort for people who might otherwise never return because they did not feel welcome and they didn't connect.

Take marriage preparation, for instance. Before we were married, my wife and I were invited (well, were *required*) to attend a weekend marriage-enrichment day as part of our preparation for the Sacrament of Marriage. We only knew one other couple among probably thirty. At various parts of the day, including lunch, we sat with a small group of other couples. The informal, small-group discussions became our favorite part of the day. We realized in talking to other engaged couples that we were not alone, that we were not the only crazy people getting ready for marriage. The small-group component enabled us to connect with the people there—connections we might not have made sitting in lines of chairs just listening to talks.

2. Participants experience a sacramental touch of Christ.

This is where one-on-one evangelization always falls short. We cannot do it on our own. We can dedicate hours and hours of meetings and discussions with the individuals we accompany along a faith journey. We can even give them books, CDs, movies, and more to try to convince them to live the Christian way of life. Sometimes, their minds will be inspired and even changed by those resources, but you cannot replicate an experience of the loving power of God felt within a faith community. In fact, it is freeing for the evangelizer to know that he does not have (and should not try) to heal, proclaim, and teach all on his own. At some point, we must extend the invitation to meet the Lord, then allow him to do the work outside of our one-on-one conversations.

Newcomers might encounter Christ in the Eucharist or in the Sacrament of Penance. They might experience an amazing and loving touch of God by reading the Bible, or encounter Christ through the invitation to pray in some new and different way. These encounters shower us with love. This is why on retreats people often feel (some for the first time in a long time) that they are loved deeply by God and others and that they are worth loving. It can be a powerful watershed moment that often compels them to turn to God in praise and thanksgiving.

All of these encounters occur in the context of a larger community, the Church. Without the Church, it is almost impossible to make any sense of life-changing spiritual encounters. Sustaining the change just would not work without the examples and support of many other people we meet who have had similar encounters with the healing love of Christ.

When I returned from my first summer youth conference with the memory of an incredible spiritual encounter with Christ, I could not have sustained my new commitment without the help and support of the local high-school youth group. Later, challenged by the many temptations of college life, I do not know what I would have done without the support of the guys in my Bible study or the encounters with people at Sunday Masses, meetings, and retreats. As a new teacher living in a small intentional community and studying with other like-minded participants in the Alliance for Catholic Education program, I cannot imagine getting through the incredible challenges of being an educator without their support. As a husband and dad today, I am so grateful for the support of the other men in my parish, especially the guys from my Christ Renews His Parish (CRHP) team. I am incredibly grateful for the spiritual experiences I had along the way that kept me focused on Christ, but it has been the communities of support that have sustained me in discipleship.

3. Groups grow only through personal invitation.

I heard the announcement to sign up for the CRHP retreat at my parish for five years before I finally decided to go. It took a personal invitation from my friend Nick to finally convince me. Actually, he went so far as to fill out the application for me, removing all possible obstacles. There were no excuses. Sometimes, that's what it takes to get even the most willing of participants. We need to remove all obstacles and objections and extend personal invitations. An advertisement in the parish bulletin or an announcement at the end of Mass are technically invitations, but they are not nearly as effective as personal face-to-face invitations.

My wife had this same realization in growing a small group she started together with some other young mothers. At the final meeting of the first year of their Wine and the Word moms' group, they talked about how they could improve the next year. They were not desperate for numbers, but they discussed how they could get more moms to come or at least feel welcome to join. They looked around and realized that every person there, except one, came because she got a personal invitation from another mom in the group. The one mom who was not personally invited said she saw the ad in the bulletin and waited months before she had the courage to call about it. She would have come much sooner if she had met someone in the group and received a personal invitation. That face-to-face invitation was all she needed to eliminate the fear she had of joining.

4. Food and drink are provided.

This may seem to be a small thing, but any experienced minister will tell you it is essential. Food is the secret weapon youth ministers have been using for years to get teens in the doors (and happy to stay). Supplying some beer and wine at adult gatherings lightens the mood and helps increase the level of comfort and community among the crowds. Jesus, after all, frequently dined with the people he met and brought his entourage of disciples with him.

One thing, oddly enough, that stuck out to me during my men's CRHP experience was the food. All the previous teams from years past returned to feed the participants and leaders of the weekend. The guys took real pride in the preparations, and—wow—did we eat well. Every meal was spectacular. It is actually one of the big selling points for recruiting new guys to come on the weekend. It was something memorable and worth talking about. The food was not life-changing (except for maybe that rack of ribs), but it set the stage for an incredible all-around life-altering experience.

What is a Theology on Tap event without drinks and hors d'oeuvres, anyway? Or a pancake breakfast? Or fish Fridays? Meals are a natural way of getting people to gather together, and they are at the core of our Faith. Remember, the early Church in the Acts of the Apostles gathered together for the "breaking of the bread." We do, too, of course, by joining together at Mass, but the Eucharist is so much more than food. We should also serve meals and break bread together in other ways so that we can create the opportunity for conversation and growth in fellowship with Christ.

5. It is easy to remember the time and place.

Meeting on a regular basis makes it much easier for participants or potential participants to fit it into their schedules. Is it a monthly meeting? If so, what day of the month is it on (i.e., the first Sunday of every month)? Is it a biweekly meeting? Then, what two days should people remember (i.e., the first and third Sunday of every month)? If it is a weekly meeting, then on what day of the week will it be held?

Knowing where to show up is also important. Having one consistent location is ideal, because people never have to check an invitation or ask the organizer where they should be. They can just show up on the day and at the time they know it is to occur. The point of having consistency of time and place is to allow newcomers to show up and to eliminate all possibility of confusion about the logistics of the gatherings. If you have to make people work to find out how they can participate, your numbers will suffer. We have to make joining as frictionless as possible.

SMALL GROUPS ARE MORE THAN IMPORTANT—THEY ARE ESSENTIAL

As I write these words, I am about three-fourths of the way through writing this book and feeling a little frustrated. I have become obsessed with creating and sharing high-quality, practical resources for ministers to use in their catechetical and evangelizing efforts, but it is hard to know how many people actually apply what I share in my books, in workshops, and on my websites. Sometimes I fall into the trap of doubt and wonder if what I am doing really makes an impact. In addition, some of the people closest to me are struggling with motivation in life and work. Other close friends with adult children want to push their kids to go to church more, not because the kids do not believe in God, but because they are just not motivated to get involved in a parish.

I brought this up to my wife, Jen, and she gave me the answer I should have known but did not realize was so important. The biggest motivating factor in almost anything we do is the people. With a supportive group of people to push us along and help us improve, we cannot help but be motivated. Trying to be a disciple all on our own simply does not work. This is what makes a CRHP group so successful. It is why Bible studies, while they may not be life-changing singular moments like retreats, can transform individuals over time in ways they could never do on their own. Consider the fact that group support is the reason why Alcoholics Anonymous is so successful. Without the AA meetings, how could a person possibly fight his addiction on his own? Belonging is key to human thriving, and helping others know they belong is key to evangelizing ministry.

I am deeply blessed to have grown up with a group of close friends who made good choices. My closest friends in high school were really great guys. We had a lot of fun and occasionally made some poor choices, but all in all, we were motivated to get good grades, succeed in sports, get into good colleges, and be loyal friends and family members. I do not know where I would be if it weren't for the example that those guys set for me and still do today. Had I run with a different crowd in school, I cannot say I would have been as motivated as I was to succeed both then and now.

People need small groups to help push them through the challenges and obstacles to living the spiritual life, too. God will help us, of course, but he also puts people in our lives to show us that we are not and do not have to feel alone. When we hit a bump in life, that supportive group of people helps us to recover and make great choices for our future. When we set out to make a change—whether it is to pray more, be nicer to someone, forgive someone who hurt us, find a new job, start a business, or serve in ministry—the support we receive from a small community of people is invaluable for our own personal growth.

Adding some aspect of small-group formation is not an optional suggestion for your evangelizing ministry. Whether you work in youth ministry, adult faith formation, young-adult ministry, college campus ministry, or ministry to children, there needs to be a small-group component not just for learning and discussion but for community and support as well. Remember, the disciples were not sent out by Jesus to minister on their own. They were sent with help, two by two. When Jesus was gone, the apostles immediately formed a community of people to help and support those in the greatest need among them. We should do the same.

DEVELOPING AN EFFECTIVE SMALL-GROUP FORMAT

Once you have a small group assembled, the kind of format you use must create an experience that is worthy of someone's time and will compel her to return and ultimately invite others to join.

Most small groups or group programs follow this format:

1. *Conversation:* Casually converse while people arrive.

2. *Opening Prayer:* Open with prayer.

3. *Content:* Watch a video or read the reading of the day, which includes an explanation of a particular topic.

4. *Discussion:* Members share how they can connect their personal lives to the topic of the day. This is a time for personal witness and testimony, not additional teaching.

5. *Closing Prayer:* Close with prayer intentions and a common prayer that all can recite together.

Now, let's break down why each of these elements is so important. First, starting with casual conversation gives people the opportunity to talk and see how things are going since the last time they met. It also allows members to welcome newcomers and introduce them to the rest of the group. We should resist the temptation to cut this time artificially short. Making sure everyone is connected together in a welcoming community is essential. It enables moments of healing to occur later during the more intimate discussion of faith.

At some point, though, there needs to be a transition from small talk to the meeting itself. Opening prayer is a great way to do this, and changing physical locations can work well, too. If everyone gathers in the kitchen, for example, moving into the living room sets a different tone in a new location in order to establish the beginning of the meeting. The prayer should mark the transition from everyday life to a meeting of fellowship and prayer.

Next, the topic of the day is introduced. At this point the group might watch a video that supports the reading or, if there is time, the group can do the reading during the meeting. If the resource is longer and the reading is done at home, then take the time to have people summarize what was read just in case some of the members have not had the chance to do the reading yet. The purpose of this time is to learn something new as a group and spark connections between the content and the joys and challenges of everyday life. That is why it is so important to pick a good inspirational resource for discussion.

During the group discussion, the key is to focus on making personal connections to the topic rather than to address additional questions about Church teaching. This discussion time should be focused on finding common challenges and success stories that will help people feel that they are not alone. It is a time where people share personal parts of their lives. They open up their hearts, not just their heads.

Group leaders have to be careful not to facilitate discussions that turn into debates about Church teachings. Talking about the reading or video is important, but the true value of this small-group time is the open sharing and not the intellectual debate. If the resource you are using does not come with reflection questions, write some to discuss that focus on application of the material without requiring additional reading or prior knowledge. If debates about Church teaching do come up, just make it clear from the outset that if you cannot find the answers today, you will do some digging and report back to the group. Always try to bring the conversation back to a mode of personal sharing rather than objective stances on ideas. Be attentive to those who hide behind that objectivity in order to avoid being vulnerable and open about what is really going on in their lives. Set an example for others by being open to sharing personal stories and applications for your life.

There are two elements to closing prayer that work really well. One is the opportunity for prayer intentions. This gives everyone a little glimpse into the hardest part of each other's personal lives and gives members something to pray about in the time in between meetings. It also offers recognition of support that is so crucial in our Church today. To feel we are not alone as we face life's struggles is an incredible gift. Second, having a specific prayer that everyone recites together is a great way to express the identity of the group and a unity of goals. It can be as simple as the Lord's Prayer, but it might also be famous prayers of Catholic saints or prayers specifically offered by the resource the group is using.

PICKING A TOPIC AND SMALL-GROUP RESOURCES

To focus on community-building in a small group is essential, but the content and focus of the group is just as important. If the group does not focus on a topic that is interesting and engaging, it is going to be difficult to convince people to show up. They might continue to come just to connect with the other members of the group, but the content itself needs to be so inspiring that it motivates members to go out and do additional reading, thinking, and praying about it. When we have fully committed disciples engaged in a small group, we are able to begin what we have referred to as "teaching" in this book. The goal is not only learning but also inspiration for people to want to learn more. A great presentation of a topic provides a new way of looking at things that may surprise even those who know a lot about the Faith already.

How do you select a resource that is inspiring and engaging? Consider the following criteria when selecting a group-study program or book for your group:

- Is the topic specifically related to something this group has in common (men's group, women's group, mom's group, youth group, college life, young adults, etc.)?

- Is the topic new and interesting to the group? (The theology of the body, for example, was a very new concept for people in recent years.)

- Does the creator of the resource present a well-known topic in a new and surprising way? (This may include a fresh, new look at the Bible or Church teachings.)

- Does the resource come with engaging questions and discussion prompts that encourage people to open up and share their personal connections?

- Have people recommended this resource before? Does their experience match with the group's identity?

For additional small-group ideas, including a downloadable checklist version of this resource-selection criteria, small-group checklists, and small-group resource ideas, visit healproclaimteach.com/chapter8.

REMARKABLE LARGE-GROUP EXPERIENCES

Most evangelizing ministries also tend to host large gatherings of people as core features of their groups. These events may include retreats, conferences, large-group gatherings, youth nights, speaker series, and social events. These gatherings usually have small-group elements integrated into them, but most of the time they are open to the public and welcome anyone to attend. While small groups give the opportunity for people to grow in intimacy and trust with members of their groups, a large-group event offers the opportunity to meet new people every time.

The goal of any large-group experience is simple: get more people to come, come back, and then (most importantly) come back with others. How do you do that? Create a *remarkable* experience. Create an experience worth talking about. Create an experience that will motivate participants not only to return but also to invite their friends. Consider the following common elements of large-group gatherings that give people an experience that will motivate them to share their experiences with others.

1. **Remarkable large groups make people feel welcome.** There should be a steady influx of new people all the time. This means we need to train our leaders and the core group of participants to seek out newcomers and start a conversation

with them. This is a simple gesture, but it is a simple expression of a form of healing ministry. We may not dramatically heal the emotional pain of the people who walk in the doors for the first time, but we can certainly hurt them by not making them feel welcome the first time they join us.

2. **Remarkable large groups are fun.** One of the most common ways to make large groups fun is with games. While often done with trepidation, ice breakers can be great ways to help people get to know each other and have fun while doing it. They make a large group feel smaller. It creates the connections between people on teams and in groups that are absolutely essential to inspire people to come back. Those connections, which can be formed in bonds of fun and competition, may lead to relationships outside of the group and can certainly motivate people to come back to see their friends.

3. **Remarkable large groups use music to set the tone for intimacy.** Music can hit people in the heart and create an intimate experience even amid a large group of people. Music breaks down barriers of uncomfortableness and draws people into an experience that touches the heart. It can put people in a position to be able to open up to others in breakout discussions that they might not have otherwise done. It sets the tone for an intimate experience despite the size of the group.

Do not force music to be a part of your gathering. Playing poorly performed or uninspiring music will deprive your efforts of credibility and obstruct people from having that intimate encounter with God and the other members of the group. Find volunteers who have real talent or use professionally created music from a music playlist or album to draw people into the mood you are trying to create.

4. **Remarkable large groups have engaging leaders.** The leaders might even take on a level of celebrity that draws people in. It may be that your ministry invites authors or popular speakers that will draw a crowd to your conference, retreat, or faith-formation series. Or it could be that the participants really like you or your colleagues as the leaders of the group. Dynamic youth-group leaders are probably the best example of this. They connect with teens in personal ways because they are so open with their personalities. They are not afraid to be themselves, and so teens feel comfortable being themselves as well. I have a hunch that the same could be true for adult meetings, if people were willing to live with a level of uncomfortableness that comes with putting their personalities out there while leading a group.

5. **Remarkable large groups have secrets to share.** Retreats are probably best known for having secrets that only those who have gone on the retreat can share. For example, "Live the Fourth!" is a phrase that leaders of Kairos retreats use throughout the three-day retreat that puzzles participants until the closing of the event. Offering surprise opportunities for affirmation both by other participants on a retreat or through letters from family and friends at home is another common secret that often gets mentioned as the most powerful part of a retreat weekend.

6. **Remarkable large groups provide opportunities for participants to serve as leaders.** Eventually, as the group grows larger, leaders need to recruit volunteers to help orchestrate the event. Partly this serves a practical purpose (we need more help), but it also creates a core group of ambassadors who are going to invite the most people to join. When someone is commissioned as a leader, she takes real ownership over the group. She really wants to see it succeed, and so she

starts inviting people to attend, sometimes more often than she did when she was only a participant.

This also provides the leader of the group the additional opportunity to engage volunteer leaders in a more intimate way. With initial training and then ongoing planning meetings, there is an opportunity for mentoring, discipleship, and faith sharing that can really inspire this group to create an engaging experience as leaders. It also may be the only opportunity this group of leaders has to focus on their own faith as disciples rather than leaders of the group. In other words, the gatherings of leaders should be about more than planning; they should be opportunities for continual formation and personal evangelization.

BRANDING MAKES A GROUP EASIER TO SHARE

Whether we realize it or not, our Church's large groups gather with a common identity that needs to be articulated. It might be the unity of a common age level (middle school, teens, college students, young adults, adults, etc.), a state of life (men, women, singles, married couples, families, etc.), or a common interest. Communicating that common identity is crucial to getting new members. You want people to hear about your gathering and know right away if it is for them or not.

One of the best ways to communicate this identity in a way that gets people excited about checking out your ministry, inspired to come back, and motivated to talk about it with friends is to express a unique name and story for your group. In other words, focus on your brand. Your brand is the reputation or feeling that your group communicates to current and potential members.

Whether you come up with a creative name for your large-group gathering or not, you will have a brand. Calling your gathering by the name of the type of people there expresses a brand whether you realize it or not. Most of our ministries use traditional names such as "youth group," "freshmen retreat," "adult faith-formation series," and "religious education." These are helpful in that they express who they are for, but they do not give members an identity, story, and purpose worth talking about. (Remember, we want to create *remarkable* large groups.)

Sometimes a name is inherited as a part of a meeting or retreat process. There are a lot of different retreats, for example, that come prepackaged with a brand: Christ Renews His Parish (CRHP), Cursillo, Kairos, Teens Encounter Christ (TEC), Search, and so on. Sometimes ministries inherit Catholic names and acronyms such as CCD (Confraternity of Christian Doctrine) or RCIA (Rite of Christian Initiation of Adults) that come with preconceived notions that we have to unlearn in order to experience these ministries more deeply.

The challenge, whether you come up with a new and creative name yourself or use one that you inherited, is to express a meaning and purpose for the gathering that establishes who it is for but goes a step further. Here we can take a lesson from the business world. Again, what is a brand? The origin of the term is the symbol used to identify ownership or membership, like the branding on a cow on a farm. Today, companies use it to describe specific product lines. Frequently, and incorrectly, the word *brand* is used to describe a logo or a type of design, but branding goes way beyond images. A brand is the story people tell about you. The best brands today help us remember the memory of a feeling or experience that we associate with a particular product. These brands communicate a purpose beyond the features of a product that is anchored in our own human experience.

Apple is probably the most commonly cited example of good branding. Apple's brand now extends beyond just computers and into other products, from phones to music to watches to TV. Apple was able to find success outside of computers because its brand communicated an experience that extended from one product to a wide variety of products. People often misinterpret Apple's branding success to its simple design. Simplicity is a common feature of Apple products, but that only feeds into the story people tell themselves about their iPhones, iPads, and Macs.

Apple communicates an identity that may be difficult to describe but rightfully connects to its tagline, "Think different." As Simon Sinek described in a popular TED Talk "How Great Leaders Inspire Action" and in his book *Start with Why*, in everything that Apple does, it challenges the status quo.[3] By associating yourself with the Apple brand, you start to see yourself in the same light: as someone who thinks differently and challenges the status quo. The simplicity of design stands in opposition to the complexity of conventional thinking or of corporate America. When you use an Apple computer, so say Apple fans, your experience frees you from the complexity of other computers and technologies. Your iPhone is not just a phone; it is an experience of simplicity and art.

The best example I have seen of branding in the Catholic Church is at the Church of the Nativity in Lutherville-Timonium, Maryland, which is the basis for the book *Rebuilt*. The parish is committed to naming things. Youth group isn't "high-school youth group"; it is Uprising. Children's Liturgy of the Word is known as Time Travelers, because by talking about the Gospel they seemingly go back in time and experience the stories of the Bible as if they were really there. I have to admit, that sounds a lot more interesting to me as a parent than something more direct, such as "religious education," "children's liturgy," or worse, "CCD." It is the difference between something my kids *have* to do or *should* do compared with what they *want* to do.

A lot of other ministers have had similar success with creative branding. Katie Prejean, a youth minister and teacher in Lake Charles, Louisiana, believes very strongly in coming up with a brand name for all her ministries. As she pointed out to me after a webinar we did together, every gathering of people within a ministry is never random. The ultimate purpose of these gatherings is to build a relationship with Jesus. A group that regularly gathers needs a name to use in conversation with each other and other potential participants. When this name expresses a purpose and common identity, it is no longer random but expresses a deeper meaning and context to how a group can help participants. Her youth group is called Teens Undivided. It was a name she inherited from her predecessor, but she continued to use it and build upon its meaning. That name helps to express a deep need for teens to find unity when they are driven apart by technology. Prejean, therefore, uses technology to her advantage. She uses social media to grow the awareness of the Teens Undivided brand so participants can invite newcomers. The brand also gives loyal participants a common language and identity that is exciting and worth talking about.

Whether we decide to use social media or not, having a brand is something we can apply to evangelizing ministries of all ages. Why is having an intentional brand so important? First, as we have just pointed out, you have a brand and a name whether you make up a creative one or not. Save yourself the time and energy of trying to explain the history of CCD as Confraternity of Christian Doctrine. Second, it is so important that you create a name that appeals to newcomers and gives loyal participants something exciting to share. Your name should tell a story about who you are as a group and what you do. If that story is not worth talking about, then you cannot expect more people to show up. Spend some time considering the common identity of the members in your ministry, and come up with a name that tells a story and gives people something worth talking about.

LEADING A LARGE GROUP

How do you, while standing in front of a large group of people, effectively heal the marginalized, proclaim the Gospel, and teach disciples? Focus first on letting yourself be evangelized (see chapter 6). That will build a firm foundation upon which you can be the leader of this large group. Next, make sure you take the time to do the important work of one-on-one ministry and in small-group participation (see chapter 7). Those conversations and relationships will feed into the work you do in large groups. In addition, keep these suggestions for becoming an exceptional leader in mind as you lead events and large-scale meetings:

1. **Be authentic.** Do not let leadership go to your head. Share the parts of you that are difficult to put on display in front of a group. Share your challenges in life and your insecurities, because by opening up your heart, you give the people in attendance the permission to open up as well. No one will think less of you for sharing a piece of your life. Remember, this is an essential quality of being a wounded healer. In the Church you have to be wounded to heal other wounds.

2. **Maintain and focus on personal connections.** Whenever you are not in front of the group or orchestrating events in the background, get out on the ground floor and talk with the people who are there. A lot of them may be there by

your own personal invitation, so making that follow-up connection is crucial. Even if someone else brought them in, though, you want to make sure they feel connected with you not just as the leader but as a person they can turn to if needed. Make sure people know you are accessible to them. It enables you to be the healer in between the large-group meetings.

3. **Make sure your message is the Gospel message.** Every message you share with this group should be grounded in the proclamation of the Gospel in some way. What does that mean? It means that every message calls the participants in the group to a transformation of their lives. That transformation will come with sacrifice—a sacrifice that you and the other leaders and core members show by the way you live your lives. It is a sacrifice that mirrors in some small way the great sacrifice of Jesus Christ on the Cross. Remember, we are motivated to share God's love because we have experienced it for ourselves. We must constantly proclaim this message of God's love, even when it requires us to share uncomfortable and personal stories about our lives as testimonies to that love.

4. **Remember who is really in charge.** Jesus was very humble about his role as teacher. He said, "My teaching is not my own but is from the One who sent me" (Jn 7:16). Likewise, we should never forget who is really in charge. It is never our show put on display; it is just our opportunity for us to pass on that which has been given to us by God and his disciples. This is a comforting realization. It relieves us from the worry that we are not doing enough or saying the right thing. Trust in the Spirit's work through you, and stay joyful about proclaiming the Gospel. If you spend all your time and energy

worrying about success, you will drain away your ability to be an effective leader of this group.

5. **Teach like Jesus did.** Remember the model of teaching that Jesus gave to us in the Sermon on the Mount (see chapter 5)? "You have heard it said . . . but I say to you . . ." We can follow a similar model when sharing our messages in front of a large group. Consider this model when coming up with a key point to share: "People think _____, but really, _____." For example:

- People think the saints were perfect people who never made mistakes, but really, many of the saints were some of the greatest sinners before their conversions.

- People think that the Church believes sex is bad, but really, the Church proclaims the need for chastity instead.

- People think Jesus was just a nice guy, but really, he could be harsh and challenging when convincing people to turn away from sin and come follow him.

- People think Catholics worship Mary, but really, Catholics revere Mary for her unique relationship with our God, Jesus Christ.

The point is to focus on commonly held beliefs and misunderstandings so you can turn them on their heads in order to garner attention and challenge people to discover more. The more you can inspire your group to go out and learn more about what you have shared, the more likely they will be to grow closer to God, come back again for more, and invite their friends to join them.

FROM GENERAL TO SPECIFIC

Now we turn to the final section of our application of Jesus' model for evangelizing ministry of healing, proclaiming, and teaching. In the remaining chapters, we will apply these three forms of ministry to the many successful forms of evangelizing ministry being carried out at various age levels in our Church today and in recent years.

Most likely, as you are reading this book, you are serving in and participating in many different ministries. Some of the following chapters will be more applicable to you than others. While we will look at evangelizing ministries that you may not be involved in today, I would encourage you to read about each one no matter what age level you serve. You may find some inspiration for your ministry as you read about the other age levels. I would also encourage you to read and share the principles in each chapter with the team involved in carrying out your evangelizing ministry. As a group, read, consider, and discuss the ways in which you can improve your ministry's efforts to heal, proclaim, and teach.

For additional resources on forming and leading small and large groups, visit healproclaimteach.com/chapter8.

PART IV

EVANGELIZING MINISTRY WITH EVERY GENERATION

9

MINISTRY WITH CHILDREN

The very idea of "evangelizing" children may seem strange. How do we convince kids to believe what we believe when they are so young that they will believe anything? Can we really preach to children? Can they really understand Church doctrine at their age? Remember, we are talking about a different understanding of evangelization in this book. If evangelization is all about getting people to understand and believe ideas, then evangelizing children will indeed be exceptionally hard. In fact, the reverse is true.

Children, with their propensity to love and their unending pursuit of play, are not only perfectly prepared to receive the evangelizing work of God's Church; they are also exceptional at evangelizing adults. Evangelization is about discovering the love God has for us and responding with as much love as we possibly can return. It is about setting a good example and showing others the joys of living the Christian life, a life of self-sacrifice and love for others. We teach people to love unconditionally just as God loves. This is why children are such excellent evangelizers. Children already love unconditionally, usually without much teaching or convincing required. They want so desperately to be loved, and they know instinctively that the way to be loved is to love others first. As kids, they know they are completely dependent on adults and, therefore, are humble in their way of life. As Jesus said, "Unless you turn and become like children, you will not enter the kingdom of heaven" (Mt 18:3). This is a lesson we can all learn as ministers to children, but it is also a lesson that the parents of those children have the opportunity to learn every single day.

The challenge we have in developing our evangelizing ministries for children, therefore, is to make sure we do not undo the gifts God has already instilled in them. We need to be careful not to numb a child's passion for play and love. We have to be careful that we set a good example for the responsibility we have toward others and to show how to redirect a passion for fun and play toward a passion for learning about God.

EVANGELIZING PARENTS THROUGH THEIR KIDS

In all the months leading up to becoming a father for the first time, I kept thinking about how I would possibly be able to do it. I had no idea how to be a dad. It was such an enormous responsibility, and they do not exactly provide you with extensive training leading up to delivery. The day our first child was born, though, it made a whole lot more sense. All my fears and worries about being a good dad didn't go away, but they didn't stop me from taking care of our little newborn girl. That is the thing about being a new parent: no one else is going to take care of that child but you. When that baby is hungry or needs a diaper change, you are all she's got. Babies are utterly at the mercy of their parents to take care of them. It is no wonder that children grow up at early ages loving unconditionally.

There are a lot of different ways we can attempt to evangelize children, but none of them come near the effectiveness of reaching the children though their parents. Or, more accurately, reaching the parents through the children. Parents have been given the responsibility to raise and educate their children.

Very often it is children who draw parents back into the Church again. After some years of being away and not seeing the value in going to church, they start to come back with their kids. They enroll their children in religious-education programs or Catholic schools. They come back to Mass on Sundays even though they were not going before they had kids.

Without doing a single thing, children evangelize their parents. That call to unconditional love leads them to bring their children to the Church. These parents may not be fully committed disciples yet, but at least they are getting in the door. For those of us who lead evangelizing ministries with children, we have an incredible opportunity to reach adults. In fact, our ministry might be the only one that even has the possibility of reaching and evangelizing these adults.

Oddly enough, though, parents are often cited as the most difficult challenge by many of the catechists and teachers I know. The most common challenge I read about through e-mails to the *Religion Teacher* website is getting parents to support catechesis at home or, to put it bluntly, just to get the parents to bring the kids to Mass on Sundays. I can definitely relate to this kind of experience when teaching and evangelizing children. Here is the thing, though: while we may see the *kids'* names on the attendance sheet and spend most of our time with them in classes and meetings as catechists and teachers, our responsibility is always to the *whole* family and never just to the kids.

We can look to the gospels for a little insight into how we can reach parents through their children. There are two examples of stories of individuals coming to Jesus for help with their children. In one story, a Canaanite woman comes to Jesus and says to him, "Have pity on me" (Mt 15:22). Then she does him homage and says, "Lord, help me" (Mt 15:25). She seeks his help for her daughter, but she calls on him to help *her* and to have pity on *her* first. In the very same way, the parents who bring their children to religious-education programs want something similar. They might want us to help their kids, but they probably want us to help *them* help their kids more.

In another story, Jairus, a synagogue official, comes to seek Jesus to heal his daughter before she dies (see Mk 5:21–43). Jesus, who healed another woman on the way to help him, arrived too late. Jairus's daughter was already dead. Jesus turned to the people there who were greatly upset and weeping and told them, "The child is not dead but asleep" (Mk 5:39). How did the people respond? They "ridiculed him" (Mk 5:40). Of course, to their astonishment, Jesus healed the young girl. Sometimes children can be going through difficult times and parents may not know what to do. While we may not be able to work miracles, we can certainly do our best to be there for the child when they need it the most. Sometimes children need someone other than their parents to confide in for support.

Ultimately, the secret to evangelizing parents is to reach them through their kids. These two people from the gospels turned to Jesus for help just as parents turn to the Church and our ministries today. If we can show them that we are welcoming their children into a community and selflessly showing their kids the kind of love they deserve, then we have the opportunity to touch the lives of the parents as well. The more we can focus on sharing our loving service to help the parents, the more the parents will respond and support the work that we are trying to accomplish within their children.

SHEPHERDING STUDENTS

After cooperating with parents, the second-biggest challenge that catechists and teachers face today is trying to keep kids interested and engaged in the lessons they have prepared. Students get bored easily, have a hard time paying attention when the teacher speaks, or simply do not do the work that they are asked to do. Often, unfortunately, they are just not excited to be there.

What if, instead, students could not wait to come to catechesis? What if, during class, they were exceptionally focused and excited to ask questions and learn more about the theme of the day? How do we make this a reality? The best way to motivate kids to want to learn is to give them ownership over the learning process. When a person has the freedom to choose what he wants to learn, he is much more motivated to participate in and engage with a topic. This is why so many students excel in their "favorite subjects" but do only moderately well in other areas. This is why adults today choose to read about their favorite topics and hobbies without anyone asking them to.

Maria Montessori founded a new educational model at the turn of the twentieth century that exemplified the ownership approach to education. The Montessori approach stood in opposition to the status quo in education because it focused on a discovery method of learning as opposed to the commonly practiced direct-instruction approach that is still in use today. Montessori's model quickly grew and is now used by more than twenty-two thousand schools throughout the world today.

Montessori, who was herself a practicing Catholic, deeply influenced Sofia Cavalletti and Gianna Gobbi, who founded what is known as the Catechesis of the Good Shepherd (CGS) in the 1950s. Cavalletti, a scripture scholar, and Gobbi, a Montessori practitioner, joined together to begin this movement in religious education, the cornerstone of which is honoring a child's innate ability to understand and accept God's love and teachings.

Consider their shepherd analogy of catechesis for a moment. If we are shepherds rather than instructors, we guide the sheep in a certain direction without force or control. The sheep may wander, but we guide them back in the right direction. The analogy implies movement and enables the sheep to proceed with some level of determination all on their own. Likewise, Christ is our one true shepherd. He does not force us to do what he wants. He guides us. He gives us freedom, but he shows us the way. Best of all, he does it with great love. Recall his promise to us: "I am the good shepherd. A good shepherd lays down his life for the sheep" (Jn 10:11).

When I asked author Ann Garrido, who trains catechists to be certified leaders in CGS, to share a little bit about what she believes sets the CGS method apart, I was surprised by her response. In fact, it had a great influence on this entire chapter. She said that the thing that distinguishes CGS from traditional religious education the most is the way it enables children to evangelize the Church: "As a CGS formation leader who trains adults to work in an atrium, I have seen adult participants have profound transformations in their lives because of how they learn to be with and receive from children in new ways—like really life-changing stuff! This is a place where the line, 'Unless you become like little children . . .' really is experienced with surprising results."

I can say that this works on parents as well. As a parent with two daughters who are now making weekly visits to a CGS atrium, the physical space in which the catechesis unfolds, I love hearing about the "works" that they do. After an initial catechetical presentation, CGS children are allowed to choose the work that they feel most excited to pursue. For example, following a presentation about the Sacrament of Baptism, a child may choose to work with a model baptismal font and the words of the Rite of Baptism, printed on a laminated card. This work helps the child commit the words, signs, and symbols of the rite to memory and contemplate their meanings. The catechists, rather than walk the children through each activity step-by-step, guide them to discover and figure things out on their own, learning to seek understanding by way of their own questions.

Traditional religious education is focused primarily on the catechist, who plans the lessons, teaches about the topics, and directs the students to complete certain predetermined activities. CGS, being modeled after a Montessori approach to education, flips the traditional model on its head and puts the student in the driver's seat. The child gets to decide and discover for herself, while the catechist helps by leading her in the right direction.

Garrido wrote an article in *America* magazine that highlights five ways CGS can be distinguished from traditional religious education. This is not to suggest that all religious education should be transformed into a CGS model, but these points do reveal some areas where traditional religious education within a classroom setting has some room to grow. Here is a short summary and application of her five points.[1]

1. **Theology of the child.** Traditional religious education is based on an assumption that we as catechists have something to teach children who for now are missing some piece of information. The CGS approach, on the other hand, recognizes the presence of the Holy Spirit already given at Baptism and encourages children to get in touch with the Spirit as they seek to learn more. For this reason the CGS curriculum is based more on the questions children ask and how they learn to explore rather than requiring them to learn rote answers to the questions adults think children should learn.

2. **Role of the adult.** Catechists who apply the CGS methodology act more as colisteners and colearners rather than as didactic teachers. They listen to the needs and questions of the children and match them up with the resources that will

best put them in a position to encounter God. The goal is to guide children to Christ so that they can get to know him better and fall in love, not teach children about a God they do not know at all.

3. **Attention to the environment.** As a religion teacher and catechist, I loathed classroom decorations. If you walked into my classrooms, you would have seen many times throughout the year that the walls were bare and bulletin boards sparsely showed students' work. Every time I tried to decorate, it always felt forced and lacked a unifying principle or reason for the things you would see on the walls. In the atrium, on the other hand, keen attention to the environment is essential. Following Montessori's belief that children absorb religious beliefs through the environment around them rather than through lessons and lectures, CGS creates a place (the atrium) in which the spiritual life is not just learned; it is lived. When CGS comes to a new location, all of the teaching materials are created and made by the catechist, the children, and usually a host of volunteers. Attention to the good order of the atrium is just as important as attention to the content of the catechesis.

4. **Spiritual methodology.** The CGS curriculum focuses on five themes: Incarnation, the kingdom of God, the paschal mystery, Baptism, and the Eucharist. During the teaching portion of CGS meetings, these five themes are interwoven regularly in a spiral approach that touches on them repeatedly each year and expands upon what has already been covered. The religious-education curricula in most dioceses also focus on the complete presentation of a series of doctrines laid out by the US Conference of Catholic Bishops, but each grade has a more explicit focus on specific subject areas (for example, second grade is sacraments, sixth

grade is Old Testament, seventh grade is New Testament and sacraments).

5. **Emphasis on essentials.** As Catholics, we believe that there is a hierarchy of truths when it comes to Catholic doctrine, meaning that some things are more essential to understand than others. According to Cavalletti, children become restless when they are presented with peripheral material. When she taught core truths about the Faith, the kids were able to concentrate more and settle down. She concluded that children have a natural inclination to seek to understand the essential rather than the details that we might find further down along the hierarchy of truths. Therefore, children's catechesis should be focused on the essentials in order to reduce the unengaging "busywork" that young people naturally resist in class.

VACATIONS ARE FUN, EVEN WHEN THE BIBLE IS INVOLVED

Since the late 1800s, Protestant churches throughout the United States have been hosting summer programs called vacation Bible school (VBS). According to some stories, a Sunday-school teacher in a Baptist church was so frustrated that she did not have enough time to teach everything she wanted to teach about the Bible during the year that she started summer classes as well. Over time, other churches heard about it and tried it, too. Today, VBS is an incredible event in Protestant and Catholic churches throughout the United States that brings joy to kids and families during the summer months outside of school.

My first real experience with VBS was as a parent. I have to admit that I never really gave it much credit before actually seeing it in action. The minute I walked in the door for my daughter's first VBS closing ceremony, I was blown away. The smiles on children's faces as they sang and praised God were heartwarming, but the joy on the faces of the parents and volunteers was even more exciting. It did not stop there, either. For the next six months, we listened to the VBS CD in our van—a very welcome departure from songs about stars, zoos, and barnyard animals.

So, what makes VBS so successful? VBS provides parents with an inviteable event (see chapter 8) in the context of their children's religious education. Sure, kids are inspired in their faith in a unique way and participate in activities that teach lessons they normally would not learn during the summer, but the real opportunity (I think) is in evangelizing the parents. Parents get to see a spark in their children that they do not see as easily during the weekly drop-off and pickup from Catholic school or parish religious education. They get to see amid the summertime fun that faith can be fun for their kids, too.

The message to the kids is clear, too: faith is fun. Children have a natural tendency toward fun and play. With any free moment they have, they actively seek ways in which they can use their creative energy to have fun and enjoy themselves. While we call VBS "school," it is not anything like the school year. The kids have fun and learn about God, the Bible, and (in Catholic versions of VBS) the lives of the saints. If our goal is to make faith relevant and engaging for all generations, then VBS does just that for young children. Children, whose lives revolve around play, get to spend their summertime having fun while also focusing on their faith.

Just as I finished writing this section of the book, my daughter started singing the words to one of her VBS songs during breakfast. It is amazing how God works through moments like this, right? I asked her what she liked about VBS that was better than her catechesis in her Catholic school. Do you know what stood out to her? You probably guessed it: the music. They have music at school, but the full-body praise and worship music she got to participate in during VBS stood out to her. Have you ever taught your young people the hand motions to a praise-and-worship song? If you haven't tried it yet, you should. When my wife taught fourth grade, she would get daily requests for praise-and-worship songs. I even taught a few songs to middle-school students when I taught in a Catholic school, and guess what? They loved it! They smiled, laughed, and had fun. The music and hand motions gave my students a chance to let go a little, to open up—even to be vulnerable—which enabled them to get in touch with their hearts in class instead of just their heads. Make the commitment to use more music to evangelize and catechize children. Music makes a huge difference for young people whether you are in a VBS, a parish religious-education classroom, or a Catholic-school Mass.

THE SUPPORT OF A COMMUNITY

The nun in full habit with a scowl on her face became a stereotype of Catholic education in the early- and mid-twentieth century. Fifty years ago religious sisters, brothers, and priests accounted for more than 90 percent of the teachers in Catholic schools. In 2014, they made up only 3.2 percent. Just a few days before writing this, I taught a lesson on vocations to second-graders, and most of the students in the class did not even know what a nun was!

What have we lost? For one, most young people will never be exposed to a vowed religious way of life. Religious sisters, brothers, and priests share housing, meals, and finances together. They set aside specific times each day to pray together. But it is not just the prayer that characterizes their way of life; it is also the fact that they pray *together*. Religious life is a commitment to the communal life. Even in monasteries where silence is observed most of the day, the men or women still gather together as a community to pray. For all religious, their communal identity and commitments drive them forward and keep them motivated to stay true to God. These allow them to be filled up by God and each other so they can give themselves more fully over to the work of their ministries.

This spirit of community, common purpose, and vision may be the greatest loss to Catholic education over the past fifty years. Children simply are not exposed to vowed religious life, which for past generations had been a visible sign of singular commitment to God and of vibrant discipleship. On the other hand, the Church is experiencing a resurgence of lay movements that focus heavily on the communal life. I am blessed to be a graduate of the University of Notre Dame's Alliance for Catholic Education (ACE). In this two-year program, we took classes at Notre Dame in the summers and taught in underresourced Catholic schools during the year. We lived together in a community of other teachers, splitting the bills, buying groceries together, and praying together at least once each week. I am grateful for the master's degree I earned through the program, but the relationships and friendships I formed with my housemates and classmates are absolutely priceless.

The ACE program is not the only service program focused on developing lay communities. ACE is now just one of many teacher-training programs servicing Catholic schools in the United States as a part of the University Consortium for Catholic Education. Notre Dame also hosts another separate program based on a similar model of living in community, but in service to parish ministry, called Echo, named for the original meaning of the Greek word for catechesis. As in ACE, the Echo students take classes at Notre Dame in the summers, and they serve in various ministries in parishes throughout the country during the year. Religious orders have also founded lay groups to serve in ministry in various capacities, most popular among them being the Jesuit Volunteer Corps. These volunteers live in community but also vow to live simply on a very small stipend in solidarity with the people that they serve.

My experience of community as a Catholic-school teacher went beyond ACE. I found that, as a teacher, I was part of a community that was unlike any other job I had up to that point or have had since. I do not think I can fully explain the experience effectively, but when you work and teach for a Catholic parish alongside a dozen others who make sacrifices to be there, you form a bond together and with the students and parents that would be difficult to find in any other profession. I do not know what it was like to be a dedicated sister or brother working in a Catholic parish or school, but I do feel that God forms a bond between teachers in a Catholic school that I have not seen in other places I have worked.

We teachers and catechists of children can all make progress in our attempts to heal, proclaim, and teach with the support of small communities of prayer. Training and education are crucial to helping us be good teachers. Prayer and a faith community are essential to helping us be good evangelists.

CATECHETICAL CONFERENCES THAT BUILD COMMUNITY

In the last few years I have attended and spoken at a number of catechetical conferences across the United States. I love meeting other passionate and dedicated people who love God and want to serve in his Church. I find in the conversations I have with them before, after, or even during my talks the same issues coming up everywhere I go. Whether it is struggles with parents or the challenge of getting kids interested and excited about learning, the stories are similar. The thing is, though, most of the time I hear the pain in their voices as if they are the only person on the planet who struggles with this problem, at least at first.

One of my favorite things about catechetical conferences is watching people share stories and share ideas. It is truly magical. The smiles on people's faces as they talk and hear new ideas are incredible. The relief I see when someone shares a story that made them feel alone and without hope only to realize that others have experienced the same thing is powerful. By opening up with their colleagues, catechists and teachers find comfort and hope.

While it may seem that catechetical conferences provide high-quality training and professional development for catechists and teachers, really the true value comes in the progress that is made in developing a community of disciples. If we really want to push through the challenges that come with children's catechesis, then we need to work together to discover new and better ideas that work. Please, catechetical leaders, continue to invite great speakers to present to your dioceses, but do not forget the true value in what you do: gathering Christ's disciples together to unite them in a common mission of evangelizing God's children.

PRINCIPLES FOR DEVELOPING EFFECTIVE EVANGELIZING MINISTRIES WITH CHILDREN

At the end of each of these chapters on evangelizing different generations of people in our Church, you will find a list of principles to help in developing your own evangelizing ministries for each age level. For this list of principles, I will start with the defining principles for catechesis that drive the work I do as a catechist and religion teacher. The first four principles presented here are also *The Religion Teacher* website's four principles for effective catechesis.

1. Make disciples, not theologians.

Jesus sent his disciples out to "make disciples of all nations" (Mt 28:19), but for some reason we feel compelled instead to form young people into novice theologians. Being a disciple means being a student of Christ for the rest of your life. Being a theologian means having an expertise worthy of sharing with those who lack it. Disciples constantly learn from the teacher, Jesus Christ. They are in a relationship with him and continue to maintain that relationship for the rest of their lives. Theologians may be disciples, but they are mostly recognized for their scholarly expertise. Disciples are not required to attain that same level of expertise in Catholic doctrine as theologians; all they need is to be engaged in an intimate relationship with Christ.

I can agree in part with the many people who complain about the negative effects of what they are calling "poorly catechized" generations of Catholics. I believe, though, that it is not catechesis that is the most detrimental cause of our shrinking Church but rather the lack of evangelization. A child who is on fire for her faith in Christ *wants* to learn about God. Disciples desire to learn more. It is not the information they hear or understand that is important; it is the desire to learn that matters most. When a child is formed in the Faith, not only to pass tests and get good grades but also to learn to love and serve God, we have formed a disciple. When a child is taught information with educational methods to help him memorize and understand the information on a test, we have simply formed a novice theologian. Do not focus solely on head knowledge; also focus on the heart. Form disciples, not theologians.

Evangelizing Ministry Method: Heal, Proclaim

2. Teach with testimony.

I was teaching a group of eighth-graders a few years back in preparation for Confirmation. We got to the end of the year, and I felt very confident that the students knew their stuff. I had taught the class for a few years in a row, and I had a good system for Confirmation prep. Plus, I already had a good idea of the questions our bishop was going to ask the kids during their Confirmation Mass. We got to the end of the year, just before Confirmation, and I came to a haunting realization. I had been so caught up in preparing the kids mentally to receive the sacrament that I had taken myself almost completely out of the process. I looked back on the year and realized that I had never once shared the major stories in my life that led me to love God and serve him as a catechist. The students had never heard my conversion story. I was a teacher, but I wasn't a witness.

Just before his Ascension into heaven, Jesus promised his apostles that they would receive the power of the Holy Spirit and be his witnesses throughout the world (see Acts 1:8). They were not sent out as teachers or expert philosophers. They were sent out as witnesses to him, his life, and his teachings. Recall Blessed Pope Paul VI's prophetic words: "Modern man listens more willingly to witnesses than to teachers, and if he does listen to teachers, it is because they are witnesses" (*Evangelii Nuntiandi*, 41).

To teach with testimony means to share our own personal faith and the stories of our encounters with Christ in the context of the lesson or message we are sharing. It means setting aside our defenses and welcoming young people into a vulnerable part of our lives. By doing so, we open up the possibility for the kids to be willing to have those encounters as well. When we take the ideas we present as catechists down from the level of the abstract and into something personal and meaningful, we enable young people to experience catechesis as more than education. When we teach with testimony, kids not only relate to us, but they also see that it is possible to relate to God.

Evangelizing Ministry Method: Heal, Proclaim

3. Plan with a purpose.

When I started my *The Religion Teacher* website (thereligion teacher.com), it was out of frustration for a lack of high-quality resources for religious educators. The textbook resources were lacking depth, and there were very few quality resources easily found on the Internet. Today, though, there are many download-able resources on websites such as mine. The question is, which activities and resources should we use, and why?

There is a temptation in all forms of education to plan activities related to the theme of the day that are fun but not effective. Sure, everything teachers and catechists plan can connect to a certain topic, but it may not contribute to achieving growth in the person who participates in the activities. When you have a clear purpose in mind for a given activity, you really start to hone in on what is important to learn and to be able to do related to a certain topic. With that purpose in mind, you might find that a very creative craft you did in the past actually just kept the kids quiet and occupied but never really taught them anything about Christ.

Planning with a purpose has two meanings. First, it means writing down a specific goal for children in your ministry to reach at the end of a given day or lesson. It is a clear description of where you want them to be. Teachers and catechists will rec-ognize this practice as a *lesson objective*. A lesson objective is a description of what the students will be able to do as a result of the activities they go through in class. It takes into account where the kids are at now and where we want them to be as a result of our work with them. Writing this down is a freeing process, because once you know what you want them to be able to do or to feel, you can start to pick not just good activities but the right activities for your group of kids.

The second meaning of this principle is to take some time to consider the purpose of the topic you are teaching in the first place. Very often, children will ask their teachers, "Do we *have* to learn this?" I used to get that question all the time as a religion teacher, and I always provided the truthful but unsatisfactory reply: "Yes, because it will be on the test." While an accurate response, it does not get to the heart of the question. Why are the things we teach even important in the first place? If we cannot provide a real answer to that question, then we need to rethink what we are teaching.

The practice I like to use in preparing to teach young people is something I call Five-Why Your Lesson Plan. The practice of asking yourself the question "why?" five times is inspired by lean manufacturing. In lean manufacturing, specifically in Toyota production systems, management would ask the question "why?" five times until they got to the root of a problem. If something broke on the assembly line, they would not just ask why it broke and fix it, they would ask why it broke, find the reason, and then ask "why?" again to discover what caused the problem. Eventually, after asking the question five times, they would usually arrive at the very core or origin of a problem and fix it.

Likewise, when you ask yourself "why?" not just once but five times, you really uncover a deeper and more powerful meaning behind the topics you teach in children's catechesis. If you are teaching a lesson on the Ten Commandments, for example, asking yourself, "Why is it important to teach the Ten Commandments?" and then digging deeper into your response four more times will greatly augment your approach. It transforms a lesson about God's law from, "Hey, you should follow these commandments because God said so," to, "God made us, he loves us, he knows what will make us happy, and if we follow these commandments, we will know joy."

Evangelizing Ministry Method: Proclaim, Teach

4. Invite parents.

Dr. Christian Smith is one of the foremost researchers and analysts of the trends in youth and religion. His landmark studies on Catholic youth in the United States have provided statistical support for what many of us working in religious education know but are afraid to admit. A clear thread throughout this research is that no other factor in retaining youth as Catholic adults even comes close to the influence of parents on the adult faith of their children.

These statistics along with the Church's teaching that parents are the primary educators of their children make it clear that we have to work with parents as partners if we really want to have an impact on the children we serve. Many parents, however, do not embrace this vocation. For some, it seems that attending religious-education classes is enough to prepare kids to be good people as adults.

We can either be upset by the lack of involvement on the part of parents or we can choose to do something about it. Think about where these parents are in their faith journeys. They are not completely distant, and they do not outright reject God and the Church. Give them some credit for bringing their children to learn about God. They have loose ties, but they just have not had the opportunity to experience Christ's healing love for themselves. If they had, they would not be so distant.

The only way to get parents to catechize their children at home is to evangelize them through the Church. As we talked about in chapter 8, we have to have something to invite them to.

It may be a meeting with you, a parish event, a retreat, or simply Sunday Mass. Plan and host events where you can invite parents in to participate in your class along with their children. The more you can invite parents into a deeper connection with your parish or school, the more likely they are to feel welcome and interested in increasing their participation in the community. The more they participate, the greater chance they will have to experience their own encounter with Christ that compels them to go deeper along their discipleship journey.

Evangelizing Ministry Method: Heal, Proclaim

5. Empower children with choices.

The temptation we have as religious educators is to give kids all the answers. We feel inclined to plan everything we can for them so they can learn as much as possible in the little time that we have together. Remember, to teach disciples we have to inspire in them a motivation and self-determination to learn on their own. A disciple never stops learning. If we focus too much on what we teach and not enough on what the students want to learn, the children are eventually going to get burned out. If we are not careful, we will give the impression that Confirmation is "graduation," even if we try to convince people otherwise.

The more we can give choices to children in the directions they would like to go in learning about their faith, the more likely they are to take ownership over their faith and practice it as adults. Catechesis of the Good Shepherd is the prime model here. A central tenet is to motivate children to choose where they spend their most time. They get to decide where they want to go deeper and learn more. The reason Catholic converts are so much more passionate about their faith compared with cradle Catholics is that those raised in their faith spent almost their whole lives being told what they should study and believe.

They rarely got the opportunity to learn and discover what they wanted to believe all on their own within the Catholic faith.

Evangelizing Ministry Method: Teach

6. Catechize within a community.

"The effectiveness of catechesis depends to a great extent on the vitality of the Christian community in which it is given."[2] We cannot expect our work in evangelization and catechesis to be effective simply because of our great ability to teach and evangelize. We might be gifted individuals, but if we are not a part of an evangelizing community that a young person's entire family is welcomed into and nourished by, then children's catechesis is destined to fail. While we develop our evangelizing ministries for children, we also have to develop our own personal relationships with others in our parishes and schools so that we can find nourishment and inspiration ourselves and so that we can make a meaningful impact on the kids we serve.

This kind of dedication to community was built into the parochial-school model run by priests, sisters, and brothers. Today, we need to cultivate that same experience of community among all teachers, catechists, and volunteers who serve in our children's ministries. The community itself has an evangelizing effect on people that we simply cannot create in a classroom all on our own. We can all be individual witnesses to the Faith, but children need to see the witness of a Christian community if we really expect them to be lifelong members of the Church as adults.

Evangelizing Ministry Method: Heal

7. Laugh, play, have fun, and be joyful.

Did you know the average adult laughs five to fifteen times per day, while some people have claimed that young children can laugh up to 300 to 400 times per day? Whether the numbers are completely accurate or not, think about your experience with children of any age. Isn't it incredible how much more they laugh and smile than we do as adults?

The veteran preschool and elementary-school teachers I know—the ones who have stayed in education for decades—are all some of the happiest and most joy-filled people I know. It is really incredible. Where some of us might find working with young children to be draining, these teachers find that the joys and smiles they see every day actually fill them up. We can all learn a little bit from this in developing our evangelizing ministries for children.

Vacation Bible school, Catechesis of the Good Shepherd, and other creative forms of children's ministry are effective because they cultivate the joy and playful hearts that already exist in children. At the same time, they influence adult and parent volunteers in ways that the adult-evangelizing ministries in a parish simply cannot do on their own. When joy and play is the focus of children's ministry, it magnifies and attracts people of all ages to grow further in their love for God.

Our challenge in catechesis is to capitalize on this creative, joyful energy. Children have a natural tendency toward play. It is in their nature to have fun with their creativity. Even the kids who pull the worst pranks are often just finding an outlet for their creative and joy-producing energy. Our task is to direct that energy and desire for joyful play into a pursuit of deeper knowledge and recognition of God in their lives. It may just be that the reason young people are bored, despite intellectually engaging activities, is due to this desire for fun and happiness.

Pope Francis, of course, wrote an entire Church document on the need to evangelize with great joy. Evangelizing ministries for children are held to an even higher standard in this regard. We have to teach young people with joy because at this point in their lives, joy is simply a part of who they are. Children play and have fun doing it. Rather than be upset about kids not paying attention, let's develop ministries that set kids up for experiences in which they can learn about God and have fun at the same time. Most of all, though, let's be joyful ourselves so that the young people will connect with us at a level in which they can grow closer with us and with God.

Evangelizing Ministry Method: Heal, Proclaim, Teach

For additional resources to help evangelize children, visit healproclaim-teach.com/chapter9.

10

MINISTRY WITH TEENAGERS

There are a lot of books and movies about the lives of teenagers. Whether the characters are vampires, wizards, or just regular high-school kids, the stories are always focused on some kind of coming-of-age moment when a person who felt like an outsider for his unique traits suddenly embraces his uniqueness, becoming fully who he is meant to be.

Being a teenager is a tough period of transition. Teens are trying to figure out their identity and aligning themselves with groups of people they want to be seen with and projecting an outward appearance that displays that identity. Teens tend to be very self-conscious and doubtful about their identity as they start to take ownership over it. This leads to all kinds of behaviors that separate them from their parents and sometimes lead them to make poor decisions.

Many teens experiment with alcohol, other drugs, sex, or crime. They can begin to form very bad habits and addictions to things such as pornography, which is a big challenge for young men, especially, to overcome. Some teens suffer so badly from abusive relationships either in their families or in new romantic relationships that they simply do not know how to understand the experiences they are going through.

At the same time, teenage years can be hopeful and exciting. Many people still look back on their time in high school as their "glory days." As high school comes to an end, teens set sights on the lives ahead of them. Their search for identity turns into a search for a vocation. They prepare to enter the adult world.

Evangelizing ministry during the teenage years is crucial, as we have the opportunity to inspire teens to be leaders and take ownership of their faith just as they are making important life choices. As mentors and guides we can take this time to lead teens to more intimate relationships with God. Or, we can inadvertently push them away by boring them with abstract ideas that they find irrelevant to their lives and to the world. We can choose either to *teach at* them or to *guide* them on a path of learning to be a better disciple.

The ministries highlighted in this chapter have found great success in recent years, and each one of them shows how to heal, proclaim, and teach in exemplary ways.

BISHOP SHEIL AND THE CYO

Benny Sheil was a talented young baseball player. When he graduated from Saint Viator's in Chicago in 1906, he had offers to come pitch for various professional baseball teams, including one from Charles Comiskey to come play for the Chicago White Sox. Yet, none of the offers really grabbed his attention. He was not ready to take on a career as a baseball player. Something else was tugging at his heart.

After another year of discernment while studying English at the University of Illinois and continuing to play baseball, he decided to return to Saint Viator's, this time to the seminary. Three years later he was ordained a priest and began his first assignment at a Chicago parish learning what it meant to be a pastor.

A few years later, Father Sheil became the chaplain of the Cook County Jail on the South Side of Chicago, and his life would never be the same. There he counseled many teenage boys who had grown up just blocks away from his own childhood home. For many of these young men—some on death row—Father Sheil was the first person who actually showed them they were loved. Growing up in broken homes, orphanages, and gangs, these young boys had never had anyone tell them they were loved. While society and the papers condemned these young boys as criminals and outcasts of society, Father Sheil stood by their sides, showed them they were loved, and offered them a path to love others as well despite what they had done.

Father Sheil never forgot those years as Cook County Jail chaplain. His heart stayed with those boys throughout the years that followed. Later, he was assigned an admirable position in the Archdiocese of Chicago offices and given a number of important responsibilities, including the organization of the first international Eucharistic Congress to take place in the United States in 1926. During that time he became close friends with the archbishop of Chicago, Cardinal Mundelein, who brought him along on his many trips to Rome. On one of these trips, the cardinal delivered a letter to Father Sheil from Pope Pius XI. Benny Sheil, the ballplayer and jail chaplain, was going to become a bishop.

It was not long before a vision took shape in the young bishop's mind to create something to help those outcasts on the streets of Chicago. What could the Church do to help get these young men off the street and on a path that led them to a better life? Out of this desperate need for change, Bishop Sheil began to share his vision for the Catholic Youth Organization (CYO), which would offer an alternative path to the one that sent so many young men to Cook County Jail.

The CYO began with a boxing tournament that would take place in Chicago's largest professional stadium. All young men in Chicago were invited to participate in the tournament. Race or religion was not a requirement. Whether you were black or white, Irish or German, Catholic, Protestant, or Jewish, you were welcome to participate in the CYO boxing tournament. While professional boxing was at the height of its popularity in the United States, Bishop Sheil put the Church in the position to welcome young men with open arms.

Next, a baseball league was formed, with parishes creating their teams from young men in their area. A school of aviation was founded as well, responding to the dreams of many young men who wanted to become pilots. Girls and boys entered into social clubs and instrumental bands. The CYO sponsored dances and social events that gave children and teens a safe place to meet and spend time with one another.

The CYO was not just a social club or a sports organization. It was created as an extension of the evangelizing mission of the Church. From its earliest charter, the CYO was "a recreational, educational, and religious program that will adequately meet the physical, mental, and spiritual needs of out-of-school Catholic boys and girls, and, without regard to race, creed, or color, assist those young people who are in need . . . while instilling in their minds and hearts a true love of God and country."[1]

Most people recognize the CYO today as the genesis of organized youth ministry in the United States. Parishes throughout Chicago adopted the model, which spread to parishes throughout the country. Today, as a national organization, the National Federation of Catholic Youth Ministers (NFCYM) and the many youth ministers who serve in the United States continue the mission of Bishop Sheil's CYO.

Like so many successful ministries and movements in the Church's history, the CYO was founded in response to a deep need. Young people, in the desperation and poverty of the Great Depression, needed to find acceptance in places other than the gangs run by bootleggers such as Al Capone. But, more importantly, as Bishop Sheil learned during his one-on-one experience as prison chaplain, these young people needed to feel accepted, loved, forgiven, and supported in good times and bad. If you think about it, not much has changed among the youth today. They struggle with acceptance and guilt. They want to be loved for who they are, but they are afraid of being rejected. They are in search of people and communities that welcome them, accept them, and walk with them on their journeys of self-discovery.

This is a challenge that all people face but especially teens— not just Catholic teens but every young person. Bishop Sheil knew this, which is why the CYO was open to all young people, not just those who were enrolled as members of a particular Catholic parish. It is a mindset shift that we could all benefit from adopting today. Bishop Sheil set out to help kids find fulfillment and healing for their difficult childhoods no matter who they were.

SEARCHING FOR MATURITY

In 1962, a few decades after the foundation of the CYO, another priest, also known for his connection to sports, started a retreat movement that spread across the country. Msgr. Peter Armstrong, known as the "Pigskin Priest" for his many years as chaplain to the San Francisco 49ers, was the head of the CYO in the Archdiocese of San Francisco when he had an incredible idea. As the story goes, he was in a room with a group of people listing all the problems with spiritual retreats for teenagers when he said, "It's too bad young people can't give the retreats." A seventeen-year-old boy in the group simply asked, "Why not?" and the Search for Christian Maturity retreat was born.

This retreat model relied on teens planning and leading retreats themselves. Teen leaders prepared, organized, and led the retreats with adults simply acting in support in the background. During these teen-led retreats today, the participants meet in groups throughout the weekend and teen leaders offer personal witness talks to inspire discussion.

Empowering teens as retreat leaders became a powerful feature of high-school retreats adopted by other dioceses, schools, and parishes throughout the country and continues to be used in dioceses today. The teens-leading-teens model also found success in other retreats that started to form about the same time in other parts of the country, including Kairos and Teens Encounter Christ. The Search retreat was so popular and so successful that it even inspired what would become one of the most popular adult-retreat processes in the country: Christ Renews His Parish.

I have been blessed to be on "the inside" of a few Search retreats, Kairos retreats, and other teen-led retreats. They all have a few common elements that make them stand out as profound experiences. Some of these same key elements can be found in chapter 9 of this book, but specifically these retreats are successful for the following reasons:

- **They welcome all.** The retreats are great examples of inviteable events that new people can feel welcome to attend because there are no prerequisites for joining. They make teens feel accepted at a time in their lives when they feel especially unsure of themselves.

- **Small groups build relationships.** The participants may know each other from school, sports, or youth group, but the small-group focus allows the teens to bond with peers whom they might have never gotten to know otherwise. The seemingly serendipitous gathering of people in these small groups often leads to friendships that last for years.

- **The personal witnesses set the tone.** To listen to peers pour their hearts out and share the difficult and joyful stories of their lives helps other teens realize that they are not alone. They are not the only ones trying to figure things out. This vulnerability opens up the possibility for participants to find healing for the wounds of sin and separation.

- **Affirmation leads to healing.** The retreats always focus heavily on affirmation either within the groups or from families and friends who support them. This out-of-the-ordinary affirmation also provides the opportunity for true healing through the realization that they are loved by others and worthy of that love.

- **There are always surprises and secrets that create memorable experiences.** Secrets such as "Live the Fourth" (a secret you only learn by attending a Kairos retreat), affirmation letters, discipleship walks, and the like create the experience of being initiated as an insider, which motivates new people to want to learn more about and discover the secrets.

- **The retreats form teen leaders and, more importantly, disciples.** Once the teens participate in the retreats, they have the opportunity to continue on as leaders of the retreat. This leadership opportunity transforms faith from passive participation to active ownership. In some ways this opportunity is what makes these retreats so great. It was the initial reason that Search was created in the first place.

Whether or not your teenage evangelizing ministry adopts wholesale a retreat process such as Search or Kairos, consider incorporating or evaluating your retreat opportunities with these elements in mind.

ENCOUNTERS AT YOUTH CONFERENCES

When I attended my first youth conference at Franciscan University in Steubenville, Ohio, I was one of those teenage guys sitting with his arms crossed wondering what planet I was on. There with me stood hundreds of teenagers who were singing, smiling, and waving their hands and bodies around in ridiculous praise-and-worship motions. Eventually, though, the other guys and I started participating, mostly to laugh at each other and to mock the other kids around us. In time, though, we were full participants, having fun and dancing along. For me, as I wrote in chapter 3, it was the eucharistic adoration that transformed me. For the first time as a teen, I felt God's true and loving presence. I never would have opened myself up to that possibility if I had not been disarmed by the example of my peers, our youth-group leaders, and the speakers onstage. The praise and worship and the willingness to let my guard down put me in a position to be open to God's love. It was a powerful experience that so many countless others have shared in retreats like that one.

Whether it is the Steubenville youth conferences, World Youth Day, National Catholic Youth Conference, or regional events such as the annual Religious Education Congress in Los Angeles, these large events can create the opportunity for transformative experiences in the lives of young people. Unlike their everyday experiences of boredom in school or unfulfilled social lives, these large events offer a unique and joy-filled experience that young people do not often have.

With motivational speeches from dynamic Catholic leaders, emotionally charged praise-and-worship music, and an experience of the sacraments that is wholly unique, teens tend to experience a "spiritual high" that kick-starts their faith life at home. For a few years, I helped to chaperone a large group of teens from the Diocese of Toledo, Ohio, on trips to Steubenville. The kids had some bonding time on the way to and from the event on large charter buses. On the way home, we took the opportunity to allow anyone who wanted to share their experiences aloud to do so. The stories were touching and powerful and recounted experiences that often led to significant life changes. Their stories almost always expressed some kind of healing of a memory or ongoing personal struggle.

Sadly, the emotional highs were not always accompanied by a commitment necessary to change lives. Too often, when the students got home, the healing encounter became only a memory. They missed the intense emotion and were unable to find it in their parish churches.

In addition to these emotional experiences of healing, the teens need to hear the Gospel proclaimed again and again. The Gospel calls us to be open to a life transformed by God's grace. Through the parables, we are called to sacrifice all that we have and turn instead to Christ and the kingdom of God. Most of all, the Gospel tells the story of a God who loved us so much he died for us and is still here with us today. That is the key to sustain a connection with Christ, even if that feeling of healing does not show up as much as the teens want it to.

The nice thing is that during these youth events, the speakers offer messages that share the Gospel in many different ways. The talks and homilies during these conferences focus on proclaiming a way of life that is very different from what teens are used to. How do you sustain the memories of these talks in the minds and hearts of the teens? Instead of making up your own version of messages they shared, constantly reiterate and repeat the exact phrases and messages you heard on the weekend.

Katie Prejean, high-school theology teacher, parish youth minister, and youth-conference speaker, suggests that youth ministers personally reach out to the speakers and ask for a few ideas to go deeper into a topic they shared. Prejean says that, as a speaker at those events, she loves it when youth ministers follow up with her for more ideas. It adds an additional hook to keep kids engaged in the postevent youth meetings. The key is to go deeper into the message and try to find something that continues to touch the heart of the kids who experienced the weekend or are hearing about it for the first time. Hopefully, this will compel the kids to learn more about certain topics and set out on a path of discovery to grow as disciples all on their own.

For the teens who are already dedicated youth-group members and veteran attendees at the youth-conference events, you have an opportunity to teach them to grow further as disciples. Encourage them to set a good example for the other teens on the weekend by showing others how to participate and encourageing those who feel they are "too cool" for the event. You can also challenge them not to approach the event looking for that "spiritual high" but instead to see it as an opportunity to experience personal healing by helping others find healing, too. The temptation of returning participants is to become consumers of the experience rather than active servants of those they participate with as peers. This is especially important for any college-age students or young adults who are returning as chaperones with your group. Serving others is a different kind of experience, but one that can be just as fulfilling and even more important for kids at that stage of their faith journeys.

DEVELOPING A LENS FOR SELF-UNDERSTANDING

In order to deal with the pain in their lives, teens tend to cope by offering cliché justifications for why bad things happen to them. It is a response that we have all had in our lives. We say things like, "Everything happens for a reason," and as a result never really enter into the emotional pain in order to deal with it in a sophisticated way. In other words, we are afraid to experience the painful path of true inner healing.

At the University of Notre Dame, a summer youth program directed by Dr. Leonard DeLorenzo called ND Vision helps teens see their lives in a different way. Hundreds of teenagers from all over the United States come to Notre Dame's campus, sleep in the dorms, and eat in the dining halls. They spend the week listening to inspirational messages and witnessing talks, and attending daily Mass and prayer services. Much of their time is spent in small groups led by volunteer college students who are trained to mentor the young people in their care.

These undergraduate "mentors in faith" receive substantial formation and theological training leading up to the summer conferences. They actually enroll in a theology course to prepare to be ND Vision mentors. The class does have a practical component, but its primary purpose is to prepare the mentors with a theological framework for understanding significant events and experiences in their lives. This framework, inspired by the writings of great saints such as Saint Augustine, informs the work they do with teenagers in the summers. It allows them to model for their younger participants how they can see their own lives in the context of faith.

Essentially, what ND Vision provides for the mentors and the teen participants is a worldview that is infused with the presence of God. Teens who attend ND Vision do not just return home with a "spiritual high" and fun stories; they return with the ability to see their own lives in the context of God's love for them and for the world. For teenagers, who are in a stage of life that is focused on discovering their identities, this new and Christian worldview comes at a critical time. They can start to make sense of all the pain and all the hopes and dreams in their lives because they have heard the proclamation of a different vision for the world, one that provides a firm foundation for how they can live their lives in service to others.

LIFE TEEN: LIFE-GIVING MINISTRY FOR TEENAGERS

How do we help teens wake up and come alive in their faith and love for Jesus Christ? Teens strive for fun and excitement. They are constantly complaining about boredom, claiming—no matter where they live in the world—that "there's nothing to do around here." That kind of apathetic way of life reveals a need that teenagers may not realize they have. They want to come alive, and, unfortunately, they are unable to find that livelihood within the Church. That is why we need to offer an experience of their religion that is not just another boring activity but something to look forward to.

Since the 1980s Life Teen's incredibly popular youth-ministry model has been adopted by parishes throughout the United States. From its beginning, the purpose of Life Teen has been to provide life-giving encounters with Christ and his Church. At its core, Life Teen developed a model of youth ministry around the celebration of the Mass. Life Teen begins with the Life Teen Masses, known for their dynamic music and youth-friendly homilies, then leads into Life Nights, which focus on particular themes throughout the year and provide opportunities for fellowship, learning, and prayerful support of one another.

You can adopt the Life Teen model and take advantage of its dynamic training materials and resources, but whether you become a Life Teen parish or not, consider some of the key principles of success that any evangelizing teen ministry can learn from it. Learning from Life Teen, all evangelizing ministries for teens can do the following:

- **Be centered on the Eucharist.** The Eucharist makes us Catholic. If we are trying to appeal to nominally Catholic kids who seldom go to church, Life Teen Masses show young people that the liturgy can be engaging. Life Teen Masses are dynamic experiences that take away objections to going to Mass and open up the opportunities for an encounter with Christ in the Eucharist.

- **Know that music makes a difference.** Ever wonder why the music you love the most is essentially the same kind of music you loved when you were a teenager? For whatever reason, teens are especially attuned to a certain taste in the music of the day (and a distaste to the churchy music). We could expect or demand that teens just deal with this music they do not like, but we cannot expect them to do so willingly. Later, they might come back to meet Jesus in the Eucharist despite the music, but only after they have become a fully committed disciple.

- **Focus on issues that matter to teens.** Life Nights follow a curriculum that addresses topics that actually matter to teens. They do not shy away from Church teachings, but they present them in the context of relevant issues of the day. This inductive approach to teaching about the Faith (see chapter 5) anchors Catholic beliefs in things they already know, understand, and live throughout their days.

- **Give teens a sense of being a part of something bigger than themselves.** Life Teen is an international brand that connects teens within a parish but also has connections among many different parishes throughout the country and the world. This sense of being a part of something bigger than weekly youth-group meetings is an additional motivation for Christian disciples.

PRINCIPLES IN DEVELOPING AN EVANGELIZING MINISTRY FOR TEENS

How do you effectively evangelize teens in our Church today? Consider the following principles and guidelines as you develop your evangelizing ministry for teens.

1. Begin with an awareness of what teens really need in their lives.

The CYO began out of a desire to get Chicago teens out of jail and off of the streets. That is a real and significant need in the world. While your evangelizing ministry might target teens without run-ins with the law, you still need to make sure you are providing the path from where they are to a deep need and goal. If you want your teens to have a more intimate relationship with Jesus Christ, what will that mean for them in their everyday lives?

Teenagers are often carrying around profoundly complex experiences and memories that are difficult to comprehend. All teens are going through an identity crisis while they figure out who they are and how they are perceived by others. Giving them the tools to understand what they really need in their lives will help them see their lives with a new perspective informed by a connection with Christ. This is why ND Vision focuses so much on training their youth mentors to help provide a model for understanding what life brings you as a teen. With this better-informed vision for life, young people can find healing in areas of their lives that they have tried to avoid rather than address. With the light of faith, teenagers can "see with a light that illumines their entire journey, for it comes from the risen Christ, the morning star that never sets" (*Lumen Fidei*, 1).

Our evangelizing ministries for teens—whether in parish youth groups, Catholic high schools, or local or national retreats—only have value in their ability to make a life-changing and long-lasting impact on the kids they serve. We do not just want our teens to walk away with an awareness of Church teachings; we want them to graduate high school with an intimate relationship with Christ that has a real and tangible influence in daily life.

Evangelizing Ministry Method: Heal

2. Align your activities with things teens like to do.

How do you get teenagers to show up? You have to sell the experience to them. How do you get kids off the streets and into an environment focused on faith? Offer them something they are looking for. Bishop Sheil gave teenagers what they were searching for: opportunities to play sports, play instruments, get an education, and join other teens at social events. The best part? It worked. There were no catechism classes required to participate in with the CYO. They offered what teens wanted and created the opportunity for personal relationships and informal mentoring to take place within the protection of the organization and within the context of Christ and his Church.

Search, Kairos, Teens Encounter Christ, and other retreats do the same. Teens do not tell other teens about how fun it was to sit in groups and talk about Jesus. Pictures on brochures and websites show smiling faces, funny costumes, ice breakers, and outside games. The retreats offer the opportunity to get to the real and difficult issues in life, but teens are convinced to come partly because of the opportunity to enjoy themselves through games and social time.

Keep in mind that while you offer these opportunities for fun, games, and socializing, you are not hosting purely social events. Youth ministry is about more than simple social hours and free pizza. You are creating the opportunity for close and personal relationships to form among teens so they can find

healing in Christ. You have to be clear about what real participation in the kingdom of God requires: self-sacrifice. You have
to proclaim a Gospel that is good news but good news with a
price. You are giving them the opportunity to meet other teens
like themselves who are committed to following Christ but need
to know they are not alone.

Evangelizing Ministry Method: Heal

3. In order to get teens to show up, you have to get out of the church and go where they go.

While you could passively sit back and hope teenagers hear
about you and come to your youth-ministry events, it is much
more effective actively to go out and spread the word about your
ministry to newbies, occasional attendees, and core members.
The key to getting the word out is getting out of your office both
physically and, today, digitally.

First, you can find out about the social events and places
teens hang out and just show up. Are there core teen leaders in
your ministry who play a sport? Act in a school play? Does anyone skateboard, ski, or bike? Find out what kinds of events you
can attend and support. Be present and social even if it feels a
little uncomfortable. Not only does it show support for your core
leaders, but it also creates the opportunity for them to point you
out or introduce you to friends who might have only heard about
you and the ministry you do without actually attending yet.

One of the advantages we have today, though, is the ability to
get out of the office in a digital way. Like it or not, teenagers are
glued to their mobile devices. They connect with friends online
and send more text messages than adults could ever imagine.
We can either choose to roll our eyes and ignore it, or we can
become active participants in the way they communicate.

Youth ministers are seeing a lot of success in adopting new
forms of media and communication. I have heard from many

youth ministers such as Katie Prejean who post inspirational messages, passages from Scripture, and eye-catching graphics that appeal to teenagers. Prejean gets on her phone and sends individual text messages to teens to remind them about events. It takes time, but once she became committed to doing it, using social media and mobile phones significantly expanded participation in her events.

Evangelizing Ministry Method: Heal

4. Proclaim before you teach.

Even if you are in a Catholic high school with textbooks, tests, and curricula to follow, it all means nothing unless everything you teach builds upon a foundation of proclaiming the Gospel. You simply cannot expect a teenager—whose modus operandi is to rebel against authority and rules—to accept Church teachings without first making the personal choice to follow Christ and the Church. The only way to do this, as we have said in this book, is to make teaching build upon the foundation of the healing and proclaiming ministry you do as well.

Every time you speak in front of a group of teens, relate your message back to the grand vision in the gospels. Make sure teens walk away with the realization that (1) God loves them, (2) he gave his life for them, and (3) he is with them today. If they do not realize or accept this message, then you cannot expect them to do anything more than answer questions correctly on a test in order to get a good grade.

Evangelizing Ministry Method: Proclaim

5. Fight doubt with authenticity and compassion.

Many teens struggle not only to come to terms with their own personal identity, but also to come to terms with their own personal faith. They suffer not only from an identity crisis but also a crisis of faith. Many of them, for the first time, question the beliefs they were raised in and choose whether they believe them or not. Some of these teens become full-fledged and passionate atheists.

Whether you are responding to attacks by teenage atheists or simply addressing some doubt being voiced by vocal young people, respond with authenticity and compassion. First, understand the motive behind the question and recognize the good things a person brings up. Do not respond as if it were a personal attack. Instead, focus on showing compassion for that young person, especially at this very difficult time of transition in life.

From there you can start to reveal the real meaning behind our beliefs. In order to do that, we have to continually make connections between what people recognize as doctrines, rules, or requirements from the Church and the core message of the Faith, or the kerygma (God loves you, he died for you, and he is with you today). Only if teens understand the foundations of our beliefs and teachings will they become disarmed. Through the proclamation, we can break down barriers and open up the possibility for a healing encounter with Christ.

After teaching middle-school religion for a couple of years, I got a job as a high-school theology teacher. But I had to teach a course on social justice, which I knew almost nothing about. I read a lot and barely kept myself a few sections ahead of the students in that first semester of teaching it. I thought the kids would completely expose my ignorance, but they didn't. In fact, they loved the course, and I rarely got into the same kinds of debates and explanations that I got into in my other courses. Why? Because teenagers have a natural tendency to seek and promote justice and freedom. They were able to understand the compassion of the Church through its social teaching. Social justice was a huge appeal to them, and for many of them it gave the Church a silver lining that they had a hard time finding in other courses.

Teenagers may seem anti-authority and anti-Church, but the positive side of that mentality is that many of them at this time in their lives have a heightened sense of justice. They want to see justice done in the world, and they feel a strong passion for making a difference for others outside of the classroom walls. If we are able to make connections between all of our Church doctrines and rules and connect them to this desire for authentic justice and mercy for those in need, we will find ourselves in a much better position to invite teens into an opportunity for a personal encounter with Christ.

Evangelizing Ministry Method: Proclaim, Teach

6. The best form of teaching comes in smaller settings.

One way in which the CYO was able to make such a deep impact on teenagers through boxing is the natural opportunity for mentoring between the trainers and the boxers. Many of the boys entering the ring did not have a positive role model or father figure in their lives whom they could look to as an example or confide in as a trusted mentor. These young people needed these relationships in their lives.

Today an organization called YDisciple is trying to do the very same thing. YDisciple was created with a recognition that little has changed in our ability to reach Catholic teens in the last few decades. They still leave the Church as adults. Rather than simply improve the resources that help youth ministers plan large-group youth nights or catechesis in a classroom, YDisciple focuses on mentoring relationships between Catholic teens and adults in the parish.

I asked Everett Fritz, director of youth- and young-adult ministry for the Diocese of Fresno, California, about his experience working with teens through YDisciple, and he made a great observation. He said, "Teens crave relationships with adults, yet they have no time to engage in meaningful relationships with people who can guide them in their life. Our culture is taking teens, at a time period in their [lives] when they are most vulnerable, and removing adult guidance from their lives. In order to make disciples, we have to put them in relationships with people who are already disciples."[2]

YDisciple has some great resources to help make these relationships between teens and adults more intentional. Whether you use their resources and this model or not, the concept itself should be applied to the way all evangelizing ministries prepare Confirmation sponsors and youth ministers. If we really want to make an impact on teens in the Church today, we need to think beyond effective group meetings and effective classrooms, and develop our ability to mentor young people one-on-one.

Evangelizing Ministry Method: Heal, Proclaim, Teach

For additional resources to help evangelize teenagers, visit healproclaim-teach.com/chapter10.

11

MINISTRY WITH COLLEGE STUDENTS

If the teenage years are about discovering who we are, then the college years are about solidifying that identity on our own. For the first time in their lives, college students set out to forge a life away from the comfort of their parents. It is a time of questioning nearly everything and testing out assumptions and beliefs about life that are now put to the test against reality.

At the same time, college is a time of incredible pressure. A lot is riding on getting good grades in college, and, as a result, many college students suffer from enormous anxiety and stress. They are overworked and overwhelmed. Parents, despite the long distance, expect the best out of their children in college, especially considering the amount of money it costs to get a college degree. College students cope with these pressures in different ways. Some simply quit or pretend not to care. Others spend countless sleepless hours in libraries and study rooms trying to get the best grades possible. This seems to give them all the more reason to let loose and party on the weekends.

For many college students, these are the first years in their lives when they drift away from the Church. Now that the choice to come to Mass is completely theirs, they are able to skip and skip again. Pretty soon skipping becomes a habit, and Church is removed from their lives altogether. Most of these young adults still consider themselves spiritual, but they do not relate well with organized religion. They pray sometimes, but they do not really have a clear connection with Christ. If they did, they would seek out others who share that faith and find ways to celebrate it.

There are beacons of hope on many college campuses throughout the United States. Passionate young students live their faith and invite others to share in celebration of God's presence in the world. The many people responsible for Catholic campus ministry at colleges are turning the tide against religious apathy and mindless partying. In this chapter, we will look at a few of the best-known models for campus ministry, what is working for them, and what they do differently to attract lost college students into an encounter with Christ and his Church.

THE SPIRIT OF BLESSED JOHN HENRY NEWMAN

Being a Catholic at a public or private non-Catholic university is common today. We might take it for granted that at many of these non-Catholic institutions there are either parishes or campus ministries serving the needs and formation of Catholic students. This, however, was not always the case. In the late 1800s, anti-Catholic sentiments were still quite common throughout the United States, especially on college campuses. Many people turned for inspiration to a very fitting Catholic figure of that century: Blessed John Henry Newman.

John Henry Newman was an intellectual and university professor in England who converted from Anglicanism to the Catholic Church in the mid-1800s. He became very well-known for his excellent apologetics and remains today one of the greatest Catholic thinkers of the last several centuries. He became the modern model for conversion to the Catholic Church despite the many doctrines that were usually intellectual stumbling blocks. Through his in-depth research and study, especially of the early Church Fathers, this Anglican priest grew more and more in sympathy with the Catholic Church and eventually decided to make a complete conversion despite the implications it would have on his career and reputation. Despite the risk, he remained respected and admired in England and throughout the world. He was later named a cardinal by Pope Leo XIII despite the fact that he was neither a bishop nor a resident priest in Rome.

Many aspiring university students turned to Cardinal Newman as a model for living as a Catholic on a university campus. First, a number of university students in Oxford, England, turned to him and requested the use of his name for their group, creating the Oxford University Newman Society. Later, Newman Societies, or Newman Clubs and Newman Centers, started to form in the United States. Beginning at the University of Pennsylvania, the organizations soon spread and expanded to the roughly 250 Newman Centers today.

Newman Centers are probably best known for their ecumenical identities and focus on social justice. Like their namesake, they do not take a defensive stance of their faith to the point of exclusion and separation from others. Instead, they focus on meeting the needs of Catholic students at every stage along their Catholic journeys. They meet the needs of intellectuals as well as those students simply in need of some spiritual guidance on their path toward God. Newman's legacy, exemplified in his personal coat of arms that read in Latin "heart speaks to heart," is felt among college campuses everywhere in the Newman Centers' balanced approach to intellectual pursuit of truth in the context of loving service to God and others.

MAINTAINING FOCUS ON CHRIST

"Be soldiers."

Those are the words Saint John Paul II said to Curtis Martin moments after he shared with the pope his vision for FOCUS, the Fellowship of Catholic University Students. Martin and his wife, Michaelann, founded FOCUS after observing a deep need for a resurgence of the Catholic faith on college campuses. Today, the organization is staffed by more than four hundred college graduates serving as missionaries and campus ministers on university campuses all across the United States. These missionaries are passionate individuals dedicated to serving God by sharing his message with young adults who so desperately need him in their lives. These men and women are truly soldiers of the new evangelization, what Pope Francis has called "missionary disciples."

The FOCUS missionaries on college campuses inspire one another to push forward in service to God and the Church. Much of this inspiration can be traced back to a special kind of inspiration coming from their founder. Martin was raised in a Catholic home, but as he grew older he drifted away from the Church. He became an atheist and a self-proclaimed "prodigal." In college, Martin's life was transformed through the influence of some Evangelical Protestant friends and members of the Campus Crusade for Christ, who encouraged him to read the Bible. Through an encounter with Christ in scripture, inspired by Evangelical friends, Martin's life was transformed.

At the time of his conversion, Martin did not have a lot of Catholic friends. The Catholics he knew did not have the same kind of passion for their faith that Evangelicals had. There certainly were no "missionary disciples" getting out of the church and into the dorms reaching the lost like him. After continued prompting from his Catholic mother, though, he agreed to attend a Catholic retreat, mostly to find material for arguments against the Catholic faith. There he met the Lord, not just in his Word but in the Eucharist. During an experience of eucharistic adoration, he realized that the Jesus Christ whom he knew and loved from his study of scripture was right there at the heart of the Catholic faith. At the time, Martin had been praying for God to lead him, but he never expected God to lead him back to the Catholic Church.

The FOCUS missionaries on college campuses set an example for what it is like to live a life passionate about the Catholic faith. Rather than sitting back, starting programs and events, and hoping people show up, they go where the students go, forming authentic friendships and relationships that sometimes blossom into spiritual friendships. FOCUS missionaries get to know students one-on-one and then invite them into Bible studies and other small-group communities of students exploring their Catholic faith.

At the core of the FOCUS approach to forming disciples is something referred to as "win, build, send." Here is how Martin described the three-step process during the 2012 Synod for the New Evangelization:

- **Win:** "We who have encountered Jesus must go out and love people because Christ first loved us. In the midst of our friendships with them, we introduce them to our greatest friend, Jesus."

- **Build:** "Once they have encountered Jesus, we build them up in the knowledge and practice of the faith. . . . Without the fullness of Catholic faith, authentic renewal is impossible. We must be transformed."

- **Send:** "As these young disciples grow in their practice of the faith, they are sent out, with our continued care, to begin the process anew. Holiness will take a lifetime, but the work of evangelization can begin shortly after an authentic encounter with Jesus."[1]

Does this sound familiar? It should. FOCUS missionaries "win" over the lost by forming relationships of love and mercy. The people they meet learn that they are loved through friendships and an encounter with Christ. These people find healing through the work of the FOCUS missionaries.

Once these young people encounter Christ, they still need to come into a full understanding of the sacrifice it takes to accept the fullness of the Catholic faith. They need to hear the Gospel proclaimed in such a way that they willingly make choices that transform their lives into something totally new.

Finally, having encountered Christ and having made the sacrifices necessary to follow him, they are sent out to learn by teaching others. They begin a lifelong process of discovering their faith with the help and teaching work of the missionaries who mentor them. Disciples—while remaining disciples—are now sent out to teach others and be witnesses as missionary disciples of Christ. The FOCUS missionaries heal (win), proclaim (build), and teach (send).

GETTING AWAY WHILE AWAY FROM HOME

Retreats are important offerings for evangelizing ministries at every age level, but I find them to be particularly important for college students. During college, people are away from home and establishing new foundations amid new surroundings. Having a retreat to develop deeper, more personal relationships with other college students while growing in love and faith in God can have a significant impact on the direction life takes during the college years.

As a student at Miami University, I coordinated all of the Catholic retreats with the campus minister. We offered several retreat options, including one at the beginning of the year for incoming freshmen and two more for any age during the fall and spring. The most popular and most important retreat we offered was Kairos, a youth retreat brought to Miami many years ago by Catholic high-school graduates and adapted for college students.

At Miami, Kairos was the glue that held our Catholic community of college disciples together. It formed close bonds between people and brought in many people who otherwise would not have been involved in campus ministry. For many students, it was an opportunity for healing that they desperately needed. The temptations and challenges college students often encounter place in their hearts a desire to talk to both God and others. The large-group time allowed for an increase in comfort amid growing friendships. The personal witness talks set the tone for small-group conversations that brought out real challenges in life. The opportunities for prayer and reconciliation made room to build a firm foundation in faith so that participants would be able to "Live the Fourth" when they arrived back home.

Kairos built a community of people at Miami who could encourage and support each other to make the sacrifices necessary to live a Christian life in college. After people attended the retreat, they maintained their relationships and got involved in other ministries at the parish where Catholic campus ministry operated. To build the kingdom of God on a college campus, sacrifices need to be made, and at times friendships need to be given up in order to live the Christian life. Many people on the Kairos retreats realized this during their weekend experience. We did not have to teach this because it was clearly "proclaimed" in witness talks, small-group discussions, and through the opportunities for prayer and discernment.

As people filtered into other ministries in our local parish, they found opportunities for personal growth and faith development. I formed some of my closest friendships with the people on my Kairos retreats (including one with the woman I would later marry) and built upon those relationships in other ministries, including Bible studies, weekend and weekday Masses, small-group events, and mission trips. Kairos was the first step that opened the doors to many other opportunities to grow in our relationships with God and with others. At Kairos we were healed, we heard the Gospel proclaimed, and we found ways we could learn and grow together as disciples afterward.

PRINCIPLES FOR DEVELOPING EFFECTIVE EVANGELIZING MINISTRIES WITH COLLEGE STUDENTS

Consider using the following principles in evangelizing college students through college campus ministries or parish ministries that reach out to people of college age.

1. Develop one-on-one relationships.

With such a large number of students on college campuses and likely a limited number of members of your ministry team, the very idea of focusing on a one-on-one approach to evangelization seems crazy. The fact is, though, that college students are excessively overloaded with responsibilities, commitments, and events. To try to convince people to attend a college retreat, Mass, prayer service, or other event when there are so many other competing interests is a very difficult thing to do. If, however, someone is personally invited to attend an event by someone whom they know, like, and do not want to let down, then they are much more likely to get involved.

This goes for campus-ministry staff as well as student leaders. There must be a clear focus on developing one-on-one relationships between staff and students, upperclassmen and underclassmen, active participants and occasional attendees. By having this strong focus on relationships over programs and events, you develop the opportunities for personal healing and increase the probability that students will choose campus ministry over their many other opportunities.

Without a doubt, this was the reason I got involved in Campus Crusade for Christ before I even realized there was anything being offered by our Catholic campus ministry at Miami University. You will recall that in chapter 7 I shared some lessons I learned from a Crusade staff alum, Scott, who developed personal one-on-one relationships with me and some other underclassmen. When he invited us to attend an overnight retreat, how could we turn him down? Eventually, I did form some relationships with the people in the Catholic campus ministry, but only after a fair amount of time had passed. It took longer to develop relationships that started to draw me into the Catholic campus ministry because their outreach was not as intentional as it was for members of the Campus Crusade for Christ.

Evangelizing Ministry Method: Heal

2. Keep the doors open.

Some of the best evangelizing ministries for college students have explicitly lived this challenge from Pope Francis: "A Church that 'goes forth' is a Church whose doors are open. Going out to others in order to reach the fringes of humanity does not mean rushing out aimlessly into the world. Often it is better simply to slow down, to put aside our eagerness in order to see and listen to others, to stop rushing from one thing to another and to remain with someone who has faltered along the way. . . . The Church is called to be the house of the Father, with doors always wide open" (*EG*, 46–47).

Working in college campus ministry, we might think it makes sense to provide dozens of events and ministry offerings to meet the diverse demands of college students. With small numbers of staff supported by dedicated student volunteers, people are often spread too thin and are trying to do too much. Some of the most successful evangelizing ministries for college students take a different approach. Again, they focus on relationships instead of programs.

This illumines most clearly the success of FOCUS. The FOCUS missionaries have no walls or doors to open. They operate purely at the level of relationships that they form with students on college campuses. They resist the temptation to look for immediate results and growing numbers of participation in events and instead build one-on-one relationships with the people who need it the most.

The Newman Center at the University of Minnesota-Duluth, led by Father Mike Schmitz, is a great example of how FOCUS and Newman Centers can work together to open wide the doors of Christ. While FOCUS has the primary objective of evangelizing college students and leading them along a path of discipleship, the Newman Center exists with "doors always wide open" to provide a Catholic context and home for the work missionaries do with students. The Newman Center is the welcoming home and center of Catholic activity on campus, focusing heavily on a dynamic and welcoming experience of Sunday Mass.

At the University of Notre Dame, campus ministers talk a lot about opening doors. Based on the inspiration and witness of Saint André Bessette, doorkeeper at Notre Dame College in

Quebec, they train their retreat leaders to be doorkeepers as well. According to campus minister John Paul Lichon, they train retreat leaders to facilitate rather than force opportunities for students to walk through the doors that open up to an experience of God.[4] Often a retreat leader can tend to orchestrate experiences for others to match their own experience by following an almost formulaic set of activities to create well-defined experiences. This approach of facilitating rather than orchestrating instead enables a retreat leader to carry on without expectations or intentions. If he simply opens doors, he makes the space for the Spirit to do the work.

Evangelizing Ministry Method: Heal

3. Do not avoid discussing the sinful behavior.

It is hard to think about college-student stereotypes without associating them with binge drinking and partying. Most people turn twenty-one in college and are legally able to drink for the first time. Even before that, though, college students are immersed in a culture of alcohol, parties, and sex, whether they choose to engage in it or not.

We have to be careful when we are dealing with culture. On one hand, we do not want to be completely written off as goody-goody Catholics out of touch with reality. On the other hand, we do not want to condone sin. At some point in their college lives, if people are maintaining a relationship with Christ, they will hit a breaking point. They will come to realize the emptiness of going too far, and when they do, we want to be there to help them. Determine not so much to be a constant whistle-blower on bad behavior but a person and community with open arms ready to catch people when they fall.

FOCUS offers a guide to virtuous living for its student leaders, which includes something called The Big Three: chastity, sobriety, and excellence. Each of these virtues applies to a specific challenge faced by college students. First, the call to selfless love is challenged by temptations of the college hookup culture. Chastity, therefore, is a virtue by which college students learn to love the right way. Coupled with the temptations to sexual sin are the poor decisions brought on by the misuse of alcohol. By valuing sobriety, college students of a legal age can consider the use of alcohol in moderation without going overboard. Finally, focusing on the virtue of excellence fights against the temptation college students experience just to go through the motions, to live comfortably without passion or purpose. Through each of these virtues, FOCUS student leaders and missionaries do not guilt others into being better people. Rather, they build relationships and live by example, showing the value of living a virtuous life.

I hit a breaking point during my college years, and I don't know what I would have done if I hadn't turned to a trusted spiritual mentor for help. After a particularly shameful weekend of partying in my senior year of college, I called Father John Ferone, who had led retreats for us over the years, and asked for help. He invited me to join him for a weekend-long silent retreat at their Jesuit residence. It was my first private retreat and one of the most uplifting experiences of my life. It turned out to be a critical experience in realizing my vocation would likely be husband and father rather than priesthood, as I sometimes considered.

I did not become a perfect person for the remainder of my college career, but I do know that the opportunity to step aside from college life for a weekend of guided, silent prayer changed my life for the better. Padre (as we all called Father Ferone) did not shame me or give me tips for living a more temperate life; instead, he led me into a deeper relationship with Christ and let God lead me into reconciliation and mercy.

Evangelizing Ministry Method: Heal, Proclaim

4. Prepare with prayer.

College is by its very nature a transition period. It is a very short amount of time in which a young person is formed to become a contributing member of society and the workforce. Unfortunately, today many young people have developed the reputation for not growing up fast enough.

As we minister to college students, we have to ask ourselves not only about how to help them now in their current life situation but also how we can lead them into a mature relationship with Christ when they have transitioned into life after college. Once they graduate, they will not have the same people who have supported them in their faith through their college years. Therefore, college campus ministries should form young adults whose foundation for faith extends beyond place and people.

As I talked with campus ministers responsible for sending college students out into the world, a common theme emerged: none of them were as concerned with involvement in campus-ministry events or offerings as they were with inspiring students to engage in a deeper prayer life on their own. Everyone I talked to while researching this chapter stressed the desire to equip their college students with the tools they needed for a healthy prayer life. In order truly to form disciples whose relationship with God extends beyond graduation, solid prayer habits are essential. Especially during the transitory college years, prayer can be an incredible gift in the discernment of next steps after graduation. If we teach nothing else to college students, let us make sure they learn how to pray.

Evangelizing Ministry Method: Teach

For additional resources to help evangelize on college campuses, visit healproclaimteach.com/chapter11.

12
MINISTRY WITH YOUNG ADULTS

Not long ago it would have been strange to include an entire chapter about ministering to young adults. The very concept of "young adult" is such a new idea in the Church that people tend to be confused by it. What does *young* adult actually mean? How young is young and how old is old? The fact that young-adult books (YA novels) actually refer to literature for teenagers doesn't help clarify the matter.

In ministry spheres, we use the term *young adults* to refer to a group of people who are mostly college graduates and still new in their careers but not yet plugged into a parish in traditional ways. Most have not married yet and do not have kids enrolled in a Catholic school or parish religious education. People of this age group today are getting married and having children later in life than previous generations. As a result, there is a group of people in the Church who do not fit in the same way as married adults with older children do. This can be experienced as a kind of limbo in the life of a young Catholic. It is a transitory time in life. Nevertheless, many ministries have formed in order to directly serve the people in this age group. This chapter highlights some of those groups seeing success today.

FROM NOTHING TO SOMETHING

I have to be honest that when my wife and I decided to move to South Bend, Indiana, we were not sure how much we would like it. We had been living in Nashville, Tennessee, which was a young and up-and-coming area with lots to do. We left a city and a group of young Catholic and Christian friends who were absolutely incredible. We did not expect to find something similar anywhere else.

When we first arrived in South Bend, we were blessed to have a group of people whom we worked with at the University of Notre Dame provide a real sense of community for us. Almost everyone we worked with was within five years of our age, and we all had similar interests. It was a built-in young-adult community with a common faith.

Around the same time, something incredible was forming in our diocese and in our parish. A new group of young, college graduates were joining together in all kinds of fun social and prayerful events that had never taken place before. I was aware of the Church referring to young-adult ministry before, but I got to experience its beginnings in our parish and diocese firsthand.

It was not long before I met the man behind the new ministry, Sean Allen. He and I were in a graduate theology course together at Notre Dame. At the time, he was a master-of-divinity student interning at the diocese in something called "young-adult ministry." Before hiring Allen, the diocese focused its energy in young-adult ministry on college campus ministry and did very little with college graduates. There just wasn't a simple way to find and reach them. After Allen finished the MDiv program, he was hired to grow young-adult ministry in the area, splitting his time between parish and diocese. It has been remarkable to see how things have developed from almost nothing to a thriving community of young Catholics.

Seeing all the things they do now, you might assume that it was the incredible programs that attracted so many young adults. There is Theology on Tap, regular picnics, happy hours, Ultimate Frisbee, pumpkin picking, prayer groups, Bible studies, retreats, service trips, married-couples date nights, and even a home-brew club. Surely, it was the wide variety of options that attracted so many people to get involved, right?

Ask Sean Allen how he built a thriving Catholic young-adult community in our parish and in the diocese, and he will tell you that there is no great marketing secret to what he did. He built relationships with people one by one and invited them to get involved in some of the few young-adult events he was planning. That is exactly how he recruited my wife and me to get involved. I talked to Allen in class and then saw him at Mass on Sunday nights. Without being pushy or overbearing, Allen would always extend invitations without any strings attached. He simply started conversations with people and mentioned his inviteable events just in case they might be interested.

As participation in the informal dinners and events grew, Allen and the young-adult leadership team he built in the parish began slowly to add more offerings for people in the parish. As needs and numbers grew, they experimented with different events, found what worked, and started extending personal invitations to people they knew to join them at the events. Since they always had something to invite people to, it was easy to get their friends and the people they met at Mass involved in the young-adult ministry.

If you are just getting started in young-adult ministry in your parish or diocese, do not be misled by the success of large young-adult gatherings. Those ministries grew one person at a time. You have to do the hard work of building one-on-one relationships with people in order slowly to grow your ministry one by one. Sean Allen grew a thriving young-adult community almost exclusively by word of mouth. There were no great marketing schemes or incredible events. He had conversations; he met people for lunch, coffee, and dinner; and he created an incredible evangelizing ministry for young adults in our parish.

TAPPING INTO THE THEOLOGICAL BEAUTY OF THE CHURCH

Children, youth, and college ministries tend to gather around pizza at their events. You always have to feed them, right? Many Catholic dioceses and parishes, recognizing the state in life of young adults, turned instead to a different setting for their regular meetings. At Old Saint Patrick's parish in the Archdiocese of Chicago, Father John Cusick started a series of lectures in the early 1980s focusing on the difficult theological and pastoral issues on the minds and hearts of young adults in his parish. Recognizing the need for a memorable brand (see chapter 8), they named it Theology on Tap to appeal to recent college graduates in the Chicago area. They created a brand that appealed to young adults in Chicago, a brand that soon spread to cities and parishes all throughout the United States.

Most Theology on Tap meetings today take place in bars and pubs rather than parish buildings. The hope is to welcome young adults in a comfortable location and show how the Church really is relevant to their regular lives. Despite the obvious criticism that meeting in a bar might bring, the Theology on Tap name has been incredibly successful in reaching young adults for decades and continues to be new and engaging for many dioceses today.

Sean Allen started using Theology on Tap as an element of the young-adult ministry in our diocese, and he has found incredible success. The meetings are often packed, and the speakers are highly engaging. Allen says that the success of

Theology on Tap comes from meeting two important needs for young adults. First, many people are drawn by the topic and the speaker and are interested in learning more about their Catholic faith. This has a great appeal for the already dedicated disciples and engaged Catholics in the diocese. Second, the Theology on Tap gatherings meet a basic human need for community and acceptance. In addition to the lecture, the meetings include the opportunity to socialize before, after, and often during the talk. This gives people the opportunity to build bonds of friendship in a faith setting that they might not normally have in their daily lives.

In recent years, RENEW International has partnered with Old Saint Patrick's Parish to offer resources for parishes and dioceses to start Theology on Taps in their own areas. At renewtot.org, you can find a number of resources to start using Theology on Tap to reach young adults in your area. Starting or improving your own Theology on Tap meetings might be a great first step in transforming your evangelizing ministry for young adults.

THE COMMITMENT TO DISCIPLESHIP

One of the best examples of a uniquely branded young-adult ministry is the i.d.9:16 community of missionary disciples in Ann Arbor, Michigan. It has a thriving model for building young-adult communities that many other parishes are adopting today. The "i.d." in its name refers to its identity as "intentional disciples"—people who have made a conscious and deliberate decision to follow Christ. The "9:16" centers its community on the evangelizing mission of the Church by referring to 1 Corinthians 9:16: "This is no reason for me to boast, for an obligation has been imposed on me, and woe to me if I do not preach it!"

The beginning of this ministry was clearly the work of the Holy Spirit. The name itself came out of a retreat that a group of young adults from Ann Arbor attended together in Harbor Springs, Michigan, in 2011. The retreat was organized by Peter and Debbie Herbeck of Renewal Ministries in response to what Pope Benedict XVI had called a "crisis of discipleship" among the millennial generation. Out of that weekend experience grew what is now a thriving model for young-adult ministry today.

I asked Pete Burak, the director of i.d.9:16, to share why he thinks his community has done so well in energizing young adults today. It was clear in his responses that the group's passion for promoting personal encounters and conversion to Christ and getting people on a path of discipleship is enabling it to attract young adults to crave something more in their lives. Burak said that he sees a lot of young adults today who fear commitment and, as a result, lack a genuine community that they can feel a part of. As he astutely observed, "Even though society is more connected than ever through social media and technology, it has become increasingly difficult to authentically share your life with others."[1] The group's community of disciples has grown because it provides the opportunities for those deep, personal connections that come along with making an encounter with and conversion to Jesus Christ as a top priority. He said that the "winning elements" of joyful, peaceful, and unified community began to flourish only after shifting to this intense focus on encounters with Christ.[2]

The organization offers an exemplary model of evangelizing ministries for young adults because it provides opportunities for all three methods of Jesus' evangelizing ministry. The intense focus on conversion and encounters with Christ enables people to seek out and experience his healing love and touch. The group's identity as missionary disciples makes it clear that by joining the group, you are called to make sacrifices for God. You are called to be "comfortable with uncomfortableness" in order to share the Gospel. Finally, the group teaches members to make a clear commitment to the "four pillars" of conversion, communion, orthodoxy, and mission, which Burak told me "lay a foundation of how a disciple acts, thinks, prays, and fulfills God's plan for our lives."[3] Through these four pillars, i.d.9:16 teaches people how to live as disciples in the modern world.

PRINCIPLES FOR DEVELOPING EFFECTIVE EVANGELIZING MINISTRIES FOR YOUNG ADULTS

1. Grow with a grassroots mentality.

When starting any new ministry, keep the words of Blessed Mother Teresa at the top of your mind: "Never worry about the numbers. Help one person at a time and always start with the person nearest you." When starting any new project, it can be tempting to focus solely on the numbers. In many areas of our Church, there are no young-adult ministries yet. Getting started can be a difficult thing, and the number of people in attendance early on can be incredibly depressing. It is almost impossible to create evangelizing ministries with huge numbers right from the start. It takes time and almost always grows just one person at a time.

In religious-education ministries, sacramental preparation, marriage preparation, and other ministries, attendance is basically built in and required. For young-adult ministry, though, people have to be convinced to join. They will not have any motivation to come all on their own. They will have to be invited.

As I wrote earlier in this chapter, Sean Allen grew the young-adult ministry in our parish one person at a time through personal invitations. It is something I have heard from everyone who has found success in growing evangelizing ministries for young adults. We have to be willing to start up conversations with strangers and develop relationships with them one-on-one.

This can sometimes be difficult for people to do, especially if you consider yourself to be an introvert. Colin Nykaza, who also found success in the word-of-mouth approach to growing a young-adult ministry in the Archdiocese of New York, tells his young-adult leaders to develop relationships by "being interested, not interesting."[4] In other words, ask a lot of questions and let other people do the talking, a system even an introvert can comfortably engage in. The more questions we ask, the more people will be willing to open up and trust us. The more we try to be interesting to others, however, the more they will perceive us as inauthentic and uninterested in who they are.

Spend the time it takes to develop relationships of trust, and invite people one by one to join your events. Create inviteable events and small-group gatherings that give you something to invite people to, but recognize that these new endeavors will only grow through your personal invitation.

Evangelizing Ministry Method: Heal

2. Engage the disciples.

There are many young adults who are already very strong in their faith but not very connected to a parish. These are people who are committed disciples, going to weekly or even daily Mass, reading the Bible and spiritual books, and developing a prayer life. They are hungry for something more than social events. They will be the first ones to join you in a young-adult happy hour, weekend picnic, or night of pumpkin picking with other young adults. They will be the ones who develop strong ties with the other people in the young-adult group. What they really need, though, are some opportunities to go further in their faith.

The i.d.9:16 community makes it clear how this can be done. Its clear focus on discipleship and evangelization draws together a group of people who are excited to be a part of a community, but more than that, they are excited to join together to celebrate a passion for their relationship with God. They make it clear that we should have no fear of being excited and open about our faith and the evangelizing mission of the Church.

We want to be careful—as with all ministries—not to let our efforts to heal overshadow the proclamation of the Gospel and the teaching mission of the Church. Young-adult ministries, therefore, need to create a firm foundation in spiritual development and discipleship in which people are given opportunities to attend retreats, join Bible studies and prayer groups, and pray together. These are the offerings that are sure to create a thriving young-adult group.

Evangelizing Ministry Method: Proclaim, Teach

3. Challenge the consumers with a vision for living the Gospel.

In a similar way, you want to make sure your young-adult ministry is more than a singles support group. Being a welcoming community, you are likely to bring in people who really do need a community that welcomes and supports them. I know this sounds elitist and judgmental, but there will always be good people in your groups who are just a little bit socially awkward. We can never be satisfied with forming a group that meets a need for socialization without challenging a person to grow spiritually as well. For some people, the young-adult community is their best source of love and acceptance. If you are not careful, it can be addicting. All are welcome—that is how our young-adult ministries heal—but all are also called to serve a higher purpose. If you are not careful, young-adult communities will create consumers of social acceptance rather than disciples.

How do you challenge people to see your community as more than an opportunity for emotional validation and social time? Challenge them with a vision. Explain to them the young-adult lifestyle you stand for and the responsibilities that come with being a member of your group. This is where proclaiming comes in. First, we offer the opportunity to come and meet new people. Some of those relationships may even develop into romantic relationships. At the same time, we want to be very clear in everything we do that our ultimate goal is to grow in relationship with Christ. In order to follow him and his commands, we must make sacrifices and love selflessly. We want to welcome people to the group and never turn anyone away, but we also want to be clear about the purpose, goal, and responsibility to pursue the challenges that come with discipleship.

This means, as a leader of a young-adult evangelizing community, you have to provide a vision for the group. You want to challenge people to go from consumers of the community to active leaders and organizers of events. Getting leaders, though, is about more than convincing people to serve on leadership teams. Anyone can make a sacrifice of their time for a group of friends whom they love. To go further, you have the responsibility to challenge your young-adult members to serve all people around them. A young-adult ministry is not a Catholic community closed off and safe from others. A thriving young-adult community should be building relationships with other young adults outside of the group. Members should be inviting new people to join all the time. This comes with the recognition that the Catholic Church offers a gift that can touch young adults in their deepest needs and desires. An encounter with Christ will be transformative. Young-adult ministry is not just a Catholic social group; it is a group of disciples dedicated to spreading the love of Christ with the world.

You may not be the pastor of the parish, but you can still share a vision. You can paint a picture for what discipleship is like in our twenties and thirties. You can explain what is required to live the Gospel in the twenty-first century. You should share this vision in every meeting with every opportunity you have. Why? Because people have to know what your community is really about. They have to know where you are going and not just where they are.

Evangelizing Ministry Method: Proclaim

For additional resources to help evangelize young adults, visit healproclaimteach.com/chapter12.

13

MINISTRY WITH ADULTS

When the Pew Forum in 2009 did its study of Christians who left their childhood religion, they found that 79 percent of the now-unaffiliated Catholics left the Church before the age of twenty-four. An additional 18 percent left before the age of thirty-five. In other words, if an adult is raised Catholic and stays Catholic through his thirties, there is only a small chance he will leave. That is the silver lining when we think about evangelizing adults in their thirties and older.

Let's focus on that group for a minute—the group of Catholics who are *staying* Catholic. (I will come back to those who left in a moment.) Some of them are passionately Catholic, deeply involved in their parishes, and living in an intimate relationship with Christ. Matthew Kelly described some research he did in Catholic parishes in his book *The Four Signs of a Dynamic Catholic*. He found that the group of highly dedicated Catholics who are actively participating in their parishes only amounts to about 7 percent of all self-identified Catholics.[1] This is the group to which most parishes direct their "adult faith formation" meetings and prayer groups. They teach these disciples by inviting them into these opportunities for faith sharing, learning, and ongoing catechesis.

What about the laissez-faire Catholics? What about the other 93 percent of Catholics who are still in the Church but only somewhat involved in their parishes? They include the 70 percent of Catholics who do not attend Mass every Sunday but do not plan to completely abandon the Church, either. These people have not yet made the full commitment to discipleship. Adult faith formation and catechesis, in the traditional sense, won't work, because they simply are not showing up yet.

To reach these groups of people, we have to make a mental shift as a Church. We have to think of ways we can proclaim the Gospel message (found most fully in the Eucharist) so that it ignites a passion in the hearts of loosely connected Catholics and compels them to learn everything they can about the Christian way of life. In this way, they can be the agents of healing for those who have abandoned their Catholic faith. They will become the agents of evangelization capable of welcoming back those who have fallen away. They will be the ones who ultimately reach that 10 percent of Americans who were raised Catholic but are now Protestant or unaffiliated with any religion at all. We cannot catechize our way to reach them. We have to take on a different approach.

This chapter is about teaching the faithful Catholic adults, proclaiming the Gospel to the "Christmas-and-Easter Catholics," and healing the many fallen-away Catholics who feel marginalized and abandoned by the Church.

OPENING THE RCIA TO ALL

About halfway through the RCIA process, my good friend Aaron, whom I was sponsoring, told me he thought everyone in the parish should have to go to the RCIA meetings. He started telling this to everyone who asked him about how RCIA was going. He said he was learning so much more than he ever thought he would. There was a ton about the Catholic Church that he thought he knew but had completely misunderstood.

The truth is, no matter how many years of Catholic education that an adult might have, there is still so much more to learn. In many ways it takes a lot of unlearning what adults thought they knew about the Church but had completely misunderstood. You do not have to be a convert, like Aaron, to learn something new. Many RCIA sponsors say at the end of the experience that they, too, learned things they never knew about their faith. Plus, many adults might know a lot from their years in Catholic schools but lack the personal connection to Christ that gives that information meaning and significance in daily life.

There are a lot of very excellent programs that assist with this need: DVD series and multipart studies to help the most dedicated of Catholics learn and grow in their faith. The people who participate in these adult faith-formation series really do grow in knowledge and understanding about their faith. I hear people talking about these opportunities in our parish all the time. They are great ways to continue to spiritually nourish the already committed disciples among the community.

What if, though, a parish placed an even greater significance on the RCIA, not just for candidates and catechumens entering the Church, but for the entire parish? Indeed, when the RCIA was formed after the Second Vatican Council, the intent was to revitalize the parish, not just create a method for converts to enter into the Church.[2] This was the starting point and inspiration for the revitalization of the Tri-Community Catholic Parish of Colorado Springs, Colorado, by pastor Father Ron Raab and associate pastor Father Andrew Gawrych.

I spoke with Father Drew Gawrych about how his parish has opened up the RCIA process to the entire parish as a way to reevangelize and recatechize the cradle Catholics of Colorado Springs.[3] The parish did this by opening up the inquiry or "evangelization" phase of the RCIA to the entire parish. During

a seven-week series that filled the room with veteran parishioners, RCIA participants, their sponsors, and the RCIA team,
Father Gawrych led the group into a reflection on the *good* news.
They looked at each of the major topics normally covered during
the RCIA—God, Jesus, Eucharist, sacraments, and so on—and
asked a simple question: "What is *good* about it?" What is *good*
about God? What is *good* about Jesus? What is *good* about the
Eucharist? The intent of these meetings was not to teach but to
proclaim the Good News as it relates to each topic. They wanted
to present the foundations of the Catholic faith with an evangelizing perspective.

Members of the parish were invited to share their personal
testimonies during these nights and relate them to the topic of
the day. They shared fifteen- to twenty-minute witnesses that
inspired all in attendance and set a level of intimacy and vulnerability that would enable true spiritual growth. Rather than
formal question-and-answer time or small-group discussions,
they spent the last thirty minutes in fellowship with food and
drinks and plenty of time for community-building to occur. Here
the RCIA team and sponsors talked with the candidates and catechumens informally about the topic of the night. This informal
fellowship time created the space needed to build bonds between
the RCIA participants, the team, and, more importantly, the
entire parish.

Father Gawrych shared with me the fruits of this heightened focus on the RCIA in his parish. First, the candidates and
catechumens, who would normally join the RCIA timidly and
unsure of what to expect, felt as if they were joining something
bigger than themselves. Rather than walking into a mostly empty
room of people considering joining, they discovered a group of
fifty, sixty, seventy, or more people who were just as interested
in learning about the Catholic faith as they were. That feeling of

being welcomed by the parish along with the inspiration found in the personal testimonies from parishioners opened up the opportunity for experiences of healing to occur on the way toward the sacraments.

Second, that initial focus on the "good news" about foundational Church doctrines enabled the participants to go back through them in greater detail during the catechesis phases of the RCIA. Father Gawrych and the RCIA team were able to effectively teach because they had laid the groundwork of faith by proclaiming the Good News. At the end, when the Easter Vigil had passed and the mystagogy sessions were over, people actually wanted to keep meeting. They did not want it to end. The content was great and they enjoyed the learning process, but it was the relationships that they formed along the way, binding the entire parish together, that made this experiment an incredible gift to the entire parish.

WHAT ADULTS REALLY WANT TO HEAR

The question remains, however: how do we get the frequent and occasional Mass-goers to come to our adult faith-formation programs? How do we get them to come to catechetical events in which they can learn (and unlearn) about the Catholic faith? What we are really talking about here is not so much how to teach disciples but how to proclaim the Good News to the crowds in our parish. We can attract new people to get involved in adult faith formation by giving them solutions to problems that bother them the most.

Think back to the way Jesus proclaimed the kingdom of God. He spoke in parables that were easy to understand. He used analogies and metaphors that were pertinent to daily life. People could relate to these parables because they already thought about those things on a daily basis.

What are the crowds in your parish thinking about on a daily basis? What are their deepest wounds caused by sin and separation from God and others? Where do they need to find comfort and the realization that they are not alone in their struggles? One helpful way to think about their biggest concerns is to look at the three Fs: finances, family, and fights.

Finances

It is inevitable, but our culture and society forces us to think about money and finances almost all the time. One thing is for certain: when it comes to both time and money, there is never enough of it. This is why the crowds in the parish can become so offended when a pastor asks for money. When most of them are struggling to make ends meet paying off student loans, car payments, and never-ending mortgage bills, it is difficult even to consider giving money to the Church.

Rather than force-feed them the value of charity and giving, why not proclaim a message of good news and help parishioners with their finances? While it is not by any means the only family-finances program, Dave Ramsey's *Financial Peace University* is used by thousands of churches throughout the country to help educate people about their finances and get them to become debt-free. Ramsey is a popular radio-show host whose message is simple, direct, and rooted in his Christian faith. Recognizing that money is on the minds of the adults in our parishes, we can provide the means to find peace through an educational series that integrates what we believe by focusing on what people want to achieve.

Family

The people in your parish who are raising families have a lot on their minds. They are worried about raising good kids and protecting them from harm. They worry about their participation in sports, their grades, and the level at which they are accepted by their peers. As the kids get older, they worry about them getting into trouble with the constant temptations of sex, alcohol, and drugs. They worry about them getting into college, getting a good job, and (someday please!) getting out of the house.

It would be great if hospitals issued parenting manuals when they send you home with your new baby, but unfortunately, parents just have to figure things out on their own. What better place to find help and support than the local parish? We have been blessed to be a part of a parish with lots of young families and kids. My wife, who currently works two part-time jobs at a local college and university, also helps to organize a number of groups for young moms. Every other Tuesday morning, young families gather for Kids of the Kingdom, where a mom leads the children in a Catholic craft and minilesson while the other moms get to socialize, share stories, and ask for help. On the first and third Sunday night of every month, these and many other moms gather for a Wine and the Word faith-sharing group, where they discuss the life of a saint and share stories about how it relates to their lives today. The no-strings-attached nature of these groups helps provide a level of support that parents need while children are young.

As children get older, life gets busier and the challenges take new forms. School, sports, dancing, and other activities start to dominate family life. Parents love these activities, and as a result, more than any other activity, children's sports interfere with a family's ability to participate in a parish. Sunday-morning Mass is all too easily replaced by soccer tournaments. Not only that, but a healthy focus on competition and hard work can easily turn into a win-at-all-costs mentality that pulls parents and coaches further and further away from the selfless requirements of the kingdom of God.

I had the wonderful opportunity to work for an organization at the University of Notre Dame that is trying to fight this problem. The Play Like a Champion Today program trains coaches and offers workshops for parents that help them see the connection between sports and faith. We meticulously evaluated every workshop by asking every coach participant to complete an exit survey after the event. After thousands of surveys, by far the biggest impact was on the way they understood their identity as coaches. For the first time, most of them started to see the work they were doing coaching in Catholic sports programs as a *ministry*. When these men and women saw coaching as a ministry, they changed the way they related to the kids and began to focus on positive, intrinsic motivation rather than simply winning the games. It helped refocus their efforts away from the scoreboard and back on each individual player instead. Best of all—and this is coming from me as a former coach—the motivational tactics that the program teaches actually work. They motivate players and improve their performance, making an impact on the final outcome of the games.

The sports culture of parents, though, is an even bigger challenge. That is why the Play Like a Champion Today parent workshops are meant to help remind people about what is really important when it comes to sports. Hosting these workshops at parishes and requiring parents to attend feels to many like just one more meeting, but without such initiatives, how will sports be put into the context of the Gospel? How else can you lead parents from self-centered competitiveness into selfless love?

Sports are just one example of ways in which a parish can focus on family issues that matter to parents. Rather than offering workshops on general parenting skills, try to think of adult faith-formation offerings that focus on issues that matter the most to families right now. The goal is to create events and small groups that meet a need in Catholic families and give participants something to talk about and invite their friends to join.

Fights

Take a quick look at the marriage statistics in the United States, and you will find numbers that are just as depressing as the statistics about Catholics leaving the Church. Some studies have found that 40 to 50 percent of marriages end in separation and divorce. While Catholics overall fare better, with only 28 percent having experienced a divorce, let's take a reality check here: three out of every ten members of your parish have experienced or are on their way to experiencing a divorce.[4]

What can we do? One of the best attempts to provide enrichment specifically to married couples in our parish has been the monthly parish-sponsored date night for married couples. The group brings in speakers, hosts social events and game nights, and offers the annual opportunity for couples to renew their marital vows—often a powerful experience for couples of all ages. They provide child care for young parents, provide food and drinks, and welcome any couples who would like to come. It has been a wonderful gift to my own marriage, and I am grateful that, whether I learn anything during the talks or not, we get the opportunity to talk with other couples who assure us, frankly, that we are not alone.

Fighting with your spouse creates wounds that are difficult to heal. Meeting with other couples even in a social context enables us to experience some healing with the relief that we are not alone. The date nights also give us the opportunity to learn what other couples do to overcome their challenges, especially those who have been married for decades longer than we have. Those couples give us hope and perspective that we would never get to experience if it were not for this ministry.

CHRIST RENEWS HIS PARISH ONE GROUP AT A TIME

After leading, planning, and attending more than seventy-five retreats as a student and young adult, I was reluctant to attend our parish Christ Renews His Parish (CRHP) weekend. I knew about the impact it could have on a person's life. It was the spark that lit up the faith of my mother- and father-in-law. I had seen friends attend, too, and knew what a great experience they had. For years I turned down invitations with excuses about having young children or being too busy with work. I dragged my feet for more than five years but finally gave in and said yes. Truth be told, my friend wouldn't let me say no and even filled out the application form for me.

The funny thing was that I was kind of underwhelmed by the retreat at first. I had been on and led retreats that followed a similar format, so the retreat itself was not very new to me. After the weekend, though, I decided to go on to take part in the planning of the next weekend despite the sacrifice my family would have to make with all the extra nights out of the house. I am so glad I said yes. I did not realize the incredible impact of CRHP until we began the formation meetings in preparation for the retreat we would put on.

CRHP started in a parish in Cleveland, Ohio, in 1969. You already read about Search in chapter 10, which was based on the concept that a retreat for teens led by teens creates a powerful experience. Well, at Holy Family Parish in Cleveland, they decided to apply that same logic to a retreat for adults in the parish: a retreat for lay adults led by lay adults. A powerful movement was born, and the CRHP retreat process was founded and grew in popularity along with other retreat movements such as Cursillo during the late twentieth century.

Now, I had been an adult leader at a Search retreat for teens and, prior to that, for many Kairos retreats for college students. In fact, I had planned, designed, and directed dozens of other retreats just like CRHP in almost every way. For me, though, CRHP was such an unexpected, incredible experience that I cannot be more grateful to my good friend who basically forced me to go. You see, unlike Search, Kairos, and all those other retreats I had helped plan, it is the many weeks of formation that really make the CRHP experience a powerful catalyst for renewal. I got to know the other men on the retreat in such deep and meaningful ways that I cannot see how the parish could replicate the experience in any other way.

During the course of those six months, I witnessed countless moments of true healing within the lives of these men that culminated in the weekend retreat. All of us, including me, were inspired to make real changes to our daily lives by praying more frequently, reading and listening to the daily readings, attending daily Mass, or going to confession. No one asked us to make these changes in our lives, and it was not an explicit part of the process. To us, it was an inherent recognition of the Gospel being proclaimed to us in the weekly discussions about scripture. We were called to make sacrifices in order to follow Christ. We all felt it. Many of the guys attested, now that they were reading the Bible during the meetings and at home, that they had already read more of that book than they had in their entire lives up to that point. CRHP lit a fire in our faith, and we were ready to share it with others.

If you really want to create a catalyst for the evangelization of adults in your parish, there is a lot you can draw from the CRHP format. You can, of course, begin offering a CRHP retreat, Cursillo, or RENEW experience in your parish. They all have incredible resources to help create the very experiences that I find to be at the heart of almost every vibrant parish I have seen.

First, gathering a group of people together in small faith-sharing groups is essential. The protection of the small-group atmosphere allows people to open up to each other in ways they never have with anyone else. It took weeks and even months for that level of trust to be built up between us, but once we got there, it was simply amazing to see what happened. True healing occurred for these men. It occurs again and again in both the men's and the women's group meetings every week in preparation for their retreat.

That small group also provided the accountability to live out the Gospel. Sure, we heard from our pastor how important it was to make sacrifices and to love one another. We all knew that we should be praying every day and never missing a Sunday Mass. But having that level of accountability each week made those habits and sacrifices a reality.

Now that my CRHP experience is over and our group enters the ranks of the alumni in our parish, I can see something I never noticed before. There is a network of strong bonds between the people who have gone on CRHP. That small-group connection built upon itself and spilled over into relationships with other people on other CRHP teams. When I attend Mass or parish events, I can now see a network of CRHP alumni who are at the core of the most dedicated members of the parish. A parish brotherhood and sisterhood has formed through CRHP to add new meaning to the letters of Saint Paul, where he addresses the congregations as "brothers and sisters."

Most of all, though, the CRHP retreat gives parishes something to invite people to. It is an incredibly effective inviteable event—the sort of thing we explored in chapter 8. CRHP is a great example of an evangelizing ministry that always welcomes new people and grows almost entirely by personal invitation. How effective was the process in evangelizing the men on our team? We had every type of Catholic in the group, from the loosely committed to the ultra-involved. We even had two non-Catholic men in our team whose wives were Catholic. A year after our retreat, both men completed the RCIA process and fully entered into the Catholic Church during the Easter Vigil. I was blessed to be one of these men's sponsors.

PRINCIPLES FOR DEVELOPING EFFECTIVE EVANGELIZING MINISTRIES FOR ADULTS

1. Turn loose ties into strong connections.

There are many adults who are present but unengaged parishioners. They bring their kids to the Catholic school or parish religious-education programs. They attend Mass occasionally or even on most weekends. They volunteer or attend social events, but as far as their faith goes, things are pretty stale spiritually. The loose ties these individuals already have with the parish offer an incredible opportunity for evangelization.

First, make sure you have a successful evangelizing activity that you can invite these people to attend. Most often this is a semiannual retreat such as Cursillo or CRHP, but monthly events can work well, too. Having these events are critical because they give you and the other engaged disciples in your parish something to invite people to. Find the ministries that offer the opportunity for the most intimate encounters with Christ and make the most disciples in your parish. Center on those events and activities as the focal point of almost everything you offer. The event should be something everybody could benefit from attending.

Adults in the parish can hear about these things during Mass announcements, parish bulletins, and the parish website, but you cannot stop there. Parents should receive invitations to these opportunities through the Catholic school or parish religious-education programs. Pancake breakfasts should be more than fundraisers; they should be times when leaders and parishioners reach out to everyone to invite them into a deeper commitment to their faith.

Most of all, though, adults need personal one-on-one relationships with other people in the parish who can invite them to attend events that were transformative for their own lives. As we discussed earlier, it is almost a rule in growing any ministry that the vast majority of people who participate come because someone personally invited them to attend. We cannot hide behind announcements, bulletins, fliers, and websites. We need to seek out the unengaged parishioners and Catholic-school parents, develop friendships, and invite them to take the chance on an opportunity of a lifetime.

Evangelizing Ministry Method: Heal

2. Baptisms, weddings, and funerals are opportunities for evangelization.

Even the fallen-away Catholics come to big family-and-friend events such as Baptisms, weddings, and funerals. These events are without a doubt focused on the people actually participating in the sacrament or being celebrated in new life; however, we should not overlook the opportunity to reach the lost who come to celebrate and honor their family and friends. This may be the only opportunity for Catholics who have fallen away to experience the Church since they were children. It is not a time to force Catholic doctrines upon them, but it can be a great opportunity to heal, proclaim, and teach.

Baptisms are celebrations of the joy of new life for families. They are joyful events and should be celebrated as such. The water of Baptism is a sacramental sign of the central goal in evangelization: to welcome all into the Body of Christ. The Rite of Baptism should also be celebrated with the intention of expressing this sentiment of welcome to all who attend. Parents of these children should be welcomed and supported as new parents in a parish, feeling confident that when they return next weekend with a crying baby in the pews they will not be turned away. The waters of Baptism heal the sin in a young child's heart, but they can also be a reminder of the healing opportunity for all people in the Church. If we are not careful, those of us responsible for Baptism ministry can get so caught up in the nuts and bolts of performing the rite that we lose the opportunity to show love to all those who attend. Baptisms are opportunities to remind people that God is not a rule-maker but a Savior. He died for us so that we can rise with him in new life. We proclaim what we believe when we renew our baptismal vows, so why not take a moment to explain in greater detail how what we pray connects with what we believe? Let the celebrations of infant Baptism in your parish be truly moments of healing, proclaiming, and teaching. Welcome, invite, illuminate.

Weddings can be incredible evangelizing opportunities as well, but they can also project the cold, harsh perception of the Church that many people carry. Of course, the approach of the pastor or priest facilitating the ceremony is key. The warm, welcoming love of the person preaching and presiding is crucial. The wedding coordinator and music ministers are just as important. If they are bossy and mean, they will project a Church that is demanding and cold instead of welcoming and warm. This may be the only connection these people will have with the Church for many years. It is without a doubt one of the most significant opportunities that we have to show that we are a Church of mercy and love, not a Church of judgment and punishment. We heal with our actions and words. We proclaim a Gospel of hope and salvation, not condemnation and judgment. We teach about the love of God through solid preaching.

Finally, funerals are the most natural opportunity for healing we have. Family and friends are suffering from the great loss. They need to know that God is with them in their suffering and that the Church is there for them as well. Planning a liturgically sound ceremony especially for those who may not be aware of the way Catholic funeral rites are conducted is essential, but instruction in the rite must be done in a way that heals rather than rejects. Funerals express the first proclamation. They are a celebration not only of a person's life but also of his life united with Christ who loves him, died for him, and rises with him. Is that person in heaven? Everyone there will have that hope. You will hear people talk about heaven and being in a better place. What may be missing, though, is the why. Why is he in heaven? Only because of Christ's passion, death, and resurrection. It is thanks to Christ that salvation is possible, not just a person's good works. This is the kerygmatic message we have to proclaim.

Evangelizing Ministry Method: Heal, Proclaim, Teach

3. Proclaim with a focus on the three Fs.

What do the adults in your parish really care about? What is really going on in their lives that is keeping them up at night or distracting them while they know they should be paying more attention during Mass? Earlier in this chapter, I suggested that in order to reach those Catholics who are not yet fully committed disciples, we have to focus on the issues that matter to them. This is why Jesus preached in parables to the crowds. How do we spark the interest of the crowds in our parish? Focus on the three Fs: finances, family, and fights.

Take a close look at your adult faith-formation offerings and other services to the adults in your parish. Are you focused too heavily on explorations of the doctrines of the Church? Do you have anything in place that is going to appeal to the concerns of people on the fringes of the parish who need real-world help? We have an incredible opportunity to proclaim the Gospel in the context of finances, family, and fights if we are willing to structure our educational series to a different audience. Seek out the resources and materials that will help address these important and timely concerns in the lives of the adults you serve.

Evangelizing Ministry Method: Proclaim

4. The Eucharist must be the centerpiece of all evangelization and catechesis.

When I talk to converts or reverts about their love for the Catholic faith, they almost always bring up the Eucharist. A good friend and fellow football coach, for example, had an incredible experience at the baccalaureate Mass for the high school where we taught together. Scott, though a non-Catholic, knelt down during the Eucharistic Prayer with the other faculty members. When it was time to stand, he could not get up. He had an overwhelming feeling that compelled him to experience Christ in the Eucharist for himself. With the same conviction and passion he showed as a coach, Scott found a way to respond to this call. He became Catholic the following year.

The Eucharist is the source and summit of the Christian life. It is the foundation of all that we do in our work of evangelization. As with so many other active disciples in the Church today, it was the Eucharist that drew me in. It was the Eucharist that compelled me to join the RCIA in the fourth grade, and it was the Eucharist during a holy hour in Steubenville, Ohio, that set me on the path to where I am today. It must be both the cornerstone of what you do as an evangelizing minister and at the core of what you offer as you serve the adults in your parish.

The Eucharist and eucharistic adoration are especially powerful in igniting the faith of the lukewarm Catholics in our Church. In the Diocese of Toledo, Ohio, Greg Schlueter realized how important the Eucharist would be to the revitalization of the Catholic faith in northern Ohio. He started something he calls Mass Impact and hosts monthly Ignite Sessions providing touching worship music, a short but deeply powerful testimony from one of the participants, Reconciliation, and eucharistic adoration. Hundreds of people attend these Ignite nights, even those who are lukewarm in their faith or not even Catholic at all. Why? Because people are talking about it. They are having powerful experiences praying before the Eucharist that they feel compelled to share, so much so that the participants are motivated to invite their friends to check it out with them.

What was at the center of the revitalization of the Church of the Nativity as told in the book *Rebuilt*? The Mass and the Eucharist. The parish realized that it had to stop trying to improve everything all at once and instead focus primarily on making the weekend experience so great that people *had* to come back. They figured that if they got the Mass right, everything else would fall into place. It worked. They grew in numbers, and parishioners grew in greater intimacy with Christ. All of their work was centered on and drawn from the experience of Christ in the Mass, in the Eucharist. It transformed laissez-faire Catholics into engaged volunteers on fire with their faith.

Evangelizing Ministry Method: Heal, Proclaim, Teach

5. Start small.

Small groups of adults are critical to the success of your evangelizing ministry. For me and my parish, the Christ Renews His Parish formation process created an opportunity for many parishioners to join small groups. As a group of men, we grew to know and trust each other, which enabled us to find healing for our wounds from sin; we offered each other a level of accountability to actually live out the Gospel in our daily lives; and we asked such challenging and interesting questions each week during our discussions about scripture that it constantly compelled us to go out searching to learn more about our Faith. Each of the three evangelizing ministry methods played out in our small-group formation meetings.

The Church of the Nativity (from the book *Rebuilt*) also highlights the importance of forming ongoing small groups, especially at the adult level, in your parish. It records weekly video podcasts that build upon the Sunday readings and weekly message series in the homilies to empower the many small groups to begin a discussion together. It was not easy for the parish staff to get these small groups started, and they still admit that they are trying to figure out the best way to continue to grow and improve them. They have seen, though, how important and effective they are. As authors Father Michael White and Tom Corcoran wrote in *Rebuilt*, "The power of small groups comes from forming relationships in which *conversations* lead to *conversion*."[5] (For more information on how to form and grow these small groups, see chapter 8 of this book.)

Evangelizing Ministry Method: Heal, Proclaim, Teach

For additional resources to help evangelize adults, visit healproclaim-teach.com/chapter13.

Afterword
GOOD SOIL

On the cover of this book is an image of the parable of the sower, sometimes called the parable of the soils. This is the first parable that Jesus proclaims to the crowds, and it causes his disciples to question why he speaks to them in parables (see chapter 5).

Just as Jesus unpacked the parable for his listeners, I want to share with you what I see on the cover of this book. The Sower plants the "word of the kingdom." Three doves fly above, representing the Holy Spirit at work in our ministries today. The seeds land on good soil, and the soil will yield much fruit. We were once the seeds; now we must understand that we are to be the fertile soil.

It is our responsibility to cultivate our hearts and minds for ministry so that Christ can sow the seeds of faith in all we do. How do we do this? What lies at the root of every effective ministry? What drives the saints and heroes of our great tradition to make disciples? Below the good soil, at the root of all effective ministries, are these three keys to evangelization: healing, proclaiming, and teaching. Commitment to these first priorities of ministry is essential to cultivating good soil and bringing forth a great harvest.

Without a doubt, the current situation in our Church calls for a renewed approach to ministry. For decades, maybe even centuries, Catholics have become too comfortable. We have lost a sense of urgency in spreading the Gospel within our communities and even among our friends and families. We have allowed our ministry fields to become infested with weeds. We have permitted the soil to become thin and rocky. We have created a path on which little is growing.

We can no longer depend on cultural Christianity to be passed from one generation to the next. The only way we can ensure survival is by standing up and working together to reenergize cradle Catholics and passive Christians through the new evangelization. It is time to prepare good soil for Christ once again.

I had two primary goals for this book. First, I wanted to answer an obvious but difficult question that both new and seasoned parish ministers are asking: "How, exactly, do we do evangelization?" To answer that question, I turned to the source, Jesus Christ himself, who carried out his ministry and mission in three ways: he healed the sick and marginalized, proclaimed the Gospel to the crowds, and taught his disciples. As parish ministers today we must do the same.

The second goal of this book was probably less explicit but far more important: inspiring others to actually do evangelize. We all need the tools and training to carry out this essential mission of the Church. The challenge is finding success as we apply what we learn. Jesus gave us a model for this, too. He prepared his disciples to carry out his mission, not on their own as isolated expert evangelizers, but as disciples joined together to support one another in their common mission.

As I look at the many amazing evangelizing ministries in the Church today, I am uplifted and excited about the work they do. Our soil is being transformed into rich soil in so many places. I have done my best in this book to share some of their approaches to evangelization so that ideas and inspiration are kindled for others who are trying to reach the same groups of people in their own parishes.

Next comes the hard part.

In order to make a real impact in the world today, we have to work together. We need to create a culture of sharing ideas, support, and inspiration as we start and lead new and exciting evangelizing ministries. We cannot wait for great charismatic leaders to come along and do this work for us; we have to look to ourselves, those around us in our parishes, and ministers in other places who are striving to achieve the same things we are. Working together, we have a real chance to transform the Church by building a movement of movements.

Here is my invitation to you. Through digital media, we can connect as we carry out Christ's call to "go and make disciples of all nations." Join me and many other evangelizing disciples at healproclaimteach.com/disciples. There you will meet others just like you, working to make the Church, and so the world, better.

I hope you find this book useful for your ministry and I hope you will share it. I hope you will try something new and see what works. Most importantly, I hope you will work together with other evangelizing disciples to remain faithful to our common mission. Jesus sent his disciples out two by two. It's time for us to do the same—to go together and make disciples.

> But the seed sown on rich soil is the one who hears the word and understands it, who indeed bears fruit and yields a hundred or sixty or thirtyfold. (Mt 13:23)

NOTES

PREFACE

1. "America's Changing Religious Landscape," *Pew Research Center*, May 12, 2015, http://www.pewforum.org/2015/05/12/americas-changing-religious-landscape.

2. Ibid.

3. Antonio Spadaro, S.J., "A Big Heart Open to God," *America*, September 30, 2013, http://americamagazine.org/pope-interview.

4. Ibid.

2. THE STAGES OF EVANGELIZATION

1. United States Conference for Catholic Bishops, *National Directory for Catechesis* (Washington, DC: United States Conference for Catholic Bishops, 2005), 49.

2. Sherry Weddell, *Forming Intentional Disciples* (Huntington, IN: Our Sunday Visitor, 2012), Kindle edition, chap. 2.

3. Ibid., chap. 5.

3. HEAL

1. Henri J. M. Nouwen, *The Wounded Healer* (New York: Image Books, Doubleday, 1979), Kindle edition, Introduction.

2. Thomas Merton, *New Seeds of Contemplation* (New York: New Direction Books, 1961), 31.

3. Teresa of Calcutta, "Acceptance Speech by Mother Teresa," *Nobelprize.org*, December 10, 1979, http://www.nobelprize.org/mediaplayer/index.php?id=1852; emphasis added.

4. Susan Conroy, *Mother Teresa's Lessons of Love and Secrets of Sanctity* (Huntington, IN: Our Sunday Visitor, 2003), 201.

5. Jean-Guy Dubuc, *Brother André: Friend of Suffering, Apostle of St. Joseph* (Notre Dame, IN: Ave Maria Press, 2010), 37.

6. Ibid, 82.

7. "Damien the Leper," *EWTN.com*, https://www.ewtn.com/library/mary/damien.htm.

5. TEACH

1. Ken Robinson, "Do Schools Kill Creativity?" *TED*, February 2006, https://www.ted.com/talks/ken_robinson_says_schools_kill_creativity.

2. Henri J. M. Nouwen, *Can You Drink the Cup?* (Notre Dame, IN: Ave Maria Press, 2006), 103.

3. Andrew Gawrych, interview by author, December 16, 2014.

4. United States Conference for Catholic Bishops, *National Directory for Catechesis*, 97.

5. Ibid.

7. ONE-ON-ONE EVANGELIZATION

1. Nouwen, *Wounded Healer*, Kindle edition, chap. 3.

2. Jim Schuster, in discussion with the author.

3. Ibid.

8. GROUP EVANGELIZATION

1. Michael Port, *Book Yourself Solid: The Fastest, Easiest, and Most Reliable System for Getting More Clients Than You Can Handle Even if You Hate Marketing and Selling* (Hoboken, NJ: John Wiley and Sons, Inc., 2011), 91.

2. Ibid., 166.

3. Simon Sinek, "How Great Leaders Inspire Action," *TED*, September 2009, https://www.ted.com/talks/simon_sinek_how_great_leaders_inspire_action.

9. MINISTRY WITH CHILDREN

1. Ann Garrido, "The Faith of a Child," *America*, September 15, 2008, http://americamagazine.org/issue/667/article/faith-child.

2. United States Conference of Catholic Bishops, *National Directory for Catechesis*, 100.

10. MINISTRY WITH TEENAGERS

1. Roger Treat, *Bishop Sheil and the CYO* (New York: Messner, 1951), 55.

2. Everett Fritz, interview by author, October 20, 2014.

11. MINISTRY WITH COLLEGE STUDENTS

1. Curtis Martin, "My Remarks at the Synod for the New Evangelization," *FOCUS*, November 5, 2012, http://www.focus.org/blog/posts/remarks-at-the-synod-for-the.html.

2. John Paul Lichon, interview by author, October 20, 2014.

12. MINISTRY WITH YOUNG ADULTS

1. Pete Burak, interview by author, October 13, 2014.

2. Ibid.

3. Ibid.

4. "Starting and Sustaining Effective Young Adult Ministries," Ave Maria Press Professional Development Webinar, February 25, 2014, https://www.avemariapress.com/webinars/parish/young-adult-ministry.

13. MINISTRY WITH ADULTS

1. Matthew Kelly, *The Four Signs of a Dynamic Catholic* (Hebron, KY: Beacon Publishing, 2012), 12.

2. Andrew Gawrych, interview by author, December 16, 2014.

3. Ibid.

4. Mark M. Gray, "Divorce (Still) Less Likely Among Catholics," *Center for Applied Research in the Apostolate*, http://nineteensixty-four.blogspot.com/2013/09/divorce-still-less-likely-among.html.

5. Michael White and Tom Corcoran, *Rebuilt: Awakening the Faithful, Reaching the Lost, and Making Church Matter* (Notre Dame, IN: Ave Maria Press, 2013) 162.

AVE
AVE MARIA PRESS

Founded in 1865, Ave Maria Press,
a ministry of the Congregation of
Holy Cross, is a Catholic publishing
company that serves the spiritual and
formative needs of the Church and its
schools, institutions, and ministers;
Christian individuals and families; and
others seeking spiritual nourishment.

For a complete listing of titles from

Ave Maria Press

Sorin Books

Forest of Peace

Christian Classics

visit www.avemariapress.com

AVE MARIA PRESS
Notre Dame, IN

A Ministry of the United States Province of Holy Cross

Jared Dees is the creator of the popular website *The Religion Teacher*, which provides practical resources and effective teaching strategies to religious educators. A respected graduate of the Alliance for Catholic Education program at the University of Notre Dame, Dees earned master's degrees in education and theology, both from Notre Dame. He has volunteered for and worked in a wide variety of Catholic ministries, including Catholic schools, parish religious education, youth ministry, campus ministry, RCIA, and adult faith formation. Dees is the digital marketing manager at Ave Maria Press and the author of *31 Days to Becoming a Better Religious Educator*. His articles have appeared in *Momentum*, *CATECHIST*, *Catechetical Leader*, and on numerous websites. Dees lives in South Bend, Indiana, with his wife and three children.